LINCOLN CHRISTIAN UNIVERSITY

# The Collected Sermons of Dietrich Bonhoeffer

The Dietrich Bonhoeffer Memorial Church in London was built on the site of Sydenham Church, where Bonhoeffer was pastor from 1933 to 1935. Sydenham Church was destroyed by bombs during World War II.

# The Collected Sermons of Dietrich Bonhoeffer

Translated from the German by

Douglas W. Stott
Anne Schmidt-Lange
Isabel Best
Scott A. Moore
Claudia D. Bergmann

*Edited by Isabel Best*

## Fortress Press
Minneapolis

For Sarah and John
and their generation in
Christian ministry

—and for those to come

THE COLLECTED SERMONS OF DIETRICH BONHOEFFER

Copyright © 2012 Fortress Press. All rights reserved. Except for brief quotations in critical articles or reviews, no part of this book may be reproduced in any manner without prior written permission from the publisher. Visit http://www .augsburgfortress.org/copyrights or write to Permissions, Augsburg Fortress, Box 1209, Minneapolis, MN 55440.

Unless otherwise identified, Scripture quotations are from the New Revised Standard Version Bible, copyright © 1989 by the Division of Christian Education of the National Council of the Churches of Christ in the USA. Used by permission. All rights reserved.

Cover art: ullstein bild/The Granger Collection, New York
Cover design: Laurie Ingram
Book design: PerfecType, Nashville, TN
Frontispiece: Josh Messner

*Library of Congress Cataloging-in-Publication Data*
Bonhoeffer, Dietrich, 1906–1945.
 [Sermons. English. Selections]
 The collected sermons of Dietrich Bonhoeffer / translated from the German by Douglas W. Stott ... [et al.] ; edited by Isabel Best.
   p. cm.
 "Bonhoeffer bibliography"—P.
 Includes bibliographical references.
 ISBN 978-0-8006-9904-8 (hardcover : alk. paper) — ISBN 978-1-4514-2436-2 (ebook)
 1. Bonhoeffer, Dietrich, 1906-1945—Sermons. 2. Sermons, German—Translations into English. I. Stott, Douglas W. II. Best, Isabel. III. Title.
 BX4827.B57A5 2012
 252'.041—dc23
                        2012005194

The paper used in this publication meets the minimum requirements of American National Standard for Information Sciences—Permanence of Paper for Printed Library Materials, ANSI Z329.48-1984.

Manufactured in the U.S.A.

# CONTENTS

FOREWORD . . . . . . . . . . . . . . . . . . . . . . . . . . . . . . . . . . . . . . . . . . ix

EDITOR'S INTRODUCTION . . . . . . . . . . . . . . . . . . . . . . . . . . . . . xiii

**God Is with Us**
*Matthew 28:20.* . . . . . . . . . . . . . . . . . . . . . . . . . . . . . . . . . . . 1

**Waiting at the Door**
*Revelation 3:20.* . . . . . . . . . . . . . . . . . . . . . . . . . . . . . . . . . . 7

**National Memorial Day**
*Matthew 24:6–14.* . . . . . . . . . . . . . . . . . . . . . . . . . . . . . . . . 13

**The Promised Land**
*Genesis 32:24–31; 33:10* . . . . . . . . . . . . . . . . . . . . . . . . . . . . 23

**God Is Love**
*1 John 4:16* . . . . . . . . . . . . . . . . . . . . . . . . . . . . . . . . . . . . . 29

**Lazarus and the Rich Man**
*Luke 16:19–31.* . . . . . . . . . . . . . . . . . . . . . . . . . . . . . . . . . . 33

**Risen with Christ**
*Colossians 3:1–4.* . . . . . . . . . . . . . . . . . . . . . . . . . . . . . . . . . 41

**The Things That Are Above**
*Colossians 3:1–4.* . . . . . . . . . . . . . . . . . . . . . . . . . . . . . . . . . 49

**Overcoming Fear**
*Matthew 8:23–27.* . . . . . . . . . . . . . . . . . . . . . . . . . . . . . . . . 59

**Gideon: God Is My Lord**
*Judges 6:15–16; 7:2; 8:23* . . . . . . . . . . . . . . . . . . . . . . . . . . . . 67

126613

The Joy of Ascension
*1 Peter 1:7b–9* . . . . . . . . . . . . . . . . . . . . . . . . . . . . . . . . . . . . .75

Who Do You Say That I Am?
*Matthew 16:13–18.* . . . . . . . . . . . . . . . . . . . . . . . . . . . . . . . . .81

Ambassadors for Christ
*2 Corinthians 5:20* . . . . . . . . . . . . . . . . . . . . . . . . . . . . . . . . .87

Turning Back
*2 Corinthians 5:10* . . . . . . . . . . . . . . . . . . . . . . . . . . . . . . . . .95

As a Mother Comforts Her Child
*Wisdom 3:3* . . . . . . . . . . . . . . . . . . . . . . . . . . . . . . . . . . . . .101

Come, O Rescuer
*Luke 21:28.* . . . . . . . . . . . . . . . . . . . . . . . . . . . . . . . . . . . . .109

My Spirit Rejoices
*Luke 1:46–55.* . . . . . . . . . . . . . . . . . . . . . . . . . . . . . . . . . . .115

Beginning with Christ
*Luke 9:57–62.* . . . . . . . . . . . . . . . . . . . . . . . . . . . . . . . . . . .123

Repent and Do Not Judge
*Luke 13:1–5.* . . . . . . . . . . . . . . . . . . . . . . . . . . . . . . . . . . . .127

Come unto Me
*Matthew 11:28–30.* . . . . . . . . . . . . . . . . . . . . . . . . . . . . . . . .133

. . . and Have Not Love
*1 Corinthians 13:1–3* . . . . . . . . . . . . . . . . . . . . . . . . . . . . . .139

What Love Wants
*1 Corinthians 13:4–7* . . . . . . . . . . . . . . . . . . . . . . . . . . . . . .147

Must I Be Perfect?
*1 Corinthians 13:8–12* . . . . . . . . . . . . . . . . . . . . . . . . . . . . .155

A Church That Believes, Hopes, and Loves
*1 Corinthians 13:13* . . . . . . . . . . . . . . . . . . . . . . . . . . . . . . .161

My Strength Is Made Perfect in Weakness
*2 Corinthians 12:9* . . . . . . . . . . . . . . . . . . . . . . . . . . . . . . . .167

Lord, Help My Unbelief
*Mark 9:23–24* . . . . . . . . . . . . . . . . . . . . . . . . . . . . . . . . . . .171

Forgiveness
*Matthew 18:21–35.* . . . . . . . . . . . . . . . . . . . . . . . . . . . . . . . . . . .177

The Betrayer
*Matthew 26:45b–50.* . . . . . . . . . . . . . . . . . . . . . . . . . . . . . . . . . .185

Loving Our Enemies
*Romans 12:16c–21* . . . . . . . . . . . . . . . . . . . . . . . . . . . . . . . . . . . .193

The Gift of Faith
*Mark 9:24* . . . . . . . . . . . . . . . . . . . . . . . . . . . . . . . . . . . . . . . . . .201

Death Is Swallowed Up in Victory
*1 Corinthians 15:55.* . . . . . . . . . . . . . . . . . . . . . . . . . . . . . . . . . .207

FOR FURTHER READING . . . . . . . . . . . . . . . . . . . . . . . . . . . . . . . .211
SOURCES. . . . . . . . . . . . . . . . . . . . . . . . . . . . . . . . . . . . . . . . . . . . .213

# FOREWORD

Dietrich Bonhoeffer is usually not remembered as a preacher. Although he preached throughout his adult life, there were only two relatively brief periods in which he actually preached every Sunday to a congregation. Both periods were in parishes outside Germany. In 1928, he served as pastoral assistant vicar to the overseas German-speaking congregation in Barcelona, Spain, and then from October 1933 to the spring of 1935 he was the pastor to two German-speaking congregations in London. In addition, he served briefly as a student chaplain in Berlin, and over the years he preached to students, confirmation classes, Sunday schools, and as the occasional guest preacher in churches, and of course he lectured extensively on preaching to his seminarians at the illegal Confessing Church seminary in Finkenwalde from 1935 to 1937. There are seventy-one complete sermons or homilies in the collected works—more, however, if we include the Bible studies and the circular letters he wrote to his students (many of which are indeed sermon-like; they are certainly reflections on Scripture and how he thought it was speaking to the concerns of his students and the issues of the times).

Bonhoeffer believed that preaching—the proclamation of the word of God as revealed in Scripture—was the very heart of Christian life and worship. But it became something more than that after January 30, 1933. During the Nazi years, Bonhoeffer understood his sermons both as a way of confessing his faith and as a prophetic means to call his church and his students to withstand the ideological spirit of the times. In addition, the act of writing and preaching a sermon became for him a source of spiritual discipline and strength—in fact, I do not think that we can understand Bonhoeffer the resistance figure or Bonhoeffer the theologian without understanding Bonhoeffer the preacher.

Simply in terms of their language and theology, many of Bonhoeffer's sermons have a beauty and power of their own. Yet when read in the immediate historical context of when they were preached—whether in Barcelona in 1928 or Berlin in 1933 or London in early 1935 or in Finkenwalde in 1938—they gain an added power and depth, for only then can we begin to understand how Dietrich Bonhoeffer was actively engaging the issues of his times and his church through his preaching.

This volume of sermons selected from the new English translations of the Dietrich Bonhoeffer Works is a significant and long-overdue addition to the literature on Bonhoeffer. Here for the first time is a carefully chosen collection of his sermons, taken from throughout his preaching life, that gives us a full portrait of Bonhoeffer the preacher. Translator Isabel Best, who translated volumes 12 (*Berlin: 1933*) and 13 (*London: 1933–1935*) of the Bonhoeffer Works and contributed to several other volumes, may be considered an expert on the sermons, their nuances and their power. In addition to selecting these sermons, she has provided a helpful introduction to the collection as well as an introduction to each sermon that gives us not only the crucial historical background for each one but also conveys how Bonhoeffer's audiences—whether they were diplomats in Barcelona or young seminarians in Finkenwalde—would have heard and understood his words.

Most importantly, she understands how we—today—might hear these words. This anthology is a powerful illustration of the extent to which these sermons, preached so long ago and in a very different world, nonetheless speak to Christians today. Bonhoeffer's writings are remarkable not only because of his poignant life and powerful message under National Socialism but also because he wrote and spoke in a language that has stood the test of time. He had a gift for expressing the very essence of the Christian message and what it means to live the Christian life of faith in this world, and as a result his writings are still read and pondered by Christians around the world and at all points of the theological spectrum.

Nowhere is that clearer than in his sermons. In October 1933, in his very first sermon in London, Bonhoeffer preached on the relationship between pastor and congregation, and he spoke at length about what it meant to preach:

> This is what makes a sermon something unique in all the world, so completely different from any other kind of speech. When a preacher opens the Bible and interprets the word of God, a mystery takes place, a miracle: the grace of God, who comes down from heaven into our midst and speaks to us, knocks on our door, asks questions, warns us, puts pressure on us, alarms us, threatens us and makes us joyful again, and free, and certain. When the Holy Scriptures are brought to life in a church, the Holy Spirit comes down from the eternal throne into our hearts, and the busy world outside sees nothing and does not realize at all that God could actually be found here.

God is with us. In the midst of our own busy and very troubled world, this book of the sermons of Dietrich Bonhoeffer will be welcomed by those who seek to understand their own path in our own times.

Victoria J. Barnett
General Editor
Dietrich Bonhoeffer Works, English Edition

# EDITOR'S INTRODUCTION

Dietrich Bonhoeffer is considered one of the foremost Protestant theologians of the twentieth century. He was a German Lutheran pastor, best known for his active part in the German Resistance movement that sought to remove Hitler from power during the Second World War. At the time of Bonhoeffer's execution by the Nazis in 1945 at the age of only thirty-nine, he was writing groundbreaking theology. He had also been a university teacher, youth leader, church leader, and director of an "illegal" seminary and other programs to train pastors for the German Protestant Confessing Church under the Nazi regime, and he was active in the international ecumenical movement.

Very close to his heart was the desire to serve his church as pastor of a local congregation. However, he only found time for a year and a half of full-time parish ministry, besides his preparatory year as a pastoral assistant in Barcelona and some months of part-time youth work in churches in Berlin and in Harlem, New York. But the sermons he preached, even as a young pastor and chaplain in his twenties, show how passionately his heart went out to ordinary people and their life struggles and search for meaningful Christian faith. This book is a selection of Bonhoeffer's sermons in English translation. The personal faith they reveal was the foundation for all his work.

Bonhoeffer was born in 1906 in the town of Breslau in the German province of Silesia, now southwestern Poland. He and his twin sister,

Sabine, were among the youngest of eight children. In 1912, their father, Karl Bonhoeffer, became head of the psychiatric clinic at the University of Berlin. Their mother, née Paula von Hase, was a pastor's daughter from a family descended from German nobility. She taught her children at home instead of taking them to church or Sunday school and prepared them herself for confirmation in the Lutheran church.

Bonhoeffer's schooling grounded him in the Latin and Greek classics, which was then still considered the finest education and preparation for university. But as a child in wartime Berlin, he also helped the family's cook search out the best buys in the market, and during holidays in the country, he gathered and dried wild berries and mushrooms and gleaned wheat and had it milled to take home to Berlin. He loved walks and outdoor games and family vacations in the Harz Mountains and along the shores of the Baltic Sea, later taking his confirmands and students there as often as he could. He was also a talented pianist and all his life enjoyed making music with family and friends.

Bonhoeffer's family remained a very strong influence in his life. They exemplified the best qualities of the German upper class, as intellectual and cultural leaders with an abiding sense of responsibility for public affairs and generous hospitality and care for anyone who was in need. This was partly the source of Dietrich Bonhoeffer's early, unquestioning willingness to be a leader in his generation. His family also supported the church resistance under Hitler as well as Dietrich's and his friends' participation in it, and later supported and participated in the conspiracy against Hitler himself.

Toward the end of the First World War, the Bonhoeffers' two oldest sons volunteered to join the infantry. Walter, the younger one of the two, died of wounds received in battle, and the family's grief, especially Bonhoeffer's mother's, was overwhelming. It deeply affected twelve-year-old Dietrich and may have influenced his decision to study theology, in contrast to his older brothers, Karl Friedrich, a physicist and chemist, and Klaus, who was studying law.

Bonhoeffer took his university entrance exams early, at age seventeen, and attended first the University of Tübingen and then the University of Berlin. Times were hard under rampant inflation in Germany, but Bonhoeffer's father was able to send him and Klaus to Rome for the Easter holiday in 1924. They visited the Forum, the Colosseum, and other classic

Roman sites, but what fascinated Bonhoeffer at age eighteen was the world-embracing grandeur and piety of the Roman Catholic Church. He kept going back for another Mass in St. Peter's.

After studying both philosophy and theology, Bonhoeffer earned his doctoral degree in 1927 with a thesis on the church as community, *Sanctorum Communio*. By 1930, he had also written his postdoctoral thesis, titled *Act and Being*, which qualified him to lecture at the University of Berlin. He always he thought for himself and was not intimidated by sometimes strongly critical reactions from his teachers at the university.

Even though Bonhoeffer was well schooled in theology, his friend Franz Hildebrandt, a Luther scholar, told him he needed to know more about Luther and about the Bible. Bonhoeffer went to work on both. He had not been a churchgoer but rather an intellectual studying theology. Now he became a believer—a deeply convinced Christian. From then on he planned not only an academic career but also one in parish ministry, taking the examinations required for ordination by his Prussian regional church. Bonhoeffer's Sunday school class at his local church was so popular that he started an evening seminar for those who outgrew it. In 1928–1929, as pastoral assistant (*Vikar*) in a German-speaking congregation in Barcelona, Spain, he also learned Spanish and got to know different sorts of people.

Bonhoeffer concluded his studies with a year at Union Theological Seminary in New York City, where he was impressed with the social gospel being explored by the students. When Frank Fisher, an African American fellow student, recruited him to work with parish youth at the Abyssinian Baptist Church in Harlem, Bonhoeffer was appalled to discover the discrimination against blacks in American society.

On returning to Germany, he went to hear the Swiss theologian Karl Barth, then teaching at the University of Bonn, whose fundamental criticisms of the church interested Bonhoeffer. Barth likewise found in Bonhoeffer someone who could have a real dialogue with him. Conversations with Barth, over the years that followed, stirred and encouraged Bonhoeffer, though he kept to his own theological path.

Back in Berlin, before he began lecturing at the university, his supervisor recommended Bonhoeffer for ecumenical work, since he had already had some experience in the United States and spoke English. At a meeting of the World Alliance for Promoting International Friendship through the Churches in Cambridge, England, Bonhoeffer was appointed youth secretary for central Europe. He participated in ecumenical organizations for years but always kept a critical stance, challenging them to make public statements only after thorough study, especially after doing their theological homework on what they wanted to say.

As a very young lecturer in theology, Bonhoeffer soon had a growing reputation, with students flocking even to his 8:00 a.m. lectures. He was highly regarded not only as a thinker who dealt with each theological issue in his own way but also as a teacher who was friendly and available in evening seminars every semester and who went on hikes and weekend retreats with his students. Bonhoeffer's third book, *Creation and Fall,* grew out of a semester's lectures and was published in 1933 at the urging of his students.

Meanwhile, in November 1931, he was ordained as a Lutheran pastor and pursued his ministry as chaplain to students at the Technical College in Berlin and by teaching a confirmation class at Zion Church in working-class north Berlin. The following autumn, Bonhoeffer helped to start a club for working-class young adults, some of whom were in the Communist labor movement. But after a few months it had to close, and he helped these young people find shelter from the fighting in the streets.

On January 30, 1933, Adolf Hitler came to power. Hitler never won a majority in a national parliamentary election. His party's plurality in summer 1932 was 38 percent. It was the Republic's elected conservatives, fearing social unrest and disorder in the country and hoping to control Hitler and his popular movement, who appointed him Chancellor, head of the government. But Hitler soon started a step-by-step plan for getting real power into his hands, breaking numerous laws along the way and rapidly dispensing with constitutional rights such as freedom of the press and the right to a fair trial before imprisonment. This would open the way for the concentration camps that followed. Meanwhile, the force of his personality and his gift for public events, such as rallies and torchlight processions, turned public discouragement into hope and enthusiasm.

The German church, following the teachings of Martin Luther, considered the authority of the state as being established by God. While the church alone had authority over its proclamation of the gospel, the state provided the legal order to which the church, along with the rest of society, owed allegiance. But what if an unjust government broke state laws? Hitler wanted either to control the German Protestant Church, particularly its influence on education and its popular youth organizations, or get it out of his way. Every aspect of society had to be bent to his single will as *Führer*. Most church people didn't grasp this at first, and they supported Hitler's National Socialist nation-building program. But fanatical "German Christians" in Hitler's party soon invented an Aryan (Nordic) Christ and wanted ethnic Jews removed from church leadership and eventually from its membership, just as they were being driven out of the civil service. For Dietrich Bonhoeffer, this discrimination immediately came close to home. The mother of his Lutheran pastor friend Franz Hildebrandt was Jewish, as was the father of his sister Sabine's husband, a professor of law. When Bonhoeffer and Hildebrandt both applied for pastorates in Berlin, Bonhoeffer realized that Hildebrandt would not be accepted, so he withdrew his own application. He eventually helped both Hildebrandt and his sister's family to emigrate to England.

Even more important to Bonhoeffer was the fact that Jesus was a Jew, and his beliefs that the Old Testament is an integral part of the Bible and that the very act of discrimination is unchristian according to the New Testament. In April 1933, he published an essay that became famous—"The Church and the Jewish Question." It declared boldly that the church must stand up against interference by the state, must aid the victims crushed by the state's relentless wheel of oppression, and ultimately must seize and stop the wheel itself. In Hitler's Germany, the victims included not only ethnic Jews and political opponents of the regime but also mentally ill and disabled people, gypsies, homosexuals, and other minorities.

Hitler illegally called a church election so the "German Christians" could put compliant church leaders in place, an election he won through pressure by local Nazi organizations. Bonhoeffer and his students and friends, calling themselves the "Young Reformation," had campaigned in vain for opposing candidates. Bonhoeffer then helped Martin Niemöller to form a Pastors' Emergency League for mutual support, which soon had thousands of members. Crude and inept "German Christian" statements did offend many. With other theologians, Bonhoeffer worked on a new confession of faith and a new catechism for those who put Christ first, ahead of patriotism.

In the midst of all this, he was offered the joint pastorate of two German-speaking congregations in London. The situation in the German Protestant Church was becoming very complex, and Bonhoeffer hoped the time abroad would give him a chance to think things through. However, while in London he spent much of his time on the telephone, encouraging like-minded friends back home to stand firm. During this time, Karl Barth and others put together the famous Declaration of Barmen, which explained the ways the German Protestant Church had become anti-Christian. Following the publication of the declaration, crucial opposition church assemblies were held, and the German Confessing Church was founded. For his part, Bonhoeffer met with other German pastors in England, and eventually most of their German-speaking congregations declared their secession from the established German Protestant Church and solidarity with the Confessing Church.

None of this activity stopped Bonhoeffer from ministering to his two small churches, however, and he especially enjoyed reviving their Sunday schools and choirs and holding Christmas pageants. His sermons were always carefully prepared, and while not explicitly political, they revealed his deep concern for what was going on in Germany. In London, he also found that he was well placed to inform ecumenical colleagues in the churches outside Germany about what was really happening under Hitler, especially to the church. Bonhoeffer's most important contact and friend was George Bell, bishop of Chichester and head of the Ecumenical Council on Life and Work (of the Churches). As bishop, Bell had resources to help German refugees who were beginning to arrive in London. However, despite Bell's support, most others in ecumenical office showed little sympathy for Bonhoeffer's viewpoint that the Confessing Church was the real Protestant church in Germany, rather than the unchristian, government-approved German Protestant Church.

Bonhoeffer took the Sermon on the Mount seriously, and he longed to found a Christian community that would seek to live according to its commandments. An opportunity came in 1935 when he was urgently called back to Germany to help the Confessing Church train its pastors. At Finkenwalde, a country manor near the Baltic port of Stettin, Bonhoeffer set up a Confessing Church seminary. For two years, he directed five semester courses, with the able help of seminarians who stayed, especially Eberhard

Bethge, who became his close friend. The "House of Brethren," the small spiritual community they established at Finkenwalde, provided continuity of leadership and a space for Bonhoeffer to try out his ideas, later described in his book *Life Together*.

Meanwhile, with help from the state, the established German Protestant Church began to crush the Confessing Church. New laws made the work at seminaries like Finkenwalde illegal and forbade Confessing pastors, on pain of prison, to raise funds, circulate publications, and even announce names for intercessory prayer. Bonhoeffer actively involved his students in resisting these rules and in ministering to many small rural parishes, which they sometimes reached by bicycle, that could no longer support pastors. Another book, *Discipleship* (first published in English as *The Cost of Discipleship*) took shape out of his lectures and discussions with the Finkenwalde students.

After the Finkenwalde seminary was closed by the Gestapo in 1937, Bonhoeffer and Bethge carried on pastoral training with small groups of students in village parishes further east, in Pomerania. Here they also managed five semester courses, under increasing difficulties. In the end, most of the students were arrested afterward or drafted into the army, and the majority died during the war. Determined to keep in touch pastorally with those who survived and even with widows of the fallen, Bonhoeffer circulated an illegal newsletter in hand-addressed envelopes. He had by now been forbidden to lecture or to publish in Germany and could stay in Berlin only at his parents' home, but he remained involved in the struggles of his colleagues in the Confessing Church. He also accepted a much less comfortable lifestyle than the one to which he was accustomed, in order to give up much of his income to help the church, his colleagues, and their families who were in need.

Bonhoeffer himself was eligible for the draft. Pastors were not exempt, and the Nazi penalty for refusing to serve was death. Bonhoeffer felt compelled to refuse. Paul Lehmann of Union Seminary and other American friends tried to save him, as war approached in 1939, by arranging for him to be offered teaching positions in the United States. He agreed to consider a one-year appointment and traveled by ship to New York in June, but he returned to Germany a few weeks later, convinced that his vocation lay in his homeland, despite the dangers.

When war broke out in August 1939, Bonhoeffer was still working in Pomerania. He applied for a military chaplaincy but was turned down. His brother-in-law, Hans von Dohnanyi, a brilliant lawyer who had worked in the justice department where he secretly documented every Nazi violation of Germany's laws, was now an assistant to Admiral Canaris, head of German Military Intelligence. Canaris and his colleagues arranged to have Bonhoeffer join the military intelligence service, within which a group was secretly planning to have Hitler arrested and put on trial for multiple offenses, including war crimes in Poland and elsewhere.

A number of high-ranking military officers objected to Hitler's conduct of the war and were in the conspiracy to take power immediately and sue for peace with the Allies. They wanted Bonhoeffer to use his ecumenical contacts to approach the Allied governments, especially Britain and the United States, regarding peace terms and willingness to allow time for a coup d'état. Canaris would send him on "intelligence-gathering" missions abroad in order to meet with these contacts. It was late 1940 by the time they had Bonhoeffer in place, based in Munich but hosted for a time by a Benedictine monastery in the Bavarian Alps, where he became one of the first modern German Lutheran pastors to have cordial and meaningful contacts with Catholic churchmen. Because Hitler was constantly shifting his military chiefs around and micromanaging their work, the plan to have him arrested became no longer possible. The objective of the plot then became assassination.

At this time, Bonhoeffer was writing a book on ethics. It was never finished, but we know the soul-searching he went through over committing himself to this conspiracy. He seriously believed it was against the Sermon on the Mount to participate in taking anyone's life, but to allow Hitler to continue his regime and his war, in which many thousands were already dying, was to deny that Germany was committing mass murder, and as a citizen Bonhoeffer shared in responsibility for it. He could help "stop the wheel" of oppression by taking upon himself the sin of disobeying the Bible and God's commandment. In his sermon on November 4, 1934, he had already spoken of "the love that . . . even gives up its own salvation in order to bring it to brothers and sisters. . . ."

Once Bonhoeffer decided that this was what he was called to do, he accepted the conditions of being a conspirator, including deception when necessary. He kept his involvement secret from most friends and colleagues, especially those in the Confessing Church, so that innocents could not be accused because of their association with him. On the face of it, the conspiracy represented treason, as did some of Bonhoeffer's own actions, notably a meeting with Bishop Bell in 1942 in Sweden; Bell was by then a member of the House of Lords. Bonhoeffer also undertook trips to the Vatican in Italy and to Norway and Switzerland, and if he had the opportunity, he continued to help Jews who were to be deported to camps to escape from Germany.

Though no signs reached the conspirators from abroad that any Allied government was willing to work with them, they remained hopeful and patient and maintained detailed plans with the utmost discretion. Still, the conspiracy had to keep regrouping after several different assassination attempts failed, including an aborted suicide bombing. The last attempt was made on July 20, 1944, when the bomb famously planted by Count von Stauffenberg in Hitler's headquarters went off but failed to kill Hitler.

By then Bonhoeffer and Dohnanyi were both in prison. They were arrested in March 1943 on charges of treason not directly connected with the plot; it remained undiscovered until it was carried out. In Bonhoeffer's case the charges included evasion of military service. The interrogations produced little evidence and were eventually suspended, but both men were kept in prison. Dohnanyi was tortured by being denied needed medical care. Bonhoeffer was only threatened with torture. He was always courteous and respectful even when his judges were not. He had been well coached by Dohnanyi, and he never revealed anything that would endanger fellow conspirators.

During his year and a half in Tegel military prison, Bonhoeffer quietly maintained a discipline of physical exercise and prayer, using the Moravian book of daily Bible texts—his childhood governess had been a devout Moravian. He read widely and he also spent time writing, especially letters. He was treated with contempt at first, until the prison staff discovered that his mother's cousin was the city commander of Berlin. From then on he was allowed regular visits from family and friends. He received care for illness in the infirmary and was soon allowed to help out there. Staff and fellow prisoners alike came to him with pastoral needs; thus, along with official prison chaplains, he quietly helped to minister to this grim community. Bonhoeffer tried to help in cases that he found especially unjust, and he got to know people he would never have met socially. Three of his guards became fast friends, and they smuggled many letters in and out for him uncensored.

Bonhoeffer's dear friend Eberhard Bethge was now a soldier on the Italian front. Their correspondence, later published in *Letters and Papers from Prison*, is the source for our knowledge of the new theology Bonhoeffer was developing. He envisioned a new church after the war that would not reach people by exploiting their weakness and suffering but rather speak to them as adults, in their strength. For Bonhoeffer, God does not meet humankind in the gap where modern science ends but rather in all our understanding, in all that we achieve. The concept of "religionless Christianity" recognized that much "church religion" had become meaningless to contemporary people. The church had to interpret its faith in new ways.

Not long before his arrest, Bonhoeffer had become engaged to eighteen-year-old Maria von Wedemeyer, but because of her youth they had not yet made wedding plans. She made many brave visits to Bonhoeffer in Tegel prison and moved into his parents' home in Berlin to help out, especially with the efforts to support family members in prison. After Bonhoeffer was moved to a Gestapo prison where letters were forbidden, Maria nevertheless managed to receive three more from him through the actions of sympathetic staff; his famous poem, "By Powers of Good," was enclosed in one of these letters. She was the inspiration for him to begin writing poetry. Their touching correspondence has been translated in the volume *Love Letters from Cell 92*.

The end of the war brought chaos, with massive bombing of civilians in Berlin and other cities. In February 1945, the Gestapo headquarters was destroyed by a direct hit, which Bonhoeffer experienced packed into the underground bunker with other inmates. From the reports of fellow prisoners who survived, we now know what happened after the bombing. But Bonhoeffer's family and friends knew nothing until long after his death. He was deported to the concentration camp at Buchenwald, where he was confined in a cellar with other political prisoners. At the time, he was still working on the manuscript of his new book on theology, and it subsequently was lost. Always he is described as a calming influence, serene in his faith and kind to everyone. One of his last acts was to lead fellow deportees in worship, at their request, on the Sunday after Easter.

One of Hitler's last acts, in his bunker on April 5, 1945, was to order specifically the executions of the conspirators around Admiral Canaris. These now included Bonhoeffer's brother Klaus and brother-in-law Rüdiger Schleicher, who had become involved at later stages. They were shot in Berlin; Von Dohnanyi was shot in the concentration camp Sachsenhausen. Bonhoeffer was taken to another concentration camp, Flossenbürg, where a sham trial was held for him, Canaris, and other conspirators. On April 9, 1945, they were hanged, cremated, and buried in a mass grave.

In postwar Germany, Bonhoeffer was considered by many to be a traitor to his country, because of his resistance activities and his execution as a conspirator against Hitler. But more than sixty years later he has come to be regarded as a martyr by countless Christians in Germany and around the world; that is, he was a witness to Jesus Christ at the cost of his own life, an example of courageous faith in action, a Christian leader who lived the ethical convictions that he proclaimed.

A reader of Bonhoeffer's sermons should expect to be challenged in his or her own ethical assumptions. For Bonhoeffer, the church was to proclaim the will of God as clearly as possible and with the greatest possible relevance to what was going on in people's lives, right now. One might study systems of ethics or catechisms from the past, but what God expects of Christians at any particular moment is to be found less in set rules than directly in the current moment itself and God's judgment upon it as revealed in Scripture. As Christians, we must read the Bible not only "for" ourselves, for nourishment and encouragement, but also "against" ourselves at times, to hear what God in Christ is really saying.

However, Bonhoeffer did not thunder threats of hell at the congregations to whom he preached. As Bonhoeffer scholar Keith Clements has pointed out, he did not shake a moralizing finger at them from his pulpit on high, but used the word "we," including himself on the same level as his hearers in terms of standing under God's judgment. Even though he was brought up with the aristocratic attitude of benevolence toward those who were poor and in need of help, as a young man Bonhoeffer in his twenties allowed his experience of other cultures and levels of society, of learning to honor human beings as he found them, to enter his heart. He had learned from the Gospels to see the need for repentance in everyone, perhaps especially the church and its leaders.

And he believed that we must learn to know and love the world in which we live, the earth that God loves to which we are to bring the message of love as well as judgment. For him, to preach a sermon was to make a way for Christ to enter the world in which his hearers were actually living. In the years between world wars—when people were trying to heal from the damage the First World War had done; struggling in poverty; pessimistic and distrustful of new and different ideas, movements, and forms of government that were emerging in the postwar chaos—Bonhoeffer spent much time listening to the people. He loved to get his students or confirmands out in the country for a walk or share a meal with them and hear what they were thinking. Often it was harder to begin a trusting pastoral relationship with their parents and with older parishioners who had suffered so much, who through war had had to give up their beloved world of the past and many former guideposts of their lives. Where was God? they asked. How could a supposedly loving Lord allow so much to be destroyed?

While Bonhoeffer mourned along with his family and friends the past good that had been lost, he fervently believed in the future. He believed the church could change and take up new tasks in a future after World War II, when all the world would strive to make and keep peace. However, in order to accomplish this, the churches had to repent that they had withdrawn and encouraged people to turn inward and to reject the wartime world of violence and suffering. Bonhoeffer believed that when Christians grow up and become able to face a changed society with all its evil as well as good, when we go out to meet that world "come of age," God is with us and in fact goes ahead of us.

Bonhoeffer himself set a Christlike example in the way he treated people wherever he was, even in the military prison and the concentration camp. But he did not preach to people there unless he was asked and unless he felt sure that he would not be taking advantage of them in their state of loss, confinement, weakness, and discouragement. The church must never do that. Bonhoeffer once said that preaching a sermon was like holding out a juicy red apple to a child and saying, "Do you want this?" The child must be in a position to refuse or accept, otherwise Christ's gift is not really a gift.

The sermons in this book were among those carefully preserved after his death, mostly as handwritten manuscripts but sometimes typed up by friends. A number of the London sermons were preserved because he sent them to a friend, Elisabeth Bornkamm, and they became part of her estate. All Bonhoeffer's surviving handwritten manuscripts were later patiently deciphered by Eberhard Bethge and prepared for publication—a true labor of love. These sermons were written in the midst of an amazingly brief and busy life, with care and concentration and often many self-corrections. The last few sermons in this book appeared in Bonhoeffer's newsletter to his former students, to encourage them in their own efforts as parish preachers.

In the decades since his death, some sermons, often excerpts, appeared in early translations into English and other languages. Beginning in the 1990s, a new English translation has been made of Bonhoeffer's entire works, based on his annotated complete works in German published by Christian Kaiser Verlag, Gütersloh, and has been published by Fortress Press, Minneapolis (see page 211). This is the source of the translations offered here. As with any book in translation (including the Bible), a reader in English must make some allowances for the fact that the author belonged to another time and a different culture from our own. In this case, the various translators themselves belong to different cultures and have brought their wealth of individual gifts and sensitivities to their work, so that the writing style may seem a bit different between one sermon and another.

For a twenty-first-century translator of Bonhoeffer, what we now call "inclusive language" becomes an issue. Though important issues in the early twentieth century included the right for women to vote and to have fair treatment as workers, the honoring of equality between women and men in language had not yet been elaborated. In German as in English, "he" was the default gender, for God and for any person not specifically identified as female. These new sermon translations as published in the Complete Works have preserved Bonhoeffer's now dated language. We know, however, that Bonhoeffer valued and honored women as members of his family, friends, coworkers, and students, although no established church in Germany at that time ordained women to the ministry. Therefore, I have felt that he would want to speak to women of the future in language that we would find respectful of us. This is consistent with his vision of a new church that would treat people as adults and also with the fact that we now have inclusive translations of the Bible. Since inclusive language is still a work in progress, however, my efforts will no doubt go too far for some readers and not far enough for others; I ask only that they be received in the ecumenical spirit in which they are offered.

As a teacher of future preachers, Bonhoeffer devoted time to making written comments on students' manuscripts, but he did not allow negative criticism in class when a student had just presented an early effort at a sermon. The future preacher too must feel accepted, must receive Christ's hope and love, in order to go forward and take them to others. Wherever that person's ministry might lead in the future, Christ's church-community must surround with prayer, sustain and uphold his servant, beginning in the seminary.

In preparing this book of Bonhoeffer's sermons, I too have felt surrounded and sustained by the community of those who devote themselves to Bonhoeffer's legacy. I especially want to thank Victoria J. Barnett, who wrote the foreword to this book. She is the general editor with whom I worked for many years as a translator for the Dietrich Bonhoeffer Works in English, and along with Clifford J. Green, executive director of the DBWE, gave me much friendly help and encouragement in working on this collection of sermons. I am honored, through them, to be associated with the International Bonhoeffer Society. I also thank my translator colleagues, especially Nancy Lukens and Martin Rumscheidt, for their friendship, and the editors I worked with on DBWE, Keith Clements, John de Gruchy, and Larry Rasmussen. My thanks to the publishing team at Fortress Press, especially Susan Johnson and Marissa Wold, with whom I worked most closely. Fortress Press made most of the sermon texts available to me, having already published them in DBWE. And I thank and bless my husband, Tom Best, who gave of his editorial and computer experience, his time, and his love. This is the kind of support that allows dreams such as this one to come true.

A sermon is an event that takes place in real time, in the actual presence of people. Bonhoeffer believed that, through the sermon, Christ is seeking entry into the world; in such a moment, the incarnation can happen anew. Bonhoeffer would pray that his words might let it happen for you, wherever you are.

# God Is with Us

## Barcelona, Quasimodogeniti
## (First Sunday after Easter), April 15, 1928

———— ⫷◉⫸ ————

Bonhoeffer preached this sermon and the next while serving as a pastoral assistant (German: *Vikar*) in a Lutheran congregation in Barcelona, Spain, as part of his training for ordination. Even though he was speaking in German to German-speaking people, Bonhoeffer found preparing and delivering his first sermons challenging. But he was eager for the experience, and his supervising pastor was happy to let him preach frequently. On this first Sunday after Easter, the twenty-two-year-old preacher began with thoughts of the ancient world, the study of which was then not far behind him: the world of legends and myths, in which most people traveled on foot and might meet divine beings on the road. It was also the world of the Bible: the Old Testament, which tells of people who had such encounters with God, and the New Testament when Jesus walked the roads of Palestine with his disciples. But as the congregation that walked with Bonhoeffer through this sermon discovered, the possibility of a walk with God exists still, even today.

Matthew 28:20: *Remember, I am with you always,*
*to the end of the world.*

Fairy tales and legends from the oldest times tell of the days when God walked among human beings. Those were splendid times, when one met a wanderer on the road who asked for lodging, then at home one recognized in this simple man the Lord God and was richly rewarded. Those were wonderful times, when God and human beings were still so close that people could walk and talk with God. Indeed, those were the days, recounted only by fairy tales and legends, that spoke of all the slumbering, secret human hopes as if they had already become reality. The beginning of our own Bible also relates how the Lord God walked about in the garden of paradise in the evening and lived and conversed with human beings. Probably very few peoples do not have similar stories. Blessed were those people permitted to experience those times when God and human beings were still close.

How quickly things changed. Our Bible recounts the story of the fall as the turning point in history. Human beings were driven from the garden in which they lived with God; now they lived separated from God in guilt and unhappiness that increased from generation to generation. The rift between God and human beings deepened. Humanity sank into the night. And as long as human beings can remember, they know only the night, the time when God no longer moves freely among us, and many look longingly back to the primal age of the fairy tale, to paradise, as if to a lost home they themselves never even knew. Or people of powerful hope speak and spoke about coming days, when God would once more dwell among human beings, when the kingdom of God would be established on earth. God and human beings somehow belong together, and God will return and be their guest.

There was one day in human history when this hope had to be radically demolished, a day on which people had to become aware of the eternal distance between human beings and God—the day humanity raised its hand against the God dwelling among them and nailed Jesus Christ to the cross—Good Friday. But there was also a day of divine response to human action, a day when God took up dwelling among human beings anew and for all eternity, the day when the outstretched but unholy hand of humanity was filled, against all hope, with divine grace, the day when Jesus Christ was raised, Easter. Remember, I am with you . . . that is the Easter message, not the distant, but the nearby God, that is Easter.

A searching, an anxious groping and questioning for divine things permeates our own age. A great loneliness has come upon our age, the kind of loneliness found only in a godforsaken age. The enormous distress of isolation and homelessness has come upon the colossal, wild activity of countless masses of people in the midst of our big cities. Yet the yearning grows for the time when once again God might abide among human beings, when God might be found. A thirst for contact with divine things has come upon people, a burning thirst demanding to be quenched. Currently a great many remedies are being offered for sale that promise to quench this thirst in a radical fashion and for which hundreds of thousands of hands greedily reach out—in the midst of this wild activity and marketing frenzy with new means and ways, we find the One Word of Jesus Christ: Remember, I am here. . . . You don't need to search very far at all, nor to question or engage in all sorts of mysterious activity. I *am* here; that is, Jesus does not promise his coming, does not prescribe paths that might take a person to him, but simply says: I am here; whether we see Jesus or not, feel him or not, want him or not—none of this makes any difference over against the fact that Jesus is here with us, that he is simply wherever we are, and that we can do absolutely nothing. I am with you always . . .

But if all this is indeed true, if Jesus really is with us, then God is also with us wherever we are, and we are no longer abandoned, homeless, lonely, then—let us follow this line of thinking to its conclusion—then the age of the legends has become reality again, and God is living among us. The only important thing now is to keep our eyes open to see where we find God—as was true for those people in the legend who had to recognize the Lord God in the foreign wanderer. God wants to be among us—do we want to make a liar of God by not believing? God is still with human beings despite Good Friday—Remember, I am with you always. . . .

But before we all start rejoicing too quickly, one serious reflection. What does it really mean to say that Jesus or God is with us? that God is in the world? Where and how are we aware of that? God lives, lives for the world, the world is filled with God, is transfigured, is meaningful, *sub specie aeternitatis* [from the viewpoint of the Eternal]—that was the Easter message. But now we ask further: Where can I sense something of this divine fullness in the world and in my own life? And we answer that today, too, God is still walking among us; today, too, we can speak with God; we are together with God, walk down the street with God, encounter God in the foreigner on the road, the beggar at the door. The world is God's world; wherever we go, we encounter God, and Jesus, the Resurrected, is with us. Remember, I am with you. . . .

But isn't all this merely metaphorical language? What can we possibly mean by saying that Jesus is with us? Isn't that merely an approximate, undefined feeling?

Not at all. It is completely clear. Jesus is with us in his words, and that means clearly and unequivocally that he is in that which he wants and in that which he thinks about us. He is with us with his will, in his words, and only in our dealings with Jesus' words do we sense his presence. The word, however, is the clearest and most unequivocal means of expression by which thinking beings connect. If we have a person's word, then we know that person's will; indeed, we know the whole person. If we have Jesus' word, then we know his will and his entire person. Jesus' word is always one and the same and yet is also always different. It tells us: You are standing under God's love, God is holy, and you should also be holy; God wants to give you the Holy Spirit that you might also be holy.

And it says this in different ways to every person in every moment. God's word is one thing to a child and another to a man, one thing to a boy and a girl, something different to a man and a woman, and yet there is no age, no moment in life when Jesus's word does not have something to say to us. Our entire life stands under that word and is sanctified by that word. From baptism to the grave, the word of the church accompanies us, places us under the assurance of the word: Remember, I am with you.

As a symbol of this situation, the church places the decisive stages of a person's life under the church's own proclamation. To young children, Jesus' word is already proclaiming how God's grace comes before all human actions; it then speaks to children of the sanctity of their parents' love. To older children at play it speaks about God's truthfulness, about God's seriousness and goodness, about service as Christ's followers, about heroic deeds and knightly deeds. To the young adult it speaks about the sanctity of the divine commission and about eternal goals, opening that person's eyes to the glory of the world, to a yearning to roam beyond the temporal; and the word tells of the purity of God and of the heart. To young people it speaks about much joy and cheerfulness, though also about what they owe to the prospect of marriage and parenthood. To mature adults the word speaks about the seriousness of work, about fate and guilt, about responsibility and loyalty and about God's will that each of us might take hold of our own life and shape it. The word also tells how God has sanctified motherhood and fatherhood. To the elderly it speaks about that world from which death separates us and about the last things. And yet it speaks one and the same thing to both the young and the elderly, namely, that God loves you and is with you, depend on it. And the other thing: God is holy, and you should also be holy; the word about God's ineffable compassion is spoken to people of all ages, as is the word about God's seriousness and beneficence in every moment of human life.

Remember, I am with you. . . . This applies *whether we want it to or not.* Are there any moments when we might not want it? Moments when God's presence is irksome to us? We all know there are such moments; these are the moments of God's judgment upon us. God is with us—suddenly the consequences of this word become transparent. If God is with us, and yet we are not with God—what happens then? Let us once more follow this notion in all seriousness all the way to its conclusion. No respected man of the world, no prophet, no prince of the earth comes to us and abides perpetually with us; but the prince of life and of the whole world is with us with his judgment and his claim on us. Can we do justice to this claim? And even if we wanted to revolt or resist, God is there always, to the end of the world. The blissful notion that God once again dwells among human beings, that God once again lends meaning to human life, that the world is full of God, this notion becomes threatening and frightening precisely because it demands responsibility. Our life and action are not to be meaningless; but what if we live our lives in apathy and thoughtlessness? Every age in life has its divine destiny. What if we ignore that destiny? Every moment of our life is related to God. What if we wish to sense nothing of that relationship?

Thus a heavy burden is suddenly placed upon us, once we take seriously the statement "Remember, I am with you. . . ." But the God who assigns also gives and forgives. Where God's judgment is, there also is God's grace. Did God come into the world and live life in the world in order to ruin that world? No. God wants to give to the life of the world as much of the divine life as the world wants; God wants to draw close, into blessed partnership, those who are lonely and all who seek life with God. "I am with you always. . . ." God lives, lives in the world, lives for the world, lends it meaning and life, makes it our home, gives our own life a relationship to eternity and a closeness to God—that is the grace we take with us from this passage.

But one more thing. One profound element in the fairy tale we mentioned earlier is that it has God move about among human beings as a human being. This promise, too, has become a reality. Jesus Christ is not only with us in lonely hours; Jesus Christ also encounters us in every step we take, in every person we meet. Remember, I am with you . . . Jesus Christ, God himself, speaks to us from every human being; the other person, this enigmatic, impenetrable You, is God's claim on us; indeed, it is the holy God in person whom we encounter. God's claim is made on us in the wanderer on the street, the beggar at the door, the sick person at the door of the church, though certainly no less in every person near to us, in every person with whom we are together daily. "Just as you did it to one of the least of these, you did it to me," Jesus says [Matt. 25:4].

I am for you, and you are for me is God's claim, God's very self; in this recognition, our gaze opens to the fullness of divine life in the world. Now life in the human community acquires its divine meaning. This community itself is one of the forms of God's revelation. God is with us as long as there is community. The most profound meaning of our ties to social life is that through it we are tied all the more securely to God. Remember, I am with you always, to the *end of the world*. Again we hear about the last things. "I am the first and the last" [Isaiah 41:4; Revelation 1:17], "Jesus Christ is the same yesterday and today and forever" [Hebrews 13:8]; such are the words we hear. Jesus is Lord of the ages and is always with his own, even when things are difficult, and will abide with us; that is our comfort. If tribulation and anxiety come upon us, Jesus is with us and leads us over into God's eternal kingdom. Jesus Christ is the breadth of our life and of our community. Jesus Christ is with us to the end of the world. This is the gift of Easter.

# Waiting at the Door

## Barcelona, First Sunday in Advent, December 2, 1928

———⇒«◉»⇐———

We know from a letter Bonhoeffer wrote to his family at this time that he was still having to work hard all the preceding week on his sermons. But he had become popular as a preacher. Attendance at Sunday services increased, and the senior pastor stopped announcing ahead of time which of them would be preaching. On this occasion, he was absent, and Bonhoeffer was responsible for the entire service.

Bonhoeffer begins with words about waiting, a traditional Advent theme, before speaking of the struggle against evil in the world. Here he was thinking back to his recent sermon on the Day of Remembrance for the dead, when his text was "Love is as strong as death," from Song of Solomon 8:6b. That sermon is not included in this book, but two sermons for later Remembrance Days are (see 101 and 207). He also returns to the motif of his sermon on April 15 of Jesus as a wanderer on the road (see 1). His hearers would have been familiar with this theme from German Christmas legends and carols, with the Christ Child calling, "Let me in, children, the winter is so cold, open your doors to me! Don't let me freeze."

Bonhoeffer also quotes from two well-loved Advent hymns, including "Lift Up Your Heads, O Gates," based on Psalm 24. At the end, he returns to the theme of waiting, and concludes with the traditional Advent refrain "Come soon, Lord Jesus" (Revelation 22:20).

Revelation 3:20 RSV: *Behold, I stand at the door, and knock.*

Celebrating Advent means being able to wait. Waiting, however, is an art our impatient age has forgotten. It wants to pick the ripe fruit even though it has hardly finished planting the seedling. But greedy eyes are all too often deceived because the apparently precious fruit is still green on the inside, and disrespectful hands ungratefully throw aside that which has disappointed them so. Those unfamiliar with the bitter bliss of waiting, of doing without while maintaining hope, will never experience the full blessing of fulfillment. Those who do not know what it feels like to wrestle anxiously with the most profound questions of life, of one's own life, and then to keep watch in anticipation and yearning until the truth is unveiled— cannot imagine how glorious is the moment when clarity emerges; and for those who do not know what it is like to court the friendship, the love of another person, to open up one's soul to the soul of that other person until it comes, till it arrives—for those people the profound blessing of the life of two intertwined souls will remain eternally concealed. We must wait for the greatest, most profound, most gentle things in life; nothing happens in a rush, but only according to the divine laws of germinating, growing, and becoming.

Of course, not everyone can wait, especially those who are sated, satisfied, and disrespectful. Only people who carry a certain restlessness around with them can wait, and people who look up reverently to the One who is great in the world. Hence only those whose souls give them no peace are able to celebrate Advent, who feel poor and incomplete and who sense something of the greatness of what is coming, before which one can only bow in humble timidity, in anticipation till God inclines toward us—the Holy One, God in the child in the manger. God is coming, the Lord Jesus is coming, Christmas is coming, rejoice, O Christendom! This is what we hear today again for the first time. And already we want to hear in the distance the song of angels about God's glory and about peace on earth; but it is not yet time, we must still learn to wait, and to wait properly. Make this time of waiting into a blessed time of preparation.

When Advent comes again and we hear and sing the traditional Christmas carols, a peculiar feeling secretly comes over us, and even the hardest hearts are softened; we sense something we felt as children when we were away from our mother, something like homesickness for past times, distant places, and yet such a blissful homesickness, without hardness, without grimness. And something in us yearns outward, farther than past years, farther than our childhood home, indeed, outward to our home beyond the clouds, to the eternal house of our Father. Something of the curse of homelessness descends upon us, the curse weighing upon the world itself, the curse of eternally having to sojourn without goal and without end. All around us we see wintry death and coldness, and we see within ourselves something uncanny, looking at us from a thousand terrible eyes; evil, evil that repeatedly banishes us to the world, evil we cannot get beyond no matter how hard we try. The two most real realities, about which we have spoken on the last two Sundays of the old church year, now, at the beginning of the new year, lay themselves anew and with all their enormous weight upon the soul: evil and death. Who can offer help here? Who can offer redemption?

The one who redeems us from evil and from death should be our Lord. A groan wrests itself from our breast, Come, God, Lord Jesus Christ, come into our world, into our homelessness, into our sin, into our death, come, you yourself, and share with us, be a human being as we are and conquer for us. Come into the midst of my evil, into my daily disloyalty, participate in my sin, the sin that I hate and yet cannot turn loose, be my brother, you holy Jesus, become my brother—in the realm of evil and suffering and death. Come along into my death, into my sufferings and struggles, and make me holy and pure despite this evil, despite death. And today his soft voice answers us: Behold, I stand at the door, and knock. And do we not tremble at this word? The spirit we have summoned, the spirit of the redemption of the world, is not far; indeed, he is standing at the door, knocking, has already been standing there a long time, waiting for the door to be opened. The Lord is coming, God is coming, coming to us.

Admittedly it is a soft voice we hear speaking there, and few people hear it. The market barkers and advertisers extol their rotten wares too loudly and noisily; everyone wants to go through the door first, hastily and impatiently. And woe to those who do not pay attention to these gates, lest all sorts of well-groomed rabble fill up the house. And amid all that pushes itself upon us, the royal sojourner stands there patiently, unrecognized and quiet. That sojourner knocks very quietly. Can you hear it? Do you think the wanderer is not knocking on your door? Ah, let all these loud voices first be quiet and then listen closely to see whether there is not also someone knocking on the door of your heart, he who would make your heart his own, who would be your quiet guest. Jesus is knocking at your door and at mine. We must but open our ears and listen within ourselves. Jesus is coming most assuredly. Coming in this year too, coming also to us.

When early Christianity spoke about the return of the Lord Jesus, it was thinking first of all about a great day of judgment. And as alien to Christmas as this thought may seem to us, it derives from early Christianity and should be taken seriously. When we hear Jesus knocking at our door, the first thing that happens is that our conscience awakens: Are we properly prepared? Is our heart capable of becoming his dwelling place? Hence the time of Advent becomes a time of introspection for us. "With seriousness, O human souls, prepare your hearts," as the old hymn goes. It is quite peculiar how calmly we contemplate God's coming, whereas earlier peoples trembled before the day of God and the world quaked when Jesus Christ walked among us. It is so peculiar because we so often encounter God's footprints in the world together with the footprints of human suffering, of the cross on Golgotha. We have grown so accustomed to the idea of divine love and of the coming at Christmas that we no longer sense the awe that God's coming should awaken in us. We have become dulled to the message; we only register what is welcome in it, what is pleasant, forgetting the powerful seriousness of the fact that the God of the worlds is approaching us on our small earth and now makes claims on us. God's coming is truly not merely a message of joy, but first of all horrifying news for every person with a conscience.

And not until we have perceived the terror of the matter can we then also appreciate this incomparable act of beneficence. God is coming, into the midst of evil, into death, judging evil in us and in the world. And by judging it, God loves us, purifies us, sanctifies us, comes to us with grace and love. God makes us happy as only children can be happy; God is with us and now intends to be with us always, regardless of where we are, in our sin, in our suffering and death. We are no longer alone; God is with us, we are no longer homeless, a bit of our eternal home has entered into us. This is why we adults can rejoice so profoundly in our hearts around the Christmas tree, more perhaps even than children can; we sense that God's goodness is once again coming near to us. We remember everything of God's goodness that we encountered during the past year, and we sense something of the strange home about which this strange tree is speaking. Jesus is coming in both judgment and grace. Behold, I stand at the door . . . Lift up your heads, O ye gates.

Christ is standing at the door, knocking. You are searching for him, would perhaps give anything to have him with you sometime, genuinely, actually with you, not just inwardly, but physically, in reality. But how could this be possible? Jesus was familiar with human beings and with their need to see, their desire to touch, and so he spoke of this need in a grand parable about how from day to day and in actual reality he is still wandering about on earth, and how we can indeed have him with us if we really want to have him and not some image conjured by our imagination. One day, at the Last Judgment, he will separate the sheep from the goats, and to those on his right he will say: Come, you that are blessed . . . "for I was hungry. . . ." To the astonished question . . . "just as you did it to one of the least of these. . . ." But here we are confronted with the terrifying reality; Jesus is at the door, knocking, in reality, asking you for help in the figure of the beggar, in the figure of the degenerate soul in shabby clothes, encountering you in every person you meet. Christ walks the earth as long as there are people, as your neighbor, as the person through whom God summons you, addresses you, makes claims on you. That is the most serious and most blessed part of the Advent message. Christ is at the door; he lives in the form of those around us. Will you close the door or open it for him?

It may seem odd to see Christ in a countenance so close to us, but he did indeed say it. Those who avoid the serious reality of the Advent message cannot speak about Christ coming into their hearts. Those who do not learn from Christ's own coming that we are all brothers and sisters through Christ, through God, have understood nothing of the meaning of that coming.

Christ is knocking; but it is not yet Christmas, nor is it yet the great, final Advent, the final coming of Christ. And through all the Advents of our lives, all the Advents we celebrate, runs a yearning for that final Advent, the Advent of the words, "See, I am making all things new." The time of Advent is a time of waiting, our entire life is a time of Advent, a time of waiting for that final time when there will be a new heaven and a new earth, when all human beings will be brothers and sisters and will rejoice with the words of the angels: Peace on earth and goodwill among people. Learn to wait, for he has promised to come. Behold, I stand at the door. . . . And we call to him: Yes, come soon, Lord Jesus. Amen.

# National Memorial Day

## Berlin, Reminiscere (Memorial Day), February 21, 1932

—————⫸《●》⫷—————

The year 1932 was a grim time for Germany. Its new postwar republican government was struggling amid inflation, unemployment, and poverty. Hitler's movement, along with Communist and socialist movements, was underway. Bonhoeffer shared in the fears for his country's future, but he also foresaw suffering for the church. German theologian Günther Dehn (whom Bonhoeffer refers to in this sermon as a "seer") had questioned the appropriateness of placing war monuments inside churches. This pacifist question had fanned the already widespread resentment among the German people over Germany's loss of honor in the Treaty of Versailles. Bonhoeffer now believed that to mourn the sacrifices of war in the church did mean proclaiming Christ's commandment in the Sermon on the Mount to be peacemakers. The church, Bonhoeffer said, was being called to Christ's way of the cross.

Bonhoeffer delivered this sermon in Berlin on Germany's National Memorial Day, observed on the second Sunday in Lent, *Reminiscere*.

---

Matthew 24:6–14: *And you will hear of wars and rumors of wars; see that you are not alarmed; for this must take place, but the end is not yet. For nation will rise against nation, and kingdom against kingdom, and there will be famines and earthquakes in various places: all this is but the beginning of the birth pangs.*

*Then they will hand you over to be tortured and will put you to death, and you will be hated by all nations because of my name. Then many will fall away, and they will betray one another and hate one another. And many false prophets will arise and lead many astray. And because of the increase of lawlessness, the love of many will grow cold. But the one who endures to the end will be saved. And this good news of the kingdom will be proclaimed throughout the world, as a testimony to all the nations; and then the end will come.*

---

The church does not leave anyone alone. None of you who have come here today in mourning, no one who is really looking for consolation and not just a ceremonial memorial service should remain alone today. You can seek consolation in all kinds of different places, in solitude, in nature, in work, in social life with friends. In all those places you can *search for* consolation. But you can only *find* consolation in the knowledge of God. Any of you, in the face of that which distresses you, which is incomprehensible to you, which keeps frightening and disturbing you all over again, who seek to know the will of God and only want to bring your suffering and your questioning obediently to a place where you can hear God yourself, you are in the right place here in the church. But *only* if you are that person. Every other person who is interested in something else besides Christian knowledge of God and God's will is in the wrong place here.

Memorial Day can be observed in very different ways. It is something different if the bereaved families, something different if the state, something different if the church is observing it. In the families on a day like this, all our thoughts may be centered on the person of the one torn from our midst by the war, and it may be that here all our love for this individual person is reawakened, and our mourning is a mourning out of love.

And if in great public or state memorial celebrations, the historically great German actions and sacrifices are commemorated, our mourning may be proud mourning. Finally, if everywhere else human beings and our achievements take a central place—and truly it is important enough that today we also are reminded of great human deeds—all of this, though, is something *different* from what the church of Christ has to say here. When the church observes Memorial Day, it must have something *special* to say. It cannot be one voice in the chorus of others who loudly raise the cry of mourning for the lost sons of the nation across the land, and by such cries of mourning call us to new deeds and great courage. It cannot, like the ancient singers of great heroic deeds, wander about and sing the song of praise of battle and the death of the heroes to the listening ears of enthralled young people. The church should not expect the laurels that decorate the great singer, for it does not itself make laurel wreaths for *any human being. How gladly* it would do so. It is hard not to be allowed to do that.

On this day the church stands here so strangely without ceremony, so little proud, so little heroic. The church is like the seer of ancient times who, when all are gathered to commemorate a great deed of the nation, is wholeheartedly present but suffers because he sees something that the others do not see and must speak of what he sees, although no one wants to hear it. We all feel it: People don't want any disturbance here. People don't want any discord. People want everyone to participate without exception. People don't want anyone to see anything different that others do not see. And if it happens anyway, you have to try to get rid of a person like that. And so it happens then that such seers are thrown out of the celebration, chased away with scorn and contempt by the very people they want to help, whom they love like nothing else in the world. But especially because they love them so much, they have become seers. The one who loves the most is the one who sees deepest, sees the greatest danger. A seer has never been popular. That is why the church will also not be popular, least of all on days like this.

Today the German people remember the years 1914–1918, the time in which millions of German men and boys showed that one can and should love one's fatherland unto death. They had to show that under conditions unheard of in human history up to then. And what would be more authentic and more human than to stand in silence here, in deep gratitude, and to affirm with great decisiveness what they intended? There are still millions living among us who, like the others, have seen death—a special, unrecognized army of men who are marked by death, in silent communion with one another and with those who have passed over into death. For us younger ones always a new reason for seriousness, for being still and becoming humble, for the older ones a source of strength when facing death, but for us all a reminder that cannot be ignored: Do not forget, never forget, that your people, that you yourself live on land that was bought with the blood of your brothers! Mourn, German people, give thanks and hope!

What Christian would not want to speak and feel this way? Who would not want to stand together in the gathering with all the brothers who know that they are united? Who would want to dare to sow discord here?

But—we must ask further—what Christian would not know that the church, which is built on the gospel of Christ, would have more to say here, because it sees more? Precisely because every human being as a human being must subscribe to what we just said earlier, that is why the church of Christ must know how to say more and say more profound things, things of more ultimate importance. The monument in the Neue Wache ["New Guardpost"] tells everyone everything we said at first: "Do not forget, and thank you"—that is what the memorial wreath says, cast from the medals of the fallen brothers. "Hope"—that is what the opening to the sky says. But no cross stands there. It is a national monument, but it is not a Christian symbol. It is not a church, in which the suffering, dying brothers are joined with those who have completed their life journey in the sign of the cross. Thus it is not Christian mourning that unites the people there; it is not Christian hope that arises out of this mourning; it is not Christian consolation that is preached here. And perhaps that, in its own way, is quite proper. But we, who perhaps just this morning stood at the Neue Wache, before one war memorial or another, and this evening came from there to the church, have a right to expect to hear in this place what Christian mourning is and what Christian consolation and Christian hope are.

Especially those among us who take things seriously are repeatedly confronted and plagued on this day by the question of where, from a Christian perspective, they should stand with regard to what happened from 1914 to 1918. We want to know how we as Christians—and not only as Germans—should see all of this. There may be some among us whose Christian conscience quakes when they think of the war and its victims and who are unsure about how they should reconcile themselves to it morally. And who among us, after all, is not among those? Who could be so clear and sure, so completely convinced of the holy cause of war if he knows of the commandment of peace, if he knows that God is a God of peace, that of Christ it is said: He is our peace [Eph. 2:14]. Who would not again and again be disturbed and would have to ask themselves: What do the events of 1914–1918, the millions of dead German men, mean for me, for us today? How is God speaking through them to me? That means once again very simply asked: How can I bring together in my mind God, Christ, and the events of the war? Should I say it was God's cause? Or shall I succumb to despair and say: Here God's power was at an end? Here Christ was far away?

For such questions we must be very determined—and what would be more natural at the beginning of the season of Lent—first of all to look at what happened on the cross of Golgotha. And now doesn't exactly the same question come up here, only incomparably more sharply and urgently: How can I bring together in my mind the cross and God?

And is not precisely here *the* answer given that stands over the whole Christian message: Christ goes through the cross, only through the cross, to life, to the resurrection, to the victory? It is the wonderful theme of the Bible, so frightening for many people, that the only visible sign of God in the world is the cross. Christ is not carried away gloriously from earth to heaven but must go to the cross. And exactly there where the cross stands, the resurrection is near. Exactly there where everyone begins to doubt God, where everyone falls into despair about God's power, there God is fully, there Christ is alive and near. Where it hangs by a thread whether one will desert the cause or remain faithful, there God is, there Christ is fully. Where the power of darkness wants to overpower the light of God, there God triumphs and judges the darkness. So it is now as well, when Christ thinks of the day his church-community will face. His disciples ask about the signs of his coming again after his death. This is not a one-time coming again but an eternal coming again. The end time in the Bible is all the time and every day between the death of Christ and Judgment Day. Yes, the New Testament sees the death of Christ as so serious, so decisive.

But Christ, who knows that his path leads to the cross, knows that the path of his disciples also does not lead peacefully and safely straight into heaven; rather, they too must pass through the darkness, through the cross. They too must struggle. That is why the first sign of the nearness of Christ—strangely enough!—is that his enemies become great, that the powers of temptation, of apostasy, of unfaithfulness become strong, that his church-community is led close to the brink of doubting in God. The first sign will be that his enemies hide behind the name of Christ and only under the guise of Christianity seek to lure us away from him. Oh, the name "Christ" doesn't do it. And how easy it is in times of confusion like today to fight in the name of Christ against the real Christ. But then, once the spirits are confused, the power of the world will break loose openly, unconcealed. The powers that want to tear the disciples away from him, that try to show them that it is madness to go with him, that Christ has no power, only words, but that they, the powers of reality, speak the language of facts; and this language is more convincing than the language of Christ. The world gangs up on the spirit of Christ. The demons rise up. It is a rebellion against Christ. And one great power of this uprising is called war! The others are called pestilence and famine. So war, sickness, and hunger are the powers that try to take Christ's dominion away from him [see Rev. 6:8], and they are all led by the archenemy of Christ the Living One, by death. It already seemed as if with Christ the victory had been won, as if Christ had conquered death. But now these powers scream: We are here. Here, see us and be terrified! We have power. Our power has not been taken from us. Christ has not conquered; *we* conquer. Christ is dead. But we are alive. Our names are war, sickness, hunger. Why are you letting yourselves be enthralled by this false prophet who speaks of peace and love, of God and his kingdom: here we are!

And they attack the nations and drag them in. And death goes around and reaps its harvest. It mows down millions.

And now comes the great disintegration of Christianity. Its ranks are broken up and torn apart. For a terrible uncertainty and fear come over the followers of Christ. They have to realize that all these attacks are basically attacks on Christ and his word and that this word apparently has no power against them. The past war caused thousands, caused millions to doubt Christ, and among them especially those who took his word seriously and now saw themselves so bitterly disappointed. Read wartime letters, read a collection of statements from our working-class people about the church and Christianity recently published by a pastor in Berlin. These things are written there so that everyone can read them. "The war has shown me that Christ is not right." "The war robbed us of our faith in God." "Since the war I know that faith is madness." Those are clear words about war, war and the church of Christ.

It's very hypocritical to simply say here: Oh, well, they didn't have real faith anyway. Dear friends, one has to have real faith to be able to notice so clearly that one's faith has been destroyed. And which of us would say that we have such real faith that it could not be threatened by anything at all? If we think we have faith like that, we should think very hard about whether this faith has not become indifference, which cannot be aroused from its lethargy by anything. So be careful with such hypocritical criticisms. Didn't those millions also have a right to Christ, who has now been torn away from them in this way? What should we say about that, we who ourselves were also dragged into these events of 1914–1918, who also share responsibility for their faith having been taken from them? And seen from here, things look very different. What a self-satisfied, hard Christianity we would be if, under such circumstances, even the most loyal, those with the strongest faith were not also struck by a nameless anxiety that Christ was being torn away from us?

If only the true people of God were not troubled to the very core, and if even the frightened church of Christ, under the plague of war, did not have to cry out: "My God, why have you forsaken me?" [Matt. 27:46; Ps. 22:1]. Even Christ himself cried out like this on the cross and, according to the story told by one Gospel writer, died with this cry. Oh, it is all too understandable that millions became unfaithful, that faced with so much hate their love grew cold.

Our situation would truly be desperate if not for the word of Christ: "When all of this comes over you, see that you are not alarmed. For this must take place." Jesus had to tell his disciples so often: "Do not be afraid, for I am with you" [see Matt. 28:20]. "Do not be afraid, for I have called you by name" [Is. 43:1]. Even the Old Testament said this already. "Do not be afraid," the angels call to the frightened shepherds [Luke 2:10]. "Do not fear, only believe" [Mark 5:36], Jesus says to the leader of the synagogue. "Do not be afraid, little flock, for it is your Father's good pleasure to give you the kingdom"[Luke 12:32]. "When you see this, see that you are not alarmed; for this must take place, but the end is not yet" [Matt. 24:36]. We ask: Why must this all take place? Because Christ himself must pass through and beyond death, because where Christ, where God himself really is, the darkness rises up most terribly and nails him to the cross. That is why we too must pass through this. This must all happen so that the end can come.

God's way in the world leads to the cross and through the cross to life. For this reason do not be alarmed, do not be afraid—be faithful! But what does being faithful mean here other than standing and falling with the word of Christ, with his preaching of the kingdom of peace, than knowing that despite everything Christ's words are stronger than all the powers of evil? What does faithfulness of the church-community of Christ mean here other than calling out into this furious raging again and again—unto exhaustion, unto humiliation, unto martyrdom—the words of Christ that there should be peace, that there should be love, that there should be blessing, and that he is our peace, and that God is a God of peace? And the more they rage, the more we should call out. And the more we call out, the more wildly they will rage. For wherever the word of Christ is truly spoken, the world senses that it is either ruinous madness or ruinous truth, which endangers its very life. Where peace is really spoken, war must rage twice as hard, for it senses that it is about to be driven out. Christ intends to be its death.

But all the more passionately, all the more loyally, the church of Christ will stand by its Lord and preach this word of peace, even though it must pass through scorn and persecution. It knows that its Lord also had to go to the cross. But now it understands the promise that Jesus has for it. The war will not be the end. Rather, it must take place so that the end can come. The gospel of the kingdom will be preached as a witness to all nations, and then the end will come. And here now our view broadens out; our eyes are suddenly drawn up to the Lord who directs all things, whom even the demons and the forces of hell must serve. War, sickness, and hunger must come, so that the gospel of the kingdom of peace, of love, and of salvation can be spoken and heard all the more keenly, all the more clearly, all the more deeply. The power of enmity and of stirring up conflict between nations must serve to cause the gospel to come to all nations and be heard by all, must serve the kingdom to which all people shall belong. War serves peace, hate serves love, the devil serves God, the cross serves life. And then, when that has been revealed, then the end will come. Then the Lord of the church will lay his hand on the church, blessing and protecting it as his faithful servant.

Memorial Day in the church! What does that mean? It means holding up the one great hope from which we all live, the preaching of the kingdom of God. It means seeing that which is past, and which we remember today, with all its terrors and all its godlessness, and yet not being afraid, but hearing the preaching of peace. It means knowing that all of that has to happen so that the end can come, so that God remains Lord. It means that we can really mourn for the dead of the world war only if we, with the same faithfulness in which they stood out there, now pass on the message of peace, for the sake of which their death had to be, and preach it all the more loudly. It means looking out beyond the borders of our own nation, across the whole world, and praying that the gospel of the kingdom, which puts an end to all war, now may come over all nations and that then the end may come, that Christ may draw near.

Memorial Day in the church! That means that God in the cross is near to us. That means pointing to Christ on the cross, who won the victory through the cross. Memorial Day in the church means knowing that Christ alone wins the victory! Amen.

# The Promised Land

## Berlin, Laetare Sunday (Fourth Sunday in Lent), March 13, 1932

In the year following his ordination on November 13, 1931, Bonhoeffer had to fulfill various pastoral assignments before he could apply for a parish of his own. A particular challenge was preparing young teenage boys for confirmation in a working-class Berlin neighborhood. The unruly class of more than forty boys was the despair of their pastor, but Bonhoeffer had experience as a youth leader in Harlem, New York, and soon won them over. He even moved temporarily to a room near their church so the boys could take turns visiting him. He also took them on retreats and hikes in the countryside and even in the mountains, where they otherwise would never have a chance to go. When Bonhoeffer preached this sermon to the boys on the Sunday of their confirmation, they were wearing new suits made from a bolt of cloth that he had bought to spare their unemployed families the expense.

Some of the boys stayed in touch with Bonhoeffer after confirmation and, according to Bonhoeffer scholar Ferdinand Schlingensiepen, one of the confirmands turned up at a Bonhoeffer conference in East Germany more than fifty years later, after seeing it announced in a newspaper.

The name for this Sunday, *Laetare,* is Latin for "I was glad," a reference to Psalm 122 ("I was glad when they said to me, 'Let us go to the house of the Lord!'"), which is traditionally read at Evening Prayer on the second Sunday in Lent. "If God is for us" is from Romans 8:31. In the second part of the text for the day, Genesis 33:10, Jacob is speaking to his brother Esau, from whom he had parted in enmity years earlier.

---

Genesis 32:24–31; 33:10: *Jacob was left alone; and a man wrestled with him until daybreak. When the man saw that he did not prevail against Jacob, he struck him on the hip socket; and Jacob's hip was put out of joint as he wrestled with him. Then he said, "Let me go, for the day is breaking." But Jacob said, "I will not let you go, unless you bless me." So he said to him, "What is your name?" And he said, "Jacob." Then the man said, "You shall no longer be called Jacob, but Israel, for you have striven with God and with humans, and have prevailed." Then Jacob asked him, "Please tell me your name." But he said, "Why is it that you ask my name?" And there he blessed him. So Jacob called the place Peniel, saying, "For I have seen God face to face, and yet my life is preserved." The sun rose upon him as he passed Penuel, limping because of his hip. . . . Jacob said, "No, please; if I find favor with you, then accept my present from my hand; for truly to see your face is like seeing the face of God—since you have received me with such favor."*

---

Dear confirmands! During the last weeks before confirmation, when I kept asking you what I should say to you in the sermon at confirmation, several times the answer came: We want a serious admonishment for our lives. And I can assure you, whoever listens well today will hear many very serious admonishments. But see here, life today gives us enough serious admonishments, more than enough. And that is why I should not make your view of the future more difficult and darker than it already is. And I know many of you are already seeing a great deal of the realities of life.

Today you should not be made afraid of life, but be given courage. That is why today in church we will have to talk more than ever about the hope that we have and that no one can take away from you.

When I look at you today, it seems to me as if I saw a crowd of young hikers before me, who after a long hike have arrived at a great, locked gate and now knock and ask to be let in. They recognize this gate and these walls from somewhere. Somehow it seems like home to them. Open up! We want to see what it looks like in there. We want to come in! So their voices call out, and they knock on the gate; some more courageously, a little more persistently, the others a little more softly; and among them probably some who have just let themselves be dragged along with the others. But now they are all there, and they all want to get in.

What kind of a strange gate is it? And what kind of a strange land that lies behind it? It is certainly a strange land these young hikers want to go into. It is the land of which it is said that there is peace and love and justice in it; the land where there is no more suffering and there are no more tears, because a wonderful Lord rules there. It is the land that is prophesied, the promised land, the land in which God rules.

Now who gave you—we might like to ask you—this great idea that there was such a thing as a land like this? And you will answer: "You yourselves, you, the Christian congregation and your pastors, and last of all, the one who visits us all, Jesus Christ. We are still at a loss about what we should do. We still don't know how it will turn out." How are you going to get through this gate, and what will you think of the land behind the gate?

And now we'll take a look at the story I read to you. Look, Jacob feels exactly the way you feel today. He had once fled from the land of Canaan, from the promised land, the land that God had given his forefathers and him, fled from his brother's anger. Then he had spent years of his life in a foreign land. But now he is drawn back. He wants to go back to his home country. He wants to go back to the land promised by the prophets. He wants to go into the land where God is the Lord and no other. And he wants to go to his brother and make peace with him. He wants to go into the land of God. Don't you want to do that, too?

And now something remarkable happens to him. Evening has come, the last evening in the foreign land. He, Jacob, knows that his brother and the promised land are near; tomorrow he will be in his home country. Now it is night. And he stays alone by the river. Just a few hours, then it will be morning, then he will cross over into his home country. But then suddenly he notices that he is being attacked. Someone steps into his path. He puts his arms around him; he wrestles with him; he will not let him go; he tries to force him down. Jacob should not return to the promised land. He should not find peace with his brother. A terrible, powerful force steps in his way and will not allow Jacob to enter; it wants to push him back into the night, into the foreign land. Stay there, where you are coming from. You may not come into the promised land; you are a foreigner, an unfaithful one. Stay away from here. And violently the great unknown one tries to push Jacob away from him into the night.

But Jacob's longing for the promised land gives him unbelievable strength, and he does not allow himself to be pushed away. He does not give way. He holds the other one fast in his arms, and now, in the struggle, he recognizes who his opponent is. It is none other than God who is guarding this land, who will not let any intruder in, who keeps this land holy, who wants to show this person that one can't just come in so simply and happily and merrily, but that only the holy and righteous cross over the borders of this land. Everyone else, every foreigner, every unfaithful one must stay away in the night of loneliness and of evil. Do you hear it, and do you understand it, too? One cannot just casually enter into the promised land. Likewise, one cannot just casually become a member of the Christian church—that is, by going to confirmation. Why not? Because God steps into the path and guards this land and keeps it holy and does not want us to enter into it unholy. Your path to the altar, too—here today and in the evening day after tomorrow, when you will go to Holy Communion—should be a path into the holy land. Take care that you don't start out on that path unholy.

But how should we become holy, so that we can enter into the land of God? Let us look at Jacob. The night is ending and morning is coming, and Jacob is still holding off his opponent. He still does not let himself be sent away. He is still holding him. Then comes a last, terrible blow from the opponent: Let me go; the day is dawning and I must leave. You stay in the night! And now Jacob's passionate determination becomes immeasurable. He dares to talk back to God, to refuse to do what he says: No, I will not let you go, unless you bless me. What else does that mean other

than that Jacob dares to reach into God's heart itself: you may not go away
from me. You may not leave me alone in the night. I cannot be without
you. I cannot. I want to see your land and live in your land. God, you will
not leave me in the night, in sin, in need. You can't leave me alone. It goes
against your heart. No, I will not let you go, unless you bless me. I want
only one thing: to know that you are not my enemy, that you no longer
reject me because of the evil things I did in the foreign land; to know that
you are with me, that you are merciful to me. I will not let you go, unless
you bless me.

And now he doesn't know how he should hold on to God, so that
God doesn't leave him. And he asks God: Tell me your name, so that I can
always call on you, so that I know who you are. But God answers: Why
do you ask me for my name? It is too wonderful for you to understand
it. "And there he blessed him." So that was God's answer, in which God
revealed the divine name, which is not an angry but a merciful name—
God blessed him there. That means God did not leave him alone in the
night. God did not push him back. God did not turn him away but was
merciful to him. God was there to be found. God promised faithfulness.
God blessed him. That means God let him come into the promised land
of God. And Jacob called the place Peniel, which means: I have seen God
face to face, and my soul is restored. And at the moment when God blessed
him, the night came to an end, the dawn broke, and the sun rose for him.
He had won victory over the night. And God had let it become day for
him. The sun came up for him, no other sun than on every day, and it
shone over a land that was not any different from any other land. But the
sun came up *for him*. Now God was there, who made it light around him
and inside him. The day of God's mercy had dawned, and the night was
over. Jacob was standing in the promised land, for he had found God and
his soul was restored.

But, of course, the signs of the night, which remind him of new nights
to come, were still there. He limped because of his hip, says the Bible. That
means he could not forget his past. It had cost him a great deal to enter
into the promised land, to receive God's blessing. One doesn't go into
God's land without scars. Have you understood? In the night where we
know that we are sinners before God, where our need becomes great and
God wants to turn away from us, there one must fight for God's blessing.

There we should scream out: I will not let you go, unless you bless me. And then morning is near; then the day breaks. Then none other than God comes and makes it light and quiet within us, and we enter into the promised land. It doesn't look any different from the day before, but God has been there and left divine mercy and blessing with us, and that is why we are in the promised land.

Now it isn't long until Jacob sees his brother coming. And now, where the day of God has dawned, he sees the face of his brother not as an enemy but "like seeing the face of God." He sees in his brother God's very self and God's love. And the brother takes him in, and he is in his home country, for he has found God and his brother. Do you understand? If you have found God, you find your brother and sister, too. You see your brother's face as if you were seeing God's face. And whoever does not find brother and sister also does not find God. It is for this reason that the very God became our brother in Christ, so that behind every brother we see God again.

And now daylight should come over you. Not so that now, from tomorrow on, suddenly everything will go smoothly and easily. But in a way that lets you know that God, who wants to bless you, will never leave you alone. That is the sun that came up for Jacob, which also will come up for you: God's love and mercy, as you see them in Christ our brother and Lord on the cross and in his resurrection. In the Christian church-community, you should find God and your brother and sister, should find your home, should have the promised land. Here one shall be the Lord, and each shall become a Christ for the other.

So you should know that in our lives all of us must again and again go into the night and through the night to the day. It is not eternally day for any mortal—indeed, we probably all see more night than day; don't be deceived about that either. But no one should ever take away from you the belief that God has prepared for you, too, a day and a sun and a dawning and that God brings to us this sun who is called Christ: that God wants to let us see the promised land in which justice and peace and love rule, because Christ rules, here from a distance, but one day for eternity. Why should we be afraid? Just go in, go through! God, Christ is the Lord, the church-community is our home.

I will not let you go, unless you bless me! If God is for us, who is against us?

# God Is Love

## Berlin, Pentecost Sunday, May 12, 1932

━━━━━━━«《◆》»━━━━━━━

Pentecost, or Whit Sunday, is the fiftieth day after Easter, often called the "birthday of the church." The text for the day—Acts 2—recalls the outpouring of the Holy Spirit on Jesus' disciples. Since ancient times, the church has observed Pentecost Sunday with the celebration of baptisms. We have here Bonhoeffer's homily when he baptized his eight-month-old nephew Thomas, son of Klaus and Emmi Bonhoeffer, on a Pentecost Sunday at his parents' home. It includes a quotation from 1 Corinthians 13, a text on which Bonhoeffer would preach a sermon series two years later.

It was quite customary at the time to hold baptisms, and even weddings and funerals, at home with family and friends. A brief homily was usual on such occasions. In 1943, when Bonhoeffer was in prison, he had been expecting to preach at the wedding of his niece Renate to his dear friend Eberhard Bethge. Bonhoeffer wrote his homily in prison, in accordance with his generation's (rather old-fashioned) concept of marriage, and it was read at the home ceremony. Thomas Bonhoeffer, by then a boy of eleven, played the piano in a trio by Mozart and took part with his sister in a traditional dance.

1 John 4:16b: *God is love, and those who abide in love abide in God, and God abides in them.*

This word is to be spoken today over this child. And not the way one might give him just any other word of one's choice—as they say—to take along on his way in life, but rather with the very particular claim that this is God's word at this time over this child; that means that this word becomes real at this moment and shows itself to be true and valid. God is love—from today on in the life of this child, that is no longer a general word of wisdom or unwisdom for his life, but is the real, only indestructible basis on which his whole life is built. It is truth, and it is reality. That is the meaning of baptism.

It is part of the role of the church that it must say such things to people, who must feel that this is either a well-meant phrase and an untruth, or else something you take for granted. The expression "God is love" is completely vulnerable to this criticism. It is extremely tempting to consider this a well-intentioned exaggeration, a phrase for use in church celebrations, and in doing so fundamentally to reject it as untrue and rob it of its seriousness. But the seriousness of this word is also destroyed if one considers it to be something one can piously take for granted. No, when the love of God is spoken about, we are speaking about something that simply cannot at all be taken for granted, something improbable, unbelievable. But what is completely improbable here is also true, so true that a person's whole life should be built on it.

God is love. That means that the beginning and the end of this child are safely in God's hands. But at the same time, it means that something has broken into the life of this child in the world, something that contradicts everything visible, understandable, and able to be experienced, something that sets this life on a foundation that lies beyond all human possibilities, on the foundation of God's own self. The laws of human life are broken through when God's love comes over a person.

For that means that the human being who we know is vulnerable to the powers of fate is bound to the One who is also Lord over fate. That human beings, whom we know life frightens, because they do not know what the immediate future will hold, are freed of this fear because they know the ultimate future, which is God's very self. That human beings, who love themselves more than God and their neighbor and therefore sin in this, are still loved by God and their neighbor, that they are forgiven. That human beings, who we know are deeply lonely in the world, can never be lonely, because God is with them and with all God's called people.

When God's love stands over a person, that means not that his or her life goes on any differently from that of any other person, but that his or her life has been stripped of its last selfish inclination and has been won for God. It is not that the fate of the person is love—that is how we often misunderstand this word—but the One who is Lord over fate is love. And these are not wishes that we give the child on his way, but realities of which the church assures him on behalf of the living God. It is good that this verse starts by speaking of God's love. That takes away the danger that later, when the text speaks of a person's love, we think something very human is meant. "Those who abide in love abide in God, and God in them . . ."; what can "abide in love" mean, at first, other than being called now to break through the laws of the world as God breaks through them?

To take the very special path that love takes, a path that is foreign and incomprehensible to the world? A path that can never lead one astray, that is completely self-sufficient, has its own laws, that is always right, even if it seems so strange? A path that is interrupted a thousand times, because it is the path, not of the priest who blindly passes by the man who had fallen into the hands of robbers, but of the one who has eyes to see and sees everywhere. To abide in love means to have open eyes, to be able to see something that only a few see, namely, the outstretched, begging hands of the others who are along the way, and now not be able to do anything else but to act, to help, to do one's duty, using everything one has. That may be here or there. Most important is that, wherever it is, one can always allow oneself to be interrupted by God.

But one can only abide in love unknowingly. Just as the eye does not see itself, love does not see itself. If I think that I am abiding in love, I am not abiding in love, because I am seeing myself. But only in blindness toward myself do I, abiding in love, walk my path with the confidence of God. I believe all things; I hope all things; I endure all things; I forgive all things. If it is really *all things* until the end, then there is no disappointment, no doubt, no stopping. Then it is true that love never ends but continues through from time into eternity.

Those who abide in love take not the prescribed path of excellence in the world but their own, often incomprehensible, often foolish paths. They lack the last bit of worldly cleverness that is called selfishness. But in these foolish, strange paths the one who has eyes to see will see some of the glow from God's own glory.

Only one person walked that path in the world completely. It led him to the cross. It leads us through the cross, but to the true life in God.

# Lazarus and the Rich Man

## Berlin, First Sunday after Trinity, May 29, 1932 (?)

———=《●》=———

Bonhoeffer did not have his own pulpit during his ministry in Berlin; rather, his opportunities to preach came when a colleague needed a substitute. For whom and in which church he was substituting was not always recorded with his sermon manuscripts, as they have been preserved. In this case, the date also is uncertain.

Bonhoeffer found preaching an awesome responsibility, and often sought to share sermon ideas with colleagues. In 1931, the Swiss theologian Karl Barth, whom Bonhoeffer had been excited to hear lecture in Bonn, had preached on this text and his sermon had become famous. However, after obtaining a copy and reading it, Bonhoeffer in his usual way decided on his own emphases in his interpretation of the text.

He quotes repeatedly in this sermon from Luke's version of the Beatitudes—both the blessings and the woes that follow. Because purple dye was very expensive in the ancient world and few besides kings could afford it, purple clothes were a sign of wealth in Jesus' time. Bonhoeffer's "woe to you who dress in purple" implicates the rich in his time as well. "Our pride, our race, our strength" echoes the rhetoric of the pro-Nazi "German Christians."

---

Luke 16:19–31: *There was a rich man who was dressed in purple and fine linen and who feasted sumptuously every day. And at his gate lay a poor man named Lazarus, covered with sores, who longed to satisfy his hunger with what fell from the rich man's table; even the dogs would come and lick his sores. The poor man died and was carried away by the angels to be with Abraham. The rich man also died and was buried. In Hades, where he was being tormented, he looked up and saw Abraham far away with Lazarus by his side. He called out, "Father Abraham, have mercy on me, and send Lazarus to dip the tip of his finger in water and cool my tongue; for I am in agony in these flames." But Abraham said, "Child, remember that during your lifetime you received your good things, and Lazarus in like manner evil things; but now he is comforted here, and you are in agony. Besides all this, between you and us a great chasm has been fixed, so that those who might want to pass from here to you cannot do so, and no one can cross from there to us." He said, "Then, father, I beg you to send him to my father's house—for I have five brothers—that he may warn them, so that they will not also come into this place of torment." Abraham replied, "They have Moses and the prophets; they should listen to them." He said, "No, father Abraham; but if someone goes to them from the dead, they will repent." He said to him, "If they do not listen to Moses and the prophets, neither will they be convinced even if someone rises from the dead."*

---

One cannot understand and preach the gospel concretely enough. A real evangelical sermon must be like holding a pretty red apple in front of a child or a glass of cool water in front of a thirsty person and then asking: do you want it? We should be able to talk about matters of our faith in such a way that the hands reach out for it faster than we can fill them. People should run and not be able to rest when the gospel is talked about, as long ago the sick ran to Christ to be healed when he was going around healing (but Christ, too, healed more than he converted). That is really no stock phrase. Shouldn't it really be that way wherever the good news of God is spoken of? But it just isn't that way—we all know that.

At the same time, one shouldn't content oneself with this state of affairs. Rather, there can be basically just one thing, namely, that one repeatedly asks oneself anew why this is so. And here is one—admittedly only one—of the reasons that we simply hesitate to accept that the gospel is as concrete, as close to life, as it is. We have spiritualized the gospel—that is, we have lightened it up, changed it. Take our gospel of the rich man and poor Lazarus. It has become common practice to see as the whole meaning of the story that the rich should help the poor. That is, it is turned into a story illustrating a moral. But this particular story especially, if one allows oneself to be affected fully by its original meaning, is something very different from that, namely, a very concrete proclamation of the good news itself. Admittedly so concretely, so powerfully worded, that we don't even take it seriously anymore.

Let us imagine how a crowd of the sick, the poor, the miserable, of poor Lazaruses, gathered around Christ, and then he began to tell the story of the poor, leprous Lazarus whom even the dogs were torturing, at the doorstep of the rich man. And when the story then took a turn with the words: "The poor man died and was carried away by the angels to be with Abraham. Lazarus received evil things in his life, but now he is comforted here," perhaps shouts of joy and hope passed through the crowd. That was the good news; that was the cool water they reached for greedily. That was the love of God itself, which spoke in this way to the poor and suffering. You outcasts, you disadvantaged, you poor and sick, you who are looked down upon shall be consoled. You have much suffering in the world, but in a short while eternal joy and eternal consolation shall come over you. Look at poor Lazarus, at how he is lying scorned before the rich man's doorstep, and then look at how he receives God's consolation with Abraham. Blessed are you, you poor, for the kingdom of God is yours. Blessed are you who are hungry here below, for you shall be filled. Blessed are you who weep here, for you will laugh. Rejoice and leap for joy, for your reward is great in heaven.

Those are the beatitudes in Luke [6:20–23]. Nothing is said here about the poor in spirit [Matt. 5:3], nothing about hunger for righteousness [Matt. 5:6], but blessed are you poor, you hungry, you who are weeping, as we know you in the world. Blessed are you Lazaruses of all the ages, for you shall be consoled in the bosom of Abraham. Blessed are you outcasts and outlaws, you victims of society, you men and women without work, you broken down and ruined, you lonely and abandoned, rape victims and those who suffer injustice, you who suffer in body and soul; blessed are you, for God's joy will come over you and be over your head forever. That is the gospel, the good news of the dawning of the new world, the new order, which is God's world and God's order. The deaf hear, the blind see, the lame walk, and the gospel is preached to the poor [see Luke 7:22].

And before we interrupt ourselves to ask questions here, let us hear the other, the terrible other side. There is the rich man, who dressed in purple and fine linen. About him it says: "The rich man also died and was buried." That already sounds very harsh. And now in hell he must suffer the torment of eternal thirst, because he was full and satisfied on earth. He has to see poor Lazarus in the bosom of Abraham and beg that Lazarus quench his thirst only for a moment. But even that can't be. "Child, remember that during your lifetime you received your good things." And behind this we hear the words: Woe to you who are full now, for you will be hungry. Woe to you who are laughing now, for you will mourn and weep. Woe to you who dress in purple and live happily in luxury, for you shall suffer eternal thirst [see Luke 6:24–26].

Blessed poor, outcast, leprous Lazarus yesterday and today, for you have a God. Woe to you who live happily in luxury and are respected yesterday and today. That is the most concretely preached good news of God for the poor.

But now we must listen to quite a few shocked objections before we continue.

There are always those in our midst who know better than the New Testament itself what the New Testament may and may not say. What we have just said here is, of course, a rough interpretation of the New Testament intended for rough, common people. It couldn't be about that. If something in the New Testament really sounds as rough as what we just said, you have to take it and spiritualize it. We call that "sublimating," that is, refining, elevating, spiritualizing, moralizing. It's not just simply the physically poor who are blessed and the physically rich who would be damned. But the main thing is always what a person's attitude is toward his poverty and toward his wealth. The external aspect doesn't matter at all, but rather the attitude matters: rich in God or poor in God. . . .

The most dangerous thing about this criticism is that it contains some truth, but basically it is intended only to provide us with an excuse. It is so terribly easy to back away from all so-called external conditions and focus on the attitude: rich on the outside but being poor in one's so-called attitude. It is so terribly easy to say that it is vulgar to understand the gospel as if it were about outward poverty and riches, while it really depends not on that but solely on the inner aspect. Now, I ask you, where in the story of the poor Lazarus does it say anything about his inner life? Who tells us that he was a man who within himself had the right attitude toward his poverty? Just the opposite, he may have been quite a pushy poor man, since he lay down in front of the rich man's doorstep and did not go away. Who tells us anything about the soul of the rich man?

That is precisely the frightening thing about this story—there is no moralizing here at all, but simply talk of poor and rich and of the promise and the threat given to the one and the other. Here these external conditions are obviously not treated as external conditions but are taken unbelievably seriously. Why did Christ heal the sick and suffering if he didn't consider such external conditions important? Why is the kingdom of God equated with the deaf hear, the blind see? . . . And where do we get the incredible presumption to spiritualize these things that Christ saw and did very concretely?

We must end this audacious, sanctimonious spiritualization of the gospel. Take it as it is, or hate it honestly!

And there was no lack of this hatred precisely because people took the gospel to be as honest as it was. The hatred comes from two different sides.

What does a gospel that was brought to the weaklings, the common people, the poor, and the sick have to do with us? We are men and women, healthy and strong. We disdain the mass of Lazaruses. We disdain the gospel of the poor. It undermines our pride, our race, our strength. We are rich, but with pride. That is certainly honestly said. But it is also said incredibly carelessly and at the same time so full of illusions. It is so easy to disdain the masses of Lazaruses. But if just one of these would really meet you face to face—the unemployed Lazarus, Lazarus the accident victim, Lazarus whose ruin you caused, your own begging child as Lazarus, the helpless and desperate mother, Lazarus who has become a criminal, the godless Lazarus—can you go up to him or her and say: I disdain you, Lazarus. I scoff at the good news that makes you glad? Can you really do that? And if you can't do that, why then do you act as if it were anything great at all to be able to do that?

But also, couldn't it possibly already be a mockery in itself to console those who live in suffering and misery with the prospect of a better future in another world? Doesn't it almost sound as if one is just trying to keep these unfortunates from rebelling here against their fate? As if one is calling them blessed just so they will stay quiet, as they are now, and not bother the others? Isn't it downright cynical to talk about consolation in heaven because one does not want to give consolation on earth? Is this gospel for the poor not basically the deception and dumbing down of the people? Does it not show that one does not take the suffering at all seriously but hides cynically behind pious phrases? Oh, countless times it has happened that way—who would deny it?—right up to our present time. And millions have become estranged from the gospel for this reason!

But a look at the Gospels shows us what is different here. Jesus calls the poor blessed, but he does heal them, too, already here. Yes, the kingdom of God is at hand, for the blind see and the lame walk. He takes suffering so seriously that in a moment he must destroy it. Where Christ is, the power of the demons must be broken. That is why he heals, and that is why he says to his disciples: If you believe in me, you will do greater works than I. The kingdom of God is still just beginning to appear. The acts of healing are like heat lightning, like flashes of lightning from the new world.

But now the good news becomes all the more powerful. Blessed are you who weep, for you will laugh; blessed are you who are hungry, for you will be filled. No cynical consolation, but the one great hope: the new world, the good news, the merciful God, Lazarus in the bosom of Abraham, the poor and the outcasts with God—yes, indeed, this may sound terribly naive and concrete. But if it were really true? If it *is* true? Is it still naive then? Is it still unspiritual then? Don't we then especially have to open our ears and hear, and hear again, about the unheard-of event that Lazarus—yesterday and today—is carried by angels to be in the bosom of Abraham? And that the well-satisfied man, the full man, who lives happily in luxury, the rich man must suffer eternal thirst?

Up until now we have spoken of these two as if they actually had nothing to do with each other. That is obviously not the case. Lazarus lies in front of the rich man's doorstep, and it is the poverty of Lazarus that makes the rich man rich, just as the wealth of the other man makes Lazarus poor. It doesn't say what the rich man nor what the poor man had done or even should have done, but the only common event that affects them equally is their death. That is the unusual light in which both of these men are shown here; they both must die, and another life awaits both of them. And this fact binds them closer together than any moral law that a rich man should help a poor man. They basically already belong together in the common fate that awaits both of them. In death the rich man is no longer rich, and the poor man no longer poor. There they are one and the same. And after death something new begins, over which all the powers of the world of death can have no more control. But this is obviously what the rich man did not see, that his whole world is a world of death and must pass away and is subject to God, that for that reason Lazarus has something to do with him, because they both must die and will live in another world, because they are brothers in death and in judgment. He did not see that behind him and behind Lazarus there stand infinities, eternities—here silent, invisible, hidden under his purple garments and the naked body of Lazarus—but that they are there and are waiting and become reality. And the conversation between the thirsting rich man and Abraham leaves no doubt as to the seriousness of what is meant here by eternity.

But now, in principle, there will also be no more revelation of this eternity in the world, as the rich man requests for his brothers, other than what is given in Moses and the prophets; today we would say: given in the preaching of the church. In their world of death, they have Moses and the prophets; let them hear them. The words about God's eternal commandment [see Matt. 5:17–19] and about the weakness and the suffering of the human being who must die [see Ps. 39:5]; about God's mercy to the humble and judgment on the strong [see Luke 1:46–55]; the words about the cross of Christ for the salvation of the poor and lost, of the curse on the satisfied and the righteous—let them hear these and remember that they all live with Lazarus in the same world of death; and if they do not hear them, they will also not hear, even if someone were to rise from the dead. Even at this most visible conquest of their world of death, they will not be afraid and not become wise. They will refuse to accept it. They will not know that the Lazarus before their door is an eternal Lazarus, and they will pass by the eternity that meets them in Lazarus.

And now, the last questions: Who is Lazarus? Who is the rich man? And finally, what should the rich man do?

Who is Lazarus? You know it yourself: Your poorer brother or sister who cannot cope with life's outward or its spiritual aspects, often foolish, often impudent, often pushy, often godless, but yet endlessly needy and—whether knowing it or not—suffering, who craves the crumbs from under your table. You may think with a little self-pity that you yourself are Lazarus. God alone knows if you are. But always keep asking if you are not perhaps after all the rich man. Who is Lazarus? Always the other one, the crucified Christ himself, who meets you in the form of a thousand people you would look down upon. Yes, he is the eternal Lazarus himself.

And now we must ask again: Who is Lazarus? And here at the end, in all humility, the last possibility must be considered, at the limits of all human and divine possibilities: We are all Lazarus before God. The rich man, too, is Lazarus. He is the poor leper before God. And only when we know that we are all Lazarus, because we all live through the mercy of God, do we see Lazarus in our neighbor.

Who is the rich man? Our story does not answer this question. Certainly we are not rich. We are not full and satisfied. We do not live happily in luxury. Really not? Do you mean that seriously? Even when you meet Lazarus? Or does he not meet you? Are we really not the rich man? Another story gives us an answer to this question: the story of the rich young man, who was very devout and very righteous, but was sad when he was told to leave his possessions, and went away [see Matt. 19:16–22]. That is the rich man. What about us?

And now: What should the rich man do? The answer to this question can be found in the story of the Good Samaritan [Luke 10:25–37]. In our story there is only this: The rich man should see that death is standing behind him and Lazarus, and that behind Lazarus God himself, Christ is standing with the eternal good news. We should see—see poor Lazarus in his full frightening misery and behind him Christ, who invited him to his table and calls him blessed. Let us see you, poor Lazarus, let us see you, Christ, in poor Lazarus. Oh, that we might be able to see. Amen.

# Risen with Christ

## Berlin, Kaiser Wilhelm Memorial Church, Third Sunday after Trinity, June 12, 1932

━━━━━━━━━━━ «◦» ━━━━━━━━━━━

Bonhoeffer preached on this occasion at the request of his friend Gerhard Jacobi. Jacobi was pastor of a church that was destroyed in the bombing of Berlin and is well-known today for having been rebuilt after World War II amid the ruins of the original church. Many of Bonhoeffer's students would have attended the service, but he was also concerned about the members of the congregation who were not studying theology. How could he make this strange text from the apostle Paul about the mystery of the resurrection—a text he had chosen himself—meaningful to all listeners?

Bonhoeffer's reference to the "government [that] issues a proclamation" is to that of Chancellor Franz von Papen, which had come to power just a few days before, on June 1. The new government hoped to restore a society more in the German tradition, with leadership from the nobility and the clergy, as had been the case under the Kaiser. Chancellor Von Papen had reintroduced the custom of invoking the name of God at the opening of parliament. But quotations such as "the cup of nothingness," from twentieth-century German poet Gottfried Benn, whose work Bonhoeffer had heard performed in an oratorio by his contemporary, German composer Paul Hindemith, show that Bonhoeffer realized that the church's message was no longer being taken seriously by much of the modern world, and was looking urgently for ways to communicate the gospel in a disillusioned and secularized society.

———

Colossians 3:1–4: *So if you have been raised with Christ, seek the things that are above, where Christ is, seated at the right hand of God. Set your mind on things that are above, not on things that are on earth, for you have died, and your life is hidden with Christ in God. When Christ who is your life is revealed, then you also will be revealed with him in glory.*

———

Dear congregation, that is certainly an extremely off-putting way to start a conversation with a person: Since you have been raised with Christ, do this and that. We have been baptized. We have been confirmed. There were times when we felt like opening the Bible. We are interested in various religious questions. Maybe we even stand by our church with loyalty and love. And finally, after all: we live in a world that over the last one and a half to two thousand years under the name of Jesus Christ has developed as a Christian world. And nevertheless: if anyone tried to start a conversation with us by just speaking to us about the fact that we have been raised with Christ, we would probably prefer not to continue to speak with them. We would see that they were moved. We would see that they were excited. We would see how intensely serious they were about what they were still going to say to us. But we would distance ourselves from this assumption that they made and from which they would not let go at any price, from this condition that they think they have to set so that we are even able to hear and understand everything else they would like to share with us; yes, we would distance ourselves from this assumption and this condition that we have been raised with Christ; we would turn away astonished and unfavorably impressed. We would shake our heads about a person like that.

*Actually*, this way of addressing us should come over us like a judgment. *Actually*, this one word should break in upon us—so powerful, so sublime, so exalted—that we grow pale in fear and trembling before it: for *this* glow, this glory of being raised with Christ is really not a part of our experience, cannot be seen anywhere in our lives, try as one might and looking as carefully as possible. Instead, we turn aside, astonished and unfavorably impressed. Instead, we shake our heads. Instead, when someone speaks to us like that, it seems to us baptized and confirmed Christians as if a representative of some mysterious secret society were coming up to us with his weird secret password. We must not delude ourselves: this address, "you have been raised with Christ," goes completely and hopelessly right over the heads of us Christians. We have long since banished this form of address into the sects (and then are surprised that there still are sects). We have long since left this form of address behind as obsolete and antiquated, in order to concern ourselves with apparently more important, more useful, more interesting, even with more Christian things.

What is it supposed to mean to us that we have been raised with Christ? It is incomprehensible for us. It seems foolish to us. It is completely uninteresting to us. It seems to us completely ill-suited for the beginning of a conversation. It seems to us completely ill-suited at the start of a work day, at the beginning of the plans that we are considering, at the beginning of important decisions we have to make. It seems to us completely ill-suited in relationships we have with one another. How should the certainty that we have all been raised in Christ affect the relationship of the teacher to the pupil, the friend to the friend, the wife to the husband, and the father to the son? If we tolerate this idea at all, then only as the crowning conclusion of a brilliant lecture. If this thought has anything to say to us, then only in the hours long after work, far removed from the immediate reality of our decisions, exalted pious hours, but to which we grant only a very limited right to affect the rest of our life. And how should the rest of our life be influenced anyway by this enigmatic and easily misunderstood assertion that we have been raised with Christ?

Dear friends, without noticing it and as if by chance, we have just laid out the whole crisis of our Christianity. For isn't it true that on the first superficial consideration, it must be unavoidably clear: if there was a time when there was a Christianity where people believed things like that, where people concerned themselves with such great thoughts, when a person could meet another person, speak to him, even close a business deal, all the while with that certainty that they have both been raised in Christ—then our time, our Christianity, our faith are greatly impoverished in comparison. Then we have suffered huge losses. For we don't even come close to understanding at all what it means that we all together have been raised in Christ. We stand here before this apostolic assurance *so* poorly prepared, with *so* little idea what it is about, that out of sheer lack of another explanation we think that it must be a whimsical eccentricity of the apostle, and we could justifiably leave it to the eccentrics, the sect members.

And then it is completely incomprehensible to us how this kind of certainty that we have been raised with Christ should even have an effect in our lives. When we are in need, in questions of politics or the economy, in questions of the education of our children, in questions of married life, when we are unsure in what form and toward which goals we should structure our whole life, would it occur to a single one of us, whether we are the questioners or those who should give the answer, to state as the first proposition of this deliberation, in all decisiveness: All of us together have been raised in Christ? You nations over here and over there—you have been raised in Christ? You men of finance, you who manage the billions of the world, and with that the savings of the small and the smallest—you have been raised in Christ? You parents and husbands and wives, you who are one another's friends, you apartment-house residents with all of your difficulties and disagreements, you employers and you employees, you who yearn to become real, strong, capable people—all of you have been raised in Christ?

Dear friends, one need do nothing more than consider something like that. One need only walk through the streets, look at the people, and ask yourself whether they accept this premise and live their lives on the basis of it, in order to see that what we call Christianity is, in human terms, hopelessly in need, that it is greatly impoverished, whether the churches are filled to overflowing as in America or almost empty as in much of Germany.

Our fathers still said: "In the name of God, Amen." They still lived under the illusion that with that, they had said something important. They still lived under the illusion that with that, they had said something that everyone had in common, that was an obligation to them all, that bound them all together. But they probably never allowed this "In the name of

God, Amen" to become too dangerous, too disturbing, too revolutionary. And why should they? This opening, this premise, could just as well mean everything as nothing. Having said these words, one could confidently draw the line and just go on, unworried and unswerving, and in the name of humankind make decisions and decrees and pass statutes, whatever one thought was good and whatever one liked. One went one's way in complete freedom, with the name of God harmlessly backing one up and the earthly well-being of human beings in view.

And did one even really need the name of God backing one up to fight for and win the earthly well-being of humankind? Should this ancient name of God, at the same time so simple and so full of meaning, be able to contribute anything to mastering the innumerable problems that had to be solved? And the richness of the human became all the more tempting and the ancient name of the ancient God slipped more and more into obscurity. So the name of God moved further and further away, and ever nearer came the fullness of concrete life standing on its own.

What if one could finally find the key to wisdom for all areas of life? The ideal form of the state? The smoothest exchange of goods between all nations of the earth, the crisis-proof monetary system from which all instability would have been removed? The best possible educational method, the most sophisticated hygiene and diet, the infallible cure? The deepest analysis of the mind and maybe also the best philosophy, the finest art, and certainly also the best of all forms of religiosity? Isn't it true that for a large segment of our people, salvation is expected from nothing other than these things? And the more this longed-for salvation eludes us, the more our plans come to nothing again and again, and the more our life falls from cliff to cliff and from crisis to crisis, the more we cry out for specialists, for experts. *They* must know; *they* must be able to do it. After all, the most exact science must be able to bring us to our goal, must bring order in our chaos. How much more trustworthy, how much more promising this scientific system is, feverishly pushing forward in all areas of our human life, than that flat, unexpressive: "In the name of God, Amen," and that antiquated, long-forgotten: "If you have been raised with Christ."

But is this world that we are rushing toward at full speed really so trustworthy and filled with promise? Will we ever really succeed in bringing together understanding and knowledge in such a way that they no longer constantly contradict each other, in integrating all our actions and work in such a way that people are not constantly acting and working against each other on this earth? And if we should succeed at that: Where should we go with it all? Is it really so that we are reeling into endlessness, into the "Never-ending", as a modern poet calls it? The "Never-ending," of which we could only be terrified—what awaits us seems *too* empty, *too* dark, *too* bottomless. Our future looks at us with hollow eyes.

Perhaps at first we are intoxicated by this grandiose prospect; we feel drunk in this gigantic freedom, without God and without hope, without a goal and without restraint, rushing violently ahead into chaos. Even the greatest futility can be intensified into pathos and art, into life and motivation. But as soon as we stop, sober up from our intoxication, come to our senses, it becomes unbelievably empty inside us: "Do you not taste the cup of nothingness, that dark drink?" And now what, what do we want now? Do we want to survive another crisis and then die, or what do we really want? We are told: "I have been through too much, I cannot be without religion anymore"; and that probably means: I have already looked too deeply into this nothingness to be able to stand being in it any longer. So go back—but back to where? We read that a government issues a proclamation that a whole nation should be rescued from collapse—by the Christian worldview. So we are all fleeing, individuals and nations, fleeing from an incomprehensible last collapse. "In the name of God, Amen" is to be used again. Religion is to be cultivated again and a Christian worldview spread.

Oh, how poor, oh, how weak, oh, how pitiful all of that sounds. Do we think that we would really let ourselves be taken captive a second time by this "In the name of God, Amen?" That we would let it really determine all our actions, that we, you and I, rich and poor, German and French, would let ourselves be bound together by this name of God? Or is there not really, hidden behind our religious tendencies, our irrepressible craving for freedom and our own will—to do in the name of God what *we* want, in the name of the Christian worldview to play off one nationality against another and stir them up to conflict with one another?

And only now does it fall like scales from our eyes; only now are we overcome by the certainty of the monstrous fact—that we are fleeing from God. Whether we dare to drink the cup of nothingness, that dark drink, or we avoid it by taking refuge in religious busyness and talk, we are fleeing from that other cup that the Bible has tasted and which it proclaims to the world in a powerful voice: the cup of the wrath of God, the cup of the consuming fire of the living God [see Jer. 25:15–29]. Our disobedience is not that we are so little religious but that we actually would like very much to be religious, find it very edifying when someone somewhere says and writes: "In the name of God, Amen," are very much reassured when some government or other proclaims the Christian worldview. It is our disobedience, it is our fleeing, it is our calamitous downfall—that we, the more pious we are, are all the less willing to let ourselves be told that God is dangerous; that God does not allow God's self to be mocked; that we human beings must die if we really want to have anything to do with the living God; that we must lose our life if we really want to gain it [Matt. 10:39]; that we must be baptized not only with water but also with fire and the spirit [Matt. 3:11]; that this "In the name of God, Amen," if it really is to have any meaning and not be just empty talk, is a majestic region that one can enter only as a completely captive slave—or not at all.

To drink this cup of God's, if one really knows what one is doing, that is serious. And to drink the cup of nothingness, that dark drink, if one really knows what one is doing, is also serious—and the eternal God with his glowing promise is infinitely closer to those who do this than they could imagine from afar.

But to stand somewhere in the middle of it all with some kind or other of harmless, naive, pious or impious talk, religious or irreligious interest, fleeing from the One who is eternally alive and fleeing from the eternally dead—that is nothingness. There is no rejoicing about this among the angels of heaven; these are the healthy people who do not need a physician [Matt. 9:12]; these are the ninety-nine righteous men [Luke 15:7]. But because we are standing there right in the middle between the two fires, because we do not know anymore, no, for good reasons do not *want* to know what it means: You have died with Christ, you have been crucified with Christ—that is why, then, we don't know anymore what it means: you have been raised with Christ. Now it is as if we had been placed under the ban, as if we *were not allowed* to know it anymore. Now it lies over us like a punishment that we must stand before these words with blind eyes and deaf ears [see Matt. 1:11–15; Isa. 6:10], completely at a loss about what they should mean and what we should do with them in our life.

Could it be possible that our ears and eyes be opened again, that we again understand dusty old words and perceive that they carry life within them? Life as no science, also no religious studies can give us, but only the eternal God, in the eternal Son? That in them we find our one and only consolation and support, whether we live or die? That we have died and our life is hidden with Christ in God. That we have been raised with Christ and for that reason can set our minds "on things that are above, not on things that are on earth?"

We must stop here for today. It is better and more salutary for us to see once in all clarity how far our private and public life is removed from this understanding than to explain just like that what an easy thing it is to regain this understanding. If it were an easy thing, then it would not be *this* understanding but once more a couple of pious, edifying human thoughts.

But because they are *God's* thoughts, they cannot remain hidden from us in eternity. Because it is God who in this Christ bends down to us, to draw us close, because God has loved us always and forever, that is why all of that cannot remain for us a riddle and foolishness for all time. It is God who will tear away the veil that now lies over these holy words; it is God who will open our astonished eyes for that glory, for it is true that we have died with Christ but have also been raised with Christ, that our true life is that which is now and always hidden with Christ in God.

And this truth of God would take us captive, would bind and be an obligation to us, would bond us together, person to person. If we come together with some "In the name of God, Amen," then we still come in our unbroken human pride, then we never really find one another, then we never really meet each other, then we always talk past each other, at the conferences and in our families. For it is simply impossible for us to give up our demands that seem so justifiable. But if we come together as the crucified and risen ones of Jesus Christ, as those who have lost our prideful human life in order to win it anew in Christ, as those who were sentenced to death but pardoned—then we will find one another, then we would look into one another's eyes and would recognize one another completely anew, as we are recognized by God. Then and only then could we love one another. Lord, our ruler, eternal God! Send a hunger into the land. Not a hunger for bread and a thirst for water, but a hunger to hear the word of the Lord [see Amos 8:11]. Amen.

# The Things That Are Above

## Berlin, Fourth Sunday after Trinity, June 19, 1932

—————————=:《①》:=—————————

Bonhoeffer had preached the previous Sunday on these verses from the apostle Paul's letter to Christians in Colossae (see page 41). But he had taken so much time that day in presenting his clear view of the contemporary world that he still had much more to say. So he asked his colleague Gerhard Jacobi, for whom he was substituting, to let him preach again on the same text.

In this sermon, Bonhoeffer refers both to literature and to world events to illustrate the conflict that arises for Christians between seeking the "things that are above" and still remaining relevant in the world. His mention of Christians being persecuted and shot refers to news from Russia that had shocked church folk in Germany. He also points to a Russian film about an educational pioneer, Makarenko, and the social problems following the Russian Revolution, but does not fail to bring in Germany's own social problems, which the Protestant churches regretted having neglected. "Stay true to the earth," is a quote from Friedrich Nietzsche's *Thus Spake Zarathustra*. His word about faith as not the "opium" that allows us to remain content refers to "opium of the people," a phrase made famous by Karl Marx, though Marx may not have said it first. Bonhoeffer's hearers may not have read Nietzsche or Marx but would have known that they were nineteenth-century philosophers opposed to the church. In the opening paragraph, Bonhoeffer quotes a line from the poem "The Limits of Human Nature" by Johann Wolfgang von Goethe (translated by Vernon Watkins). Later he mentions the familiar German poets Friedrich Hölderlin (1770–1843) and Rainer Maria Rilke (1875–1926), whose works are still taught in German schools today.

———— ◈ ————

Colossians 3:1–4: *So if you have been raised with Christ, seek the things that are above, where Christ is, seated at the right hand of God. Set your mind on things that are above, not on things that are on earth, for you have died, and your life is hidden with Christ in God. When Christ who is your life is revealed, then you also will be revealed with him in glory.*

———— ◈ ————

Dear congregation, it is as if our whole life were carried, raised up, and protected in these words. Say what you will against this "Seek the things that are above." You may suspect that those who are constantly seeking things above may lose contact with the ground under their feet. "If he reaches up and raises his head to touch the stars, then his unsure feet will have no foothold, and he will be the plaything of clouds and wind." No matter how the individual feels about it, human society suspects with good reason that people with their heads in the clouds like that might be useless extra mouths to feed, instead of using burning hearts and a strong arm to create order and progress here on earth; that they would dream of a better afterlife and would be unfit for the great revolutionary action that each generation must take, smashing old tablets and setting up new and better ones.

Because of sentences like this, "Set your mind on things that are above and not on things that are on the earth," Christians are being stood up against the wall and shot. Because of sentences like this, Christianity is accused of betraying the earth. "Stay true to the earth"; set your mind on things that are on earth. For countless people that is a holy cause—and we understand their zeal. We understand the jealousy with which they want to bind the planning and work and efforts of human beings to this earth. For we are bound to this earth. It is the place where we stand and fall. An accounting is demanded for what happens on earth. And woe to us Christians if we should fail there; if at the end of all things, it should have to be said of unbelievers: Well done, good and trustworthy slave, you have been trustworthy in a few things; I will put you in charge of many things, enter into the joy of your master; because they were faithful in an earthly way in the earthly tasks that were given them, because they had invested the talents that were entrusted to them, while it would have to be said of us Christians: As for this worthless slave, throw him into the outer darkness, because we had buried our talent in the ground—for all our setting our minds on things that are above. [See Matthew 25:14–30.]

The Russian film *The Road to Life* probably made a shocking impression on many people. There you saw how whole bands of neglected, criminal boys and young men were gathered by a superior leader and through voluntary and orderly work were changed from vagabonds into human beings. And the shocking part of it was this: the building where this working group was living was a cloister church. The clergy had been driven out; worship services and prayer had come to an end. But now a new era and a great earthly goal flooded through these rooms: to lead people out of earthly night and into earthly light. Set your mind on things that are on earth!

Today, immensely important things will be decided by whether we Christians have strength enough to show the world that we are not dreamers and are not those who walk with their heads in the clouds, that we don't just let things come and go as they are, that our faith is really not the opium that lets us stay content in the midst of an unjust world, but that we, especially because we set our minds on things that are above, only protest all the more tenaciously and resolutely on this earth. Protest with words and action, in order to lead the way forward at any price. Must it be that Christianity, which began in such a tremendously revolutionary way long ago, is now conservative for all time? That each new movement must forge a path for itself without the church, that time after time the church does not see what has actually happened until twenty years after the fact?

If that really is the way it must be, we should not be surprised if for our church, too, times will come again when the blood of martyrs will be required. But this blood, if we really still have the courage and honor and faithfulness to shed it, will not be as innocent and untarnished as that of the first witnesses. On our blood would lie great guilt of our own: the guilt of the worthless slave, who is thrown into the outer darkness.

And yet, however grave the danger that lies in these words—"Seek the things that are above, where Christ is seated at the right hand of God"—the danger that we could misunderstand it, the danger that we might become useless servants, the danger that people accuse us of betraying the earth, we feel nevertheless that in these words our life is carried, raised up, and protected, that only in these words our life acquires a meaning that it would not have at all, however much we were faithful to the earth, however eager for action we were, and with however holy an urge to improve the world we would storm ahead. There may be innumerable things that are urgent and necessary, but there is only one thing that is needed: just this, that our whole life be protected by God. And just that, for which we human beings did not even dare to ask from afar, is simply assured to us: You have been raised with Christ, and your life is hidden with Christ in God.

We would really like to say all of that in a more modern, plain, and simple way, wouldn't we? The way it is preached in some churches and as it is believed by all too many Christians: Set your mind on things that are above, for your life is hidden in God. That is after all what we really would like to hear on Sunday: We bring all the fullness, the whole richness of our life along with us into church. And here the clergy should do their duty, should bless and consecrate, should, over the depths and heights of our days, over suffering and joy, over sorrow and tears, over work and worries, speak the one word of salvation: that all of it is protected and hidden in God, the Creator of the world.

Outside in the world, of course, we are told something different. We are told that with our work and with our plans we are descending into a crisis, that with all our efforts we are only pushing ahead into the dark and boundless void. Perhaps we are told that our life is hopeless, that we must be suffocated by illness, misery, and guilt. Maybe the enticing call breaks in on the life of a happy family: Set your minds on things that are below, for the human being comes from the animals and must become an animal.

And from all these frightening things in the real world, we could flee into the church as into an old, familiar home. There, there everything would be bright and light: see, everything you plan and do and suffer is protected in God, the Creator of the world. For that reason, set your minds on things that are above.

Haven't we all already felt that the frightening truth of the world simply swallows up this church talk? If the animal in us insists on its rights, what good does it do us to talk of the godliness of human beings? If the voice in us calls to us, "Set your mind on things that are below," what help to us is the most urgent warning, "Set your mind on things that are above"? When catastrophic demonic forces attack us and tear the rudder out of our grip, so that we feel as if the fate of our world were driven by a raging hurricane, what consolation for us is the thought that all this is God's will? And if even death is reaching out for us, what good is all our talk about immortality?

Set your minds on things above, for our life is hidden in God—that may be a nice, pious, edifying sentence, but it doesn't stand up to the reality of the world. And this sentence must be contradicted by the world. It must be suspected of tempting us to betray the earth, of lulling us into a false sense of being protected in God, of robbing us of the initiative of the fighter and allowing us to be at rest in the midst of the most screaming injustice in the world.

But no such thing is in the Bible. The apostle knows very well what he is doing when—completely without concern for our cries that it was not modern enough, that it was too hard to understand, that it was not plain and simple enough—he holds fast with all tenacity to this: Set your minds on things that are above, where Christ is seated at the right hand of God, for your life is hidden with Christ in God. And as we eagerly crowd around this with all our common sense, and maybe also with a great deal of human wisdom, to find out what this "hidden with Christ in God" might mean—there, like a cherub with a flaming sword [Genesis 3:24], stands that other word in the middle of the passage: "You have died." That is the strange part about it, that wherever there is talk of the living God, this death always comes in between; that wherever there is talk of gaining life, this losing of life always comes in between. What does that mean anyway, this dying or even this having died in the midst of life?

Here an impassable boundary is proclaimed with respect to our whole life, a barrier and boundary that we not only do not want to know anything about, but about which we also, frighteningly, cannot know anything. You have died—that does not mean only something like: You all without exception are headed for death; you are captive to death at every step. Rather, it must mean: Life has already become captive to the power of that riddle which is the essential riddle of death. That last, deepest human destiny to which our dying gives such strange witness is also the destiny of our life. There is a power that stands behind our living and our dying—and this power is really not to be compared to life, as we are always tempted to do, but rather, if one is to find something comparable to it, it is more comparable to death.

Only if one could see through God's own eyes could one view death and life along the same line in this way, that is, from the perspective of death. Because for us human beings the differences between life and death are unbelievably great, while for God they fall together into one. For God a person is not more and not less, not farther away and not nearer, whether he or she lives or dies. But when speaking in human words and for human understanding about how it is for a human being, whether living or dying, whether in the eyes of God even human death is like continued living—in that case our text admonishes us with the greatest firmness to think about just the opposite case. What if it were so that in God's eyes even our life was like death? Precisely not the triumphant "Life," which we human beings make such a big thing of, but actually and fundamentally a completely unstable, futile, hopeless, and godforsaken "Death." "You have died."

The Bible still dares to think that frightening thought, for which we modern people are much too weak, that it is not "nothing" that we face there, whether we live or die, that we do not simply sink into emptiness, free of all responsibility, but that we come to ruin, confronted with the very God, and are shattered by God, who is closer to us than our own blood, that we are confronted by the wrath of God. "You have died"— that means in the final analysis nothing other than: you are lost, godforsaken, whether you die or live. That is the frightening boundary that is proclaimed to us here.

That is the message against which we rebel in our innermost being. We are glad to let ourselves be taught, we even let ourselves be taught about religious matters, but we want all of that to happen in such a way that we who speak and we who hear walk back and forth together in the beautifully decorated, cozy, warm rooms of our life. We let ourselves be preached to; we let ourselves be scolded; we let ourselves be advised and helped. But no one may lead us up to that boundary. We decided that for ourselves long ago. The boundary—that whether we live or die, we could be godforsaken people—we long ago discovered that to be an antiquated, false doctrine. We, of course, know so much better that it is just the other way around, that we, whether we live or die, actually are hidden in God; that it is only one step from us over to God; that it is as if God lives in the room next door, as Rilke occasionally hinted.

Because we know that our life in the final analysis is life sheltered in God, divine life, for that reason we also know what expectations we can have of the church. Our visible life should be talked about. It should be examined down to its divine depths; it should be transfigured by divine consecration and divine blessing. But where does our knowledge of all that come from? Have the sciences brought us to the understanding that the human being's standing before God is not so bad? Or should that possibly be true because Goethe and Hölderlin were of that opinion?

"You have died," says the apostle, and he certainly knows: If it is really true that our living and dying are nothing before God, then our thinking is also of no use. Then we could think a thousand times about how much nicer and simpler and more edifying it would be to have a God with whom we could not be lost—but these thousand thoughts would go astray. If it is true that we have died, we will have to let God himself tell us that we have died. For a lost way of thinking doesn't realize it is lost. Neither Paul nor we would know anything about this line of death, about this boundary, this being lost, if it were not God who told us all this. It is God who speaks to us; it is God who comes to us; it is God who tells us that we are lost. But when God does that, then God, the one we have lost, is of course already with us; then we have already long been helped; there God scoffs at all our lostness; there God triumphs over everything that could separate us from God's love. There God's love has drawn us close, and no power in the world can tear us out of God's hand.

The apostle wants to tell us this incomprehensible, wonderful message. You have died—he doesn't say that to us to torture us, not to cast us into despair, but simply and only because he can say in the next breath: "And your life is hidden with Christ in God." We have not been left alone at all in our lostness; instead, there is One who has stepped across the boundary that separates us from the Creator and from true life, has broken into our territory of death, has tasted all our living and dying to its deepest depths, and has still broken through this death, broken through to the eternal Father, to eternal life, where he is seated at the right hand of God. And he has pulled up the whole world with him to life and to the light, has swallowed up death in victory, has taken our whole prison captive and brought us freedom, the glorious freedom of the children of God.

Dear friends, we don't want to give the impression that we understood all that. That is the one event that takes place beyond the boundaries of all that is human and for that reason also beyond the boundaries of our understanding. That Jesus, the great wise man of Galilee, should be the Christ who breaks through the whole line of death, of human dying and living, and leads us in triumph to the Father—no human being yet has understood that. There would be a thousand objections and doubts. There would be insurmountable difficulties.

But Christ came into the world not so that we should understand him but so that we should cling to him, so that we simply let him pull us into the unbelievable event of the resurrection, so that we simply have it said to us, said to us in all its incomprehensibility: You have died—and yet you have been raised! You are in the darkness—and yet you are in the light. You are afraid—and yet you can be glad. Right next to each other the completely contradictory; right next to each other, just the way the two worlds, our world and the world of God, are right next to each other.

"You have died, and your life is hidden with Christ in God." That is the one glowing promise that is given to us. However our visible life may be: whether it leads us to the heights and brings a rich harvest of recognition, honor, and fame; whether it has to take a lower path through humiliation and collapses under the heavy burden of misery and guilt; whether it is heroic and noble and great or petty, foolish, and dull; whether our conscience rejoices in blissful joy or throbs in terrible self-accusation: This life should not be glorified and not be raised to the heavens by us human beings. If we tried to do this, we could only come to ruin before God. But precisely that, coming to ruin before God, does not have to happen to us—however our visible life may be—if we give it up, give it up before God, if we lose it, lose it for the sake of Christ, this whole visible life that is at the same time so elevated and so hopeless.

For close by us in that majestic hiddenness where God is all in all, where the Son is enthroned at the right hand of the Father—there, oh wonder of wonders, our true life has been prepared. Our life is hidden with Christ in God. We ourselves are already at home in the midst of our homelessness.

Our visible life flows away like a dream and often like a curse. Dominated by demonic ideas, involved in crises, laden with misery and guilt—this life is a life that has died. It takes its all-too-familiar dark paths, but all of that is taken care of in God. As that which has come under the power of death, it is torn away from death by God; as the lost, it is saved by God.

Oh, God certainly would have the power to destroy us sinful human beings and to create new human beings. He certainly would have the power first to extinguish our life and afterward to have a completely new, redeemed life ready for us. But no, he lifts up our life, just as it is, into his majestic hiddenness; just as it is, it is glorified in his boundless glory. Our visible life, with its joys and successes, with its worries and its sorrows and its painful disobedience: holy and blameless and perfect it stands now, for the sake of Jesus Christ, in that hidden world of God before the eyes of the Almighty, today and tomorrow and in all eternity. And no tear falls in vain, and no sigh goes unheard; no pain is ignored, and no rejoicing is lost. The visible world strides brutally and heartlessly and violently past all of this. But out of grace and mercy and great kindness, God gathers our burning, blazing life; he glorifies it for the sake of Jesus Christ; he builds it up new and good in that hidden world where the line of death that separates us from God has been taken away. Our true life is hidden—but it is grounded firmly in eternity. "When Christ who is your life is revealed, then you also will be revealed with him in his glory." Amen.

# Overcoming Fear

## Berlin, Second Sunday after Epiphany, January 15, 1933

In January 1933, shortly before Hitler came to power, Bonhoeffer preached this sermon at a vespers service on the evening of the second Sunday after Epiphany. It was a time of great tension in Berlin, and of widespread fear. The Hindenburg government was tottering, indeed was about to go under, and with it Germany's fragile first republic, created at Weimar after World War I. There was fear of Communism—the "Red Tide from the East"—and other extremist movements, and danger from open fighting in the streets. In the midst of this storm, Bonhoeffer was no more certain of the future than anyone else, but he was sure that followers of Christ should know where to turn. "God stands above all . . . his Word unstayed," Bonhoeffer assured the congregation, quoting a verse from "The Golden Sun," a beloved hymn by Paul Gerhardt.

Matthew 8:23–27: *And when he got into the boat, his disciples followed him. A windstorm arose on the sea, so great that the boat was being swamped by the waves; but he was asleep. And they went and woke him up, saying, "Lord, save us! We are perishing!" And he said to them, "Why are you afraid, you of little faith?" Then he got up and rebuked the winds and the sea; and there was a dead calm. They were amazed, saying, "What sort of man is this, that even the winds and the sea obey him?"*

The overcoming of fear—that is what we are proclaiming here. The Bible, the gospel, Christ, the church, the faith—all are one great battle cry against fear in the lives of human beings. Fear is, somehow or other, the archenemy itself. It crouches in people's hearts. It hollows out their insides, until their resistance and strength are spent and they suddenly break down. Fear secretly gnaws and eats away at all the ties that bind a person to God and to others, and when in a time of need that person reaches for those ties and clings to them, they break and the individual sinks back into himself or herself, helpless and despairing, while hell rejoices.

Now fear leers that person in the face, saying: Here we are all by ourselves, you and I, now I'm showing you my true face. And anyone who has seen naked fear revealed, who has been its victim in terrifying loneliness—fear of an important decision; fear of a heavy stroke of fate, losing one's job, an illness; fear of a vice that one can no longer resist, to which one is enslaved; fear of disgrace; fear of another person; fear of dying—that person knows that fear is only one of the faces of evil itself, one form by which the world, at enmity with God, grasps for someone. Nothing can make a human being so conscious of the reality of powers opposed to God in our lives as this loneliness, this helplessness, this fog spreading over everything, this sense that there is no way out, and this raving impulse to get oneself out of this hell of hopelessness.

Have you ever seen someone in the grip of fear? It's dreadful in a child, but even more dreadful in an adult: the staring eyes, the shivering like an animal, the pleading attempt to defend oneself. Fear takes away a person's humanity. This is not what the creature made by God looks like—this person belongs to the devil, this enslaved, broken-down, sick creature.

But the human being doesn't have to be afraid; we should not be afraid! That is what makes humans different from all other creatures. In the midst of every situation where there is no way out, where nothing is clear, where it is our fault, we know that there is hope, and this hope is called: Thy will be done, yes, thy will is being done. "This world must fall, God stands above all, his thoughts unswayed, his Word unstayed, his will forever our ground and hope." Do you ask: How do you know? Then we name the name of the One who makes the evil inside us recoil, who makes fear and anxiety themselves tremble with fear and puts them to flight. We name the One who overcame fear and led it captive in the victory procession, who nailed it to the cross and committed it to oblivion; we name the One who is the shout of victory of humankind redeemed from the fear of death—Jesus Christ, the Crucified and Living One. He alone is Lord over fear; it knows him as its master; it gives way to him alone. So look to Christ when you are afraid, think of Christ, keep him before your eyes, call upon Christ and pray to him, believe that he is with you now, helping you . . . Then fear will grow pale and fade away, and you will be free, through your faith in our strong and living Savior, Jesus Christ.

Let's say there is a ship on the high sea, having a fierce struggle with the waves. The storm wind is blowing harder by the minute. The boat is small, tossed about like a toy; the sky is dark; the sailors' strength is failing. Then one of them is gripped by . . . whom? what? . . . he cannot tell himself. But someone is there in the boat who wasn't there before. Someone comes close to him and lays cold hands on his arms as he pulls wildly on his oar. He feels his muscles freeze, feels the strength go out of them. Then the unknown one reaches into his heart and mind and magically brings forth the strangest pictures. He sees his family, his children crying. What will become of them if he is no more? Then he seems to be back where he once was when he followed evil ways, in long years of bondage to evil, and he sees the faces of his companions in that bondage. He sees a neighbor whom he wounded, only yesterday, with an angry word. Suddenly he can no longer see or hear anything, can no longer row, a wave overwhelms him, and in final desperation he shrieks: Stranger in this boat, who are you? And the other answers, I am Fear. Now the cry goes up from the whole crew; Fear is in the boat; all arms are frozen and drop their oars; all hope is lost, Fear is in the boat.

Then it is as if the heavens opened, as if the heavenly hosts themselves raised a shout of victory in the midst of hopelessness: Christ is in the boat. Christ is in the boat, and no sooner has the call gone out and been heard than Fear shrinks back, and the waves subside. The sea becomes calm and the boat rests on its quiet surface. Christ was in the boat!

We were along on that voyage, weren't we? and the call, Christ is in the boat, was once our salvation too. And now, strangely enough, all of us are at sea again, on that voyage without faith, without hope, overwhelmed, in chains, in bondage, paralyzed by fear; we have lost heart, lost the joy of living, our limbs heavy as lead; each of us knows what it's like. Perhaps, or most likely, we don't even quite realize what has happened to us; we are already so used to this state of affairs that it seems natural to us, and we almost like it that way, all this misery around us and in our own lives. What would we do if we couldn't even complain anymore?

And that's the worst of it: we don't even want to find a way out. That is the final triumph of Fear over us, that we are afraid to run away from it, and just let it enslave us. Fear has conquered us; it can be found among us in various forms. Some persons have become dull and insensitive and just live from one day to the next, brooding gloomily and doggedly along, but too apathetic to take their own lives. Others are noisy about their fear, pouring it out to everyone else in the form of crying and complaining. Still others, on the other hand, think they can drive out their fear with fine words and bold fantasies, and if they shout these words loudly enough it may seem to take care of things for awhile. But those who know can recognize in such empty words the horrifying power of fear all over again. Fear is in the boat, in Germany, in our own lives and in the nave of this church—naked fear of an hour from now, of tomorrow and the day after. That is why we become apathetic, why we complain, why we intoxicate ourselves with this and that. What else is all the razzle-dazzle and drunkenness of New Year's Eve, other than our great fear of a new era, of the future? Fear is breathing down our necks.

Those who would try to keep up their pride, as if all this had nothing to do with them, as if they didn't understand what it's all about, would hardly be human. No one human could fail to understand what the people of the world have to be afraid of today.

But look here, right in the middle of this fearful world is a place that is meant for all time, which has a peculiar task that the world doesn't understand. It keeps calling over and over but always anew, in the same tone, the same thing: Fear is overcome; don't be afraid [John 16:33]. In the world you are frightened. But be comforted; I have conquered the world! Christ is in the boat! And this place, where this kind of talk is heard and should be heard, is the pulpit of the church. From this pulpit the living Christ himself wants to speak, so that wherever he reaches somebody, that person will feel the fear sinking away, will feel Christ overcoming his or her fear.

You of little faith, why are you so fearful? In these words we must hear all the disappointment of Jesus Christ in his disciples and all his love for them. Do you still not know that you are in God's hands, that where I am, God is? Why are you so fearful? Be of good courage, strong, firm, adult, sure, confident, not shaking with fear. Don't hang your heads; don't complain about what bad times these are . . . I am in the boat. And Christ is here, too, in the nave of this church. So why not hear him and believe him?

We have come here, very probably, because somehow or other we know that something in our lives needs to change, and because we think perhaps the church can somehow help us with this. We are aware of how meager, how poor, how petty and short-sighted our lives have become. All of us see only our own worries and difficulties and no longer those of others that may be a thousand times worse. Our affairs seem so enormous and infinitely important to us that we have become dulled toward anything else. This is the work of fear in us. And now we sense that we can't bear to be hemmed in like this anymore; it's suffocating. The call of the church cuts through this questioning and foreboding. There is one thing we are lacking: to believe that the Almighty God is our father and our Lord. To believe that for God, our greatest cares are like the worries of small children in their parents' eyes; that God can turn things around and dispose of them in no time at all; for God it's easy, not hard at all. We must believe that a thousand years in God's sight are like a day [Ps. 90:4], that God's thoughts are higher than our thoughts [Isa. 55:8–9], that God is with us in spite of everything. Let us receive the call of the church once again: You of little faith, why are you so fearful? In the midst of the storm, Christ is in the ship. Away with you, Fear! Let us see you, Lord Jesus, strong helper, Savior!

But now comes a host of objections and excuses. We say we would like to believe, but we simply can't anymore. The suffering is too great. Oh, but let's not take this kind of talk too seriously. You cannot believe? Well, neither can we. Do you want to believe?—in that case you already do, in a way, perhaps not very strongly, only a beginning, but perhaps a thousand times stronger than many others who think they are able to believe. Don't worry about your faith, whether it is weak or strong. Just look to him in whom you believe, and speak to him: Lord, increase our faith! [See Luke 17:5].

We say that it is not life's misery that frightens us, but rather our own sin that we fear; and that we need to fear it, so we won't be overcome by it! Again, that sounds so right, but it is really only a trick of fear itself. No, it is not true that we must be afraid of sin. Those who are afraid of it are already up to their necks in it. Fear is evil's net, spread to catch us. Once evil has made us afraid, confused us, we are in its clutches. Don't be afraid, be of good courage . . . How can you meet the enemy with fear in your heart? You of little faith, why are you so fearful? Isn't God greater than your sin? Let God grow strong in you; then sin is knocked down. Believe in God . . . Lord, strengthen our faith!

Now, finally, let the most depressed and despairing people speak, those who ask: Isn't our time up? Aren't the years of catastrophe, of utter decline and breakdown, the chaos of our lives in both great and small things, which no one can ignore, the sign that God has let us go? God doesn't want us anymore. There's no more mercy coming our way from God. God is against us, and we have to accept it. It won't do to keep clinging if we aren't wanted. This is the cry out of the very depths of despair. There is only one thing that helps, and it is what the church does with any of us who thinks and feels this way. It takes the cross and places it before our eyes and asks: Did God abandon him? And since God did not abandon Jesus, we will not be abandoned by God, either.

Learn to recognize this sign in your own life. Learn to recognize and understand the hour of the storm, when you were perishing. This is the time when God is incredibly close to you, not far away. Right there, when everything else that keeps us safe is breaking and falling down, when one after another all the things our lives depend on are being taken away or destroyed, where we have to learn to give them up, all this is happening because God is coming near to us, because God wants to be our only support and certainty. God lets our lives be broken and fail in every direction, through fate and guilt, and through this very failure God brings us back; we are thrown back upon God alone. God wants to show us that when you let everything go, when you lose all your own security and have to give it up, that is when you are totally free to receive God and be kept totally safe in God. So may we understand rightly the hours of affliction and temptation, the hours in our lives when we are on the high seas! God is close to us then, not far away. Our God is on the cross.

The cross is the sign that stands in judgment on all the false security in our lives and restores faith in God alone. Be of good courage, be valiant, be confident, be certain—that is what it says. Yes, but everything depends here on making sure that one last, terrible misunderstanding does not arise. There is such a thing as false courage, false confidence . . . and this false confidence is itself only the most subtle form in which fear disguises itself. Let us return to our story.

When the disciples were climbing aboard the boat, they seemed quite confident; they seemed not at all afraid. Why were they confident? They looked at the lovely calm sea and saw no reason to worry. But as the wind and waves increased in force, the disciples lost their calm and fear grew in them. They gazed apprehensively at the wild sea. Its appearance had made them feel safe, but now fear was gaining the upper hand. The story says that Jesus was asleep. Only faith can sleep without a care—that is why sleep is a reminder of paradise—faith finds its safety in God alone. The disciples couldn't sleep; their security was gone; their confidence had been misplaced and now was lost. It was a false sense of security—it was only fear in disguise. This sense of security does not overcome fear and soon breaks down. Only the faith that leaves behind all false confidence, letting it fall and break down, can overcome fear. This is faith: it does not rely on itself or on favorable seas, favorable conditions; it does not rely on its own strength or on other people's strength, but believes only and alone in God, whether or not there is a storm. It is the only faith that is not superstition and does not let us slip back into fear, but makes us free of fear. Lord, make this faith strong in us who have little faith!

But the other side of the coin is also true. When Christ is in the boat, a storm always comes up. The world tries with all its evil powers to get hold of him, to destroy him along with his disciples; it hates him and rises up against him. Christians surely know this. No one has to go through so much anxiety and fear as do Christians. But this does not surprise us, since Christ is the Crucified One, and there is no way to life for a Christian without being crucified. So we will suffer and make our way through together with Christ, looking always to him who is with us in the boat and can soon stand up and rebuke the sea, so that it becomes calm.

However, it does seem to be true, what you have surely all been quietly wanting to say for some time, that today Christ is no longer doing such amazing things. He is so strangely hidden away that we often think he is no longer there at all! Dear brothers and sisters, what do we know about what Christ can do and wants to do for us, this very evening, if we will only call upon him as we should, if we call out, "Lord, save us! We are perishing!" That was fear all right, but it was faith in the midst of fear, because it knew where help comes from, the only place. We say there are no miracles anymore . . . but what do we know really, you and I? We will certainly be ashamed of ourselves if one day we are allowed to see what God can do.

They were amazed, saying, "What sort of man is this, that even the winds and the sea obey him?" We can well understand their amazement. What sort of person is this on whom fear has no effect, who overcomes the fear in human life and takes away its power? By asking this question, we are already on our knees before him, praying to him, pointing to him, the wonder worker, and saying, This is God! Amen.

# Gideon: God Is My Lord

## Berlin, First Sunday in Lent,
## February 26, 1933

<hr/>

In this sermon, the first that he preached after Hitler's takeover of power, Bonhoeffer was concerned to put things in place, to proclaim at this moment when even German cathedrals were hung with swastika flags that for Christians there is only one Lord. He took as his text the Old Testament story of Gideon, a young man chosen by God to save the Israelites from their enemies and to turn them away from the worship of false gods. As Bonhoeffer scholar Larry Rasmussen has said, Bonhoeffer "contrasted the reluctant Gideon with Siegfried, the unconquered Germanic hero figure of the Nibelung saga, who was already being idealized in Nazi propaganda." Bonhoeffer quotes from both Old and New Testaments in describing God's power in contrast to human might, and finally from Martin Luther's hymn "A Mighty Fortress," to assure his hearers that even now the power, and the victory, are God's alone.

Judges 6:15–16; 7:2; 8:23: *[Gideon] responded [to the Lord], "But sir, how can I deliver Israel? My clan is the weakest in Manasseh, and I am the least in my family." The Lord said to him, "But I will be with you, and you shall strike down the Midianites, every one of them." . . . The Lord said to Gideon, "The troops with you are too many for me to give the Midianites into their hand. Israel would only take the credit away from me, saying, "I have delivered myself." . . . Gideon said to them, "I will not rule over you, and my son will not rule over you; the Lord will rule over you."*

This is a passionate story about God's derision for all those who are fearful and have little faith, all those who are much too careful, the worriers, all those who want to be somebody in the eyes of God but are not. It is a story of God's mocking human might [Gal. 6:7], a story of doubt and of faith in this God who makes fun of human beings, who wins them over with this mockery and with love. So it is no rousing heroic legend—there is nothing of Siegfried in Gideon. Instead it is a rough, tough, not very uplifting story, in which we are all being roundly ridiculed along with him.

And who wants to be ridiculed, who can think of anything more humiliating than being made a laughingstock by the Lord of the world? The Bible often speaks of God in heaven making fun of our human hustle and bustle, of God's laughter at the vain creatures he has made. Here it is the powerful, Sovereign One whose strength is unequalled, the living Lord, who carries on this way about his creatures. For him, who has all power in his hands, who speaks a word and it is done [Ps. 33:9], who breathes forth his spirit and the world lives, or takes it away and the world perishes [Ps. 104:29, 30], who dashes entire nations to pieces, like potters' vessels [Ps. 2:9]—for this God, human beings are not heroes, not heroic, but rather creatures who are meant to do his will and obey him, whom he forces with mockery and with love to be his servants.

So that's why we have Gideon and not Siegfried, because this doubter, mocked by God, has learned his faith in the school of hard knocks.

In the church we have only *one* altar—the altar of the Most High, the One and Only, the Almighty, the Lord, to whom alone be honor and praise, the Creator before whom all creation bows down, before whom even the most powerful are but dust. We don't have any side altars at which to worship human beings. The worship of God and not of humankind is what takes place at the altar of our church. Anyone who wants to do otherwise should stay away and cannot come with us into God's house. Anyone who wants to build an altar to himself or to any other human is mocking God, and God will not allow such mockery. To be in the church means to have the courage to be alone with God as Lord, to worship God and not any human person. And it does take courage. The thing that most hinders us from letting God be Lord, that is, from believing in God, is our cowardice. That is why we have Gideon, because he comes with us to the one altar of the Most High, the Almighty, and falls on his knees to this God alone.

In the church we also have only *one* pulpit, from which faith in God is preached and not any other faith, not even with the best intentions. This again is why we have Gideon—because he himself, his life story is a living sermon about this faith. We have Gideon because we don't want always to be speaking of our faith in abstract, other-worldly, unreal or general terms, to which people may be glad to listen but which they don't really take note of; because it is good once in a while actually to see faith in action, not just hear what it should be like, but see how it just happens in the midst of someone's life, in the story of a human being. Only here does faith become, for everyone, not just a children's game, but rather something highly dangerous, even terrifying. Here a person is being treated without considerations or conditions or allowances; he has to bow to what is being asked, or he will be broken. This is why the image of a person of faith is so often that of someone who is not beautiful in human terms, not a harmonious picture, but rather that of someone who has been torn to shreds. The picture of someone who has learned to have faith has the peculiar quality of always pointing away from the person's own self, toward the One in whose power, in whose captivity and bondage he or she is. So we have Gideon, because his story is a story of God glorified, of the human being humbled.

Here is Gideon, one person no different from a thousand others, but out of that thousand, he is the one whom God comes to meet, who is called into God's service, is called to act. Why is he the one, or why is it you, or I? Is it because God wants to make fun of me, in coming to talk with me? Is it God's grace, which makes a mockery of all our understanding? But what are we asking here? Isn't God entitled to call whomever God chooses, you or me, the highly placed or the lowly, strong or powerless, poor or rich, without our being entitled to start arguing about it straight away? Is there anything we can do here other than hear and obey?

Gideon is supposed to liberate Israel from its bondage at the hands of the Midianites, an enemy nation with superior power. He, who is just like any of a thousand others, is called upon to do a phenomenal deed. He looks at himself and his own strength and then at the unconquerable might of the opposing side. He has nothing on his side—the enemy has it all. "He responded, 'But Lord, how can I deliver Israel?'" How am I supposed to accomplish this thing that you are calling me to do? Lord, it's too big a job, don't be cruel. Take it back, or let me see some help, give me armies, weapons, riches! God, you don't realize how wretched we are; look at this starving, weakened people, see how homelessness and lack of bread makes them doubt you, look how they bow down to other gods and not to you. "How can I deliver Israel?" This Gideon is someone we know, isn't he? He has suddenly become very much alive for us. Gideon, we recognize your voice only too well; you sound just the same today as you did then.

The call comes to our Protestant church, just one like many others in the world: you are to redeem Israel; you are to set the people free from the chains of fear and cowardice and evil that bind them. This call startles the church and troubles it profoundly, this church without influence, powerless, undistinguished in every way—why is it the one to be burdened with this call? It looks at the hopelessness of its proclamation; it looks at the apathy and the misery of those who are supposed to be listening and recognizes that it is not equal to the task. It looks upon its own inner emptiness and barrenness, and it says fearfully and reproachfully, *with what* am I supposed to redeem this people? How am I supposed to do this phenomenal thing? And then suddenly the call comes to us: put an end to the bondage in which you are living, put an end to the mortal fear that gnaws at you, to the power of human desire that is burning you up, to your tormented and self-satisfied keeping to yourself. Put an end to your fear of other people and your vanity; set yourself free. Who would be willing to say that he or she has never heard this call and has never answered, as Gideon did: Lord, *with what* am *I* supposed to do such great things?

But then Gideon is silenced; today as just as in those days, he's told to shut up. You're asking, "With what?" Haven't you realized what it means that this is God calling to you? Isn't the call of God enough for you; if you listen properly, doesn't it drown out all your "with what" questions? "I will be with you"—that means you are not asked to do this with any other help. It is I who have called you; I will be with you; I shall be doing it too. Do you hear that, Gideon of yesterday and today? God has called you, and that is enough. Do you hear that, individual doubting Christian, asking and doubting Christian? God has plans for you, and that does mean you. Be ready and see to it. Never forget, even when your own powerlessness is grinding you down to the ground, that God has phenomenal, immeasurable, great plans for you. I will be with you.

*What does Gideon do?* He goes out and has the trumpets blown, calls up an army from all the tribes, gathers around him whatever fighting forces he can find. Compared to the superior forces of the enemy it is still only a small army, and Gideon hesitates to go into battle. Then, just as he is pitching his tents opposite those of the enemy, there comes God again, blocking his path. Gideon, what have you done? Gideon, where is your faith? Look at this army of yours; it's too big; Gideon, it was fear and doubt that made you call up this army. The troops with you are too many for me. I'm not going to give you the victory this way. Then you would only take the credit for yourselves and say, we have delivered ourselves, we have gained the victory. But I will have none of it. Fall down before your God and let God be your Lord; know that only God can save you. This is God's promise, and the word of God is more powerful than all the armies in the world.

Here the crucial question has been put: Gideon, do you seriously believe in God your Lord, even here face-to-face with this terrifyingly dangerous enemy—then, Gideon, send your massive army home; you don't need it. God is with you; the victory belongs to God and not to your army. What a phenomenal thing to ask, what a confusing encounter with the living God! There stands Gideon with his little army, hesitating to go out against the enemy's superior forces, and then God comes and laughs rudely in his face, makes fun of him: Gideon, the troops with you are too many for me. Instead of bringing on huge amounts of weapons and armies, he calls for disarmament, meaning faith, faith; let your armies go home! How cruelly God makes fun of all human might; it's the bitterest of all tests of faith and makes God an incomprehensible lord and despot over the world. Isn't it crazy? Wouldn't Gideon have been torn apart inwardly, to have to give up the only forces that, from a human viewpoint, he could count on, here in the face of the enemy? What kind of wild God is this, zealous for his own honor, always standing in human beings' way and frustrating their plans, before they know it? Why does God frustrate us? Because God is opposed to the proud [Prov. 3:34; 1 Pet. 5:5], because humans keep getting it wrong, however they do it? Why do we always get it wrong? Because we are always trying for our own credit, and don't want to believe in God.

*But Gideon believed and obeyed*; he let his troops go home, and with every man who left him, his faith grew in this God who had made fun of him. And when they had all gone except for a tiny remnant, the victory was given into his hands. He believed, he obeyed, he gave God the glory, he renounced the honor for himself, and God kept the promise made.

Is this a tall tale like all the others? Anyone who says so has failed to understand that Gideon is still with us, that the old story of Gideon is being played out in Christendom every day. I will be with you in the face of the enemy. . . . What does Gideon do? What do we do? We rustle up all our own forces; we reach out for every means of help; we calculate, we weigh, we count; we arm ourselves with offensive and defensive weapons. Until then, suddenly and unexpectedly—nobody knows the hour—the living God is there and assails us again: if you have faith, lay down your weapons; I am your weapon. Take off your armor; I am your armor. Put away your pride; I am your pride. Do you hear that, church of Gideon? Let God alone; let the word and the sacraments and the commandment of God be your weapons; don't look around for other help; don't be frightened. God is with you. Let my grace be sufficient for you [2 Cor. 12:9]. Don't try to be strong, mighty, famous, respected, but let God alone be your strength, your fame and honor. Or don't you believe in God?

It does seem crazy, doesn't it, that the church should not defend itself by every means possible in the face of the terrible threats coming at it from every side. What madness brought this Gideon into the world? But all this is only the foolishness of the Christian faith itself; that is what this story is about. It's not about the particular command that was given; it's not that which is valid for all the ages, but rather the foolishness, the stumbling block of living faith, which confesses, "With might of ours can naught be done, soon were our lost effected . . ."

And you as an individual, you who have heard the call to free yourself from bondage, to loosen its chains and the grip of fear, you are already right back into acting from lack of faith. You think that by straining to exert all your energies, you can do it yourself, by putting all you have into it, because you want to control your own destiny. Then suddenly there is God standing in your path, and there go all your fine plans again. Lay down your weapons, for I am your weapon, and a thousand of your weapons are not equal to one of mine. Let me do what you cannot do. You want the honor of saying, I have delivered myself, but this is not for you; give me the honor and the glory, believe in me. Let my grace be sufficient for you, for my power is made perfect in weakness.

Gideon's warriors must have been flabbergasted; they must have shuddered when he gave them the order to go home. The church is always astounded, and shudders, when it hears the voice of the One who commands it to renounce power and honor, to let go of all its calculations and let God alone do God's work. We shake our heads and are scandalized as we watch many a Gideon going his way among us. But how can that confound *us* who see in the midst of our church the cross, which is the sign of powerlessness, dishonor, defenselessness, hopelessness, meaninglessness, and yet is also where we find divine power, honor, defense, hope, meaning, glory, life, victory? Do we now see the direct line from Gideon to the cross? Do we see that the name of this line, in a word, is "faith"?

Gideon conquers, the church conquers, we conquer, because faith alone conquers. But the victory belongs not to Gideon, the church, or ourselves, but to God. And God's victory means our defeat, our humiliation; it means God's derision and wrath at all human pretensions of might, at humans puffing themselves up and thinking they are somebodies themselves. It means the world and its shouting is silenced, that all our ideas and plans are frustrated; it means the cross. The cross over the world—that means that human beings, even the most noble, go down to dust whether it suits them or not, and with them all the gods and idols and lords of this world. The cross of Jesus Christ—that means God's bitter mockery of all human grandeur and God's bitter suffering in all human misery, God's lordship over all the world.

The people approach the victorious Gideon with the final trial, the final temptation: "Be our lord, rule over us." But Gideon has not forgotten his own history, nor the history of his people. . . . The Lord will rule over you, and you shall have no other lord. At this word, all the altars of gods and idols fall down, all worship of human beings and human self-idolization. They are all judged, condemned, cancelled out, crucified, and toppled into the dust before the One who alone is Lord. Beside us kneels Gideon, who was brought through fear and doubt to faith, before the altar of the one and only God, and with us Gideon prays, Lord on the cross, be our only Lord. Amen.

# The Joy of Ascension

## Berlin, Ascension Day, May 25, 1933

―――――――――《◐》――――――――――

Ascension Day is a traditional religious holiday in Europe, observed forty days after Easter, on the Thursday ten days before Pentecost. In Bonhoeffer's time, schools and most workplaces were closed, and many faithful Christians went to church on that day. On Ascension Day 1933, Bonhoeffer didn't try their patience with a long sermon, but gave them a cheering word to take away with them. He quoted the first line of the familiar German chorale "Jesu, meine Freude" ("Jesus, my Joy") by Johann Franck, which we know as "Jesus, Priceless Treasure." The refrain "Rejoice, o Christendom" that he repeats several times is from "O sanctissima," another Christmas carol that was very familiar to his hearers as "O du fröhliche" ("O How Joyfully"). Mindful, however, that Jesus' ascension had not been a joyful moment for his disciples—in fact, they felt abandoned!—Bonhoeffer recalled a story he had told to one of his first Sunday school classes in 1926—the parable in Luke's Gospel about servants keeping watch by night for the return of their master.

1 Peter 1:7b–9: . . . *when Jesus Christ is revealed. Although you have not seen him, you love him; and even though you do not see him now, you believe in him and rejoice with an indescribable and glorious joy, for you are receiving the outcome of your faith, the salvation of your souls.*

"Jesus, my joy"—that is what we have just sung, and to be able to say that honestly, from the heart, is the meaning of a life lived with Christ. If there is someone to whom it sounds very foreign, or who hears nothing in it but mushy enthusiasm, then that person has never yet heard the gospel. Jesus Christ was made a human being for the sake of humankind in the stable at Bethlehem—rejoice, o Christendom. Jesus Christ became the companion of sinners and sat among tax collectors and prostitutes—rejoice, o Christendom. Jesus Christ became a convicted criminal for the sake of convicts, on the cross at Golgotha—rejoice, o Christendom. Jesus Christ rose from death to life for the sake of all of us—rejoice, o Christendom. Jesus Christ, for the sake of his church, went from this earthly home to his heavenly kingdom—rejoice, o Christendom. Jesus Christ coming from God and returning to God—that is not a new world of problems, of questions and answers. That means it is not a new moral law, not a new burden added to the burdens people already have to carry. What it really means, above all, is the joy of God in the world, the joy of God catching fire in humanity, which is hungry for joy. In a thousand ways people today ask, where can we find joy? Church of Christ, you alone know the answer; say it out loud: Christ, my joy.

Christ's ascension has two meanings. It is Jesus's farewell to his disciples, to the world which he loved. It was a long and hard road they had walked together. He had told them many things, but now the time had come when he had to leave them alone. Now they had to be able to walk without always looking to him. Now the end of his time on earth had come. They had gone one last stretch of road together—then came the final moment; he laid his hands on them in blessing, and then he was taken from their sight. They were alone. The curtain had fallen. He had left this world of evil and gone home to his heavenly Father. Lord, have mercy on us. Rejoice, o Christendom; he has gone home to his Father; he is preparing a place for you, a home in his kingdom [John 14:2–3]; he will take you home when his time comes. Just wait—and rejoice. He will come again.

But how can people rejoice when they have been abandoned? How can those who are left orphans be comforted? How can those who are torn by homesickness be cheerful? You orphaned church, left alone in your homesickness for Jesus Christ and his ascension, your ascension, rejoice! For you are allowed to love him whom you cannot see; you are allowed to believe in him who is lost to your sight. And nobody can take your love and your faith from you. It is our church, the church living between Christ's ascension and his coming again, of which our text says: although you have not seen him, you love him; and even though you do not see him now, you believe in him. It is the church that stands alone in its waiting, alone in its faith, and that finds its joy in faith alone. Lord, teach this church, which does not see you, the true joy in Christ. Without rejoicing, there is no church. Let us talk today about joy in Christ.

Luther once said something like this: While Christ was on earth he was far away from us, but now that he is in heaven, he is close to us. What does that mean? It means that now he is no longer king of the Jews but rather king of the whole world; it means that from heaven he reigns over his whole kingdom and is near, though not visible, and present to his whole church, wherever it is scattered, among Jews and heathen, through all the world. He is close to us in his church, in his Word, in his sacrament, in the love among brothers and sisters. Here he comforts us who are abandoned; here he soothes our homesickness ever anew; here he takes us who are estranged from God, who are in barren, empty places, who don't know the way, who are alone, and makes us joyful in his Christly presence. Joy in the sermon, joy in the sacraments, joy in brothers and sisters—that is the joy of the believing church in its unseen, heavenly Lord.

Joy in the sermon—how hard that is for us people of today. That's because we are listening to the preacher and not to Christ. We turn our own joy sour because we confuse earthly joy with heavenly joy. Our poor Protestant church doesn't offer us much earthly joy. Don't come looking for it here. But heavenly joy Christ can give us, even through his frail church, and we should look for it only from him, not from the preacher. In the sermon it is Christ who wants to visit us and wants to be himself our heavenly joy.

Joy in the sermon—joy in the sacraments—how much more we have lost of the latter than of the former. Joy in the sacraments—one might say that sounds Catholic. Maybe it does sound Catholic, but mainly it sounds archetypically Christian. Here the sacrament, the Lord's Supper with our heavenly Lord, is inexpressible joy in his presence; here the sacrament is the feast of joy for which a congregation of redeemed sinners gathers together, in the midst of this world of evil, and prays for the return of its heavenly king. Here the sacrament is the communion among brothers and sisters whose joy is in one another. Joy in the sacraments—that is the joy of the heart full of longing and desire for its God whom it has found; that is the anticipation in the hearts of strangers and homeless people, as they look forward to their eternal home and pray that it may come.

King of the church, Master of joy beyond compare, give us great longing and desire, a mighty homesickness for you—and then come and comfort us with your ascension; make us certain of your promise, that one day the curtain that separates us from you will fall. We cannot see you, but we love you; we do not have you before our eyes, but we believe in you; we have plenty of sorrows and troubles, but your sermon and sacraments make us joyful. Lord, give more joy to your church; without joy in the sermon and joy in the sacraments, there is no church. Without the church, the whole world is joyless and miserable, and there is no end to hunger and thirst.

Joy of Ascension Day—we have to become very quiet inwardly before we can even hear the soft sound of this word. Joy comes to life in the quiet and the mystery. Indeed, this joy cannot be comprehended. But it is never what we can understand that brings us joy—it is that which we cannot understand but is true, real, and alive, that sets us alight with joy. That is why real joy itself is always somewhat incomprehensible, both for others and for the person who feels it. Joy is simply there; the joy of Ascension Day is simply there, where the church speaks of Christ being exalted over all the world and of his return, where he himself meets his joyfully expectant church in the sacraments. That joy is there, not loud but soft and subdued, fearful of the world, fearful of sin—but it is there like the heavenly joy of servants who are up at night watching by candlelight until their beloved master comes home [see Luke 12:35–40]. All our joy in Christ in this world is joy of anticipation—and who will admit out loud that he or she is looking forward to something? And yet what joy is stronger than the joy of anticipation?

Joy of anticipation—in expectation of what? In the expectation of the last things. For the Lord of heaven, who stills the hunger and thirst, the longing of his church-community, through the sacraments by faith—this Lord whom we cannot see, but whom we love nonetheless—he will come again. The curtain is opening. We shall see him face to face [1 Cor. 13:12]. He will come back once again to this earth on which we are strangers, and he will lead the homeless, who in the church, through faith, have been hoping in God's new land, home to our heavenly Father. ". . . when Jesus Christ is revealed. Although you have not seen him, you love him . . . and rejoice with an indescribable and glorious joy, for you are receiving the outcome of your faith, the salvation of your souls." Then the church's time of waiting will be over, then the end of the time of faith will have come; then joy will no longer be veiled in fear and holding back; then will come the time of fulfillment, the time of everlasting seeing, when blessedness breaks in. Then he will appear, our brother the Lord, and his church will fall down before him in holy joy. "You . . . rejoice with an indescribable and glorious joy." Then the world and the church will fall away, and Jesus himself will be our joy. For here we have no lasting city [Heb. 13:14], but we are looking for the city that is to come.

Christ's ascension—the curtain falls, the church of faith waits, and its joy is the sacrament. Christ's coming again—heaven opens up. Home at last, our thirst is slaked—the community of the blessed sees the incomprehensible mystery. Its joy is Jesus Christ, none other than God. At present we are still strangers, wandering in the time between his ascension and his second coming, waiting long in hope and fear. But the ransomed of the Lord shall return with singing, and everlasting joy shall be upon their heads [Isa. 35:10]. Rejoice, o Christendom. Amen.

# Who Do You Say That I Am?

## Berlin, Sixth Sunday after Trinity, July 23, 1933

B onhoeffer preached his last sermon in Berlin on a day of great tension in the Protestant church. On short notice and in defiance of German law, Hitler had called national church elections for that very day, to allow the German Christians to put in place church leaders more to his liking. Bonhoeffer and his Young Reformation students and friends campaigned hard for opposing candidates under the slogan "Church must remain church," but the network of Nazi organizations, plus a radio speech by Hitler himself the evening before, gained two-thirds of the vote for the "German Christians."

As always, Bonhoeffer refrained from making direct political statements in his sermon. Instead, he sought to let his hearers feel the very ground, the rock on which the church of Christ is built. He speaks here of Peter, the disciple who confessed Jesus as Christ, but later denied him and wept in remorse. Bonhoeffer contrasts Peter with Judas, on whom he would preach later to his seminarians (see page 185). "You are Peter," Jesus says in the text for this day, "and on this rock I will build my church."

These words, in Latin *Tu es Petrus et super hanc petram aedificabo ecclesiam meam*, are inscribed in the dome of St. Peter's in Rome.

———

Matthew 16:13–18: *Now when Jesus came into the district of Caesarea Philippi, he asked his disciples, "Who do people say that the Son of Man is?" And they said, "Some say John the Baptist, but others Elijah, and still others Jeremiah or one of the prophets." He said to them, "But who do you say that I am?" Simon Peter answered, "You are the Messiah, the Son of the Living God." And Jesus answered him, "Blessed are you, Simon son of Jonah! For flesh and blood has not revealed this to you, but my Father in heaven. And I tell you, you are Peter, and on this rock I will build my church, and the gates of Hades will not prevail against it."*

———

If we had our way, we would prefer to keep detouring around the decisions confronting us. If we had our way, we would prefer not to be dragged into this fight over the church. If we had our way, we would rather not have to keep insisting on our cause, and would gladly avoid the terrible danger of self-righteousness over against other people. If we had our way, we would remove ourselves tomorrow or better yet, today, join the quiet folk in the countryside, and leave the quarrel and self-righteousness to other people. But—God be thanked—it is not up to us. With God, we get just what we don't want. We are challenged to come out and make the decision; we cannot get out of it. Wherever we take our stand, we must also allow ourselves to be suspected of being self-opinionated, of speaking and acting against the others out of arrogance. We will not be spared any of this—making a decision means that we differ with others. Therefore, if we are honest, we will not hide from the significance of this day, today.

In the midst of the creaking and groaning of the church structures, which have been profoundly shaken and are collapsing and crumbling away here and there, we can still hear the promise of the eternal church, against which the gates of hell shall not prevail, the church on the rock, which Christ has built and continues to build through all the ages. Where is this church? Where can we find it? Where can we hear its voice? Come, all of you who are asking this seriously, you who are left alone and lonely, who have lost your church. Let us go back to the Holy Scriptures, let us look together for the eternal church. Let anyone with ears to hear listen!

It is a lonely place where Christ has gone with his disciples, on the edge of a heathen region, where he can be alone with them. This is the place where, for the first time, he promises them, as his legacy, his eternal church. Not in the midst of the people, not at the visible climax of his ministry, but rather out here far away from the right-thinking scribes and the Pharisees, from the crowds who will sing "Hosanna" to him on Palm Sunday and then on Good Friday shout, "Crucify him," he speaks to his disciples about the mystery and the future of his church. Evidently he meant that the building of this church could not begin with the scribes, the priests, or the crowds, but it was rather this little group of disciples, his followers, who were called to do it. Evidently he also did not consider Jerusalem, the city of the temple and the center of the people's life, as the right place for it, but instead he went to a quiet place where he could not hope for his announcement to make waves in any outward, visible way. And finally, he did not consider any great day of celebration as the proper time to speak about his church. Instead, he gave the promise of his church in the face of death, immediately before his first foretelling of his passion. So it is a church of a little flock, a church far out in a quiet place, a church in the face of death, about which we must be speaking here.

Jesus himself asks the decisive question, for which the disciples must have been waiting for some time, "Who do people say that the Son of Man is?" The answer is: "Some say you are John the Baptist, but others say you are Elijah, and still others say you are Jeremiah or one of the prophets." Opinions, nothing but people's opinions. The list of them could be extended as long as one wants. . . . Some say you are a great man, others, that you are an idealist, others, that you are a religious genius, others, that you are a hero, the greatest of leaders. Opinions, more or less serious opinions—but Christ doesn't want to build his church on opinions.

So now he asks them directly, "But who do you say that I am?" In this unavoidable, face-to-face situation with Christ, there is no "perhaps," no "some say," no opinions anymore, but only silence, or else the one answer that Peter now gives: "You are the Messiah, the Son of the Living God."

Here in the midst of the whirl of human opinions and perspectives, something truly new is visible. Here the name of God has been named; the name of the Eternal has been spoken; the mystery has been brought to light. This is no longer human thinking but rather the very opposite; this is divine revelation and confession of faith. "Blessed are you, Simon son of Jonah! For flesh and blood has not revealed this to you, but my Father in heaven . . . you are Peter, the rock, and on this rock I will build my church."

What is the difference between Peter and the others? Does he have such a heroic nature that he rises head and shoulders above them? He does not. Does he have unmatched strength of character? He does not. Does he have such unshakeable loyalty? He does not. Peter is nobody really, nobody but a person who confesses, a person who has met Christ standing in his path and has recognized him, and who now confesses his faith in Christ. And this Peter, this confessing person, is now named as the rock on which Christ will build his church.

The church of Peter—that means the church on the rock, the church of confessing Christ. The church of Peter is not the church of opinions and views but rather the church of revelation; not the church that talks about "what people say" but the church in which Peter's confession is always being made and spoken anew, the church that does nothing else but always and only make this confession, whether in singing, praying, preaching, or action. It is the church that only stands on the rock as long as it keeps doing this, but becomes the house built on sand [Matt. 7:26–27] that the wind blows down if it dares to think of going another way, for whatever reason, or even to look away for a moment.

But being the church of Peter is not only something to be claimed with unalloyed pride. Peter, the confessing, believing disciple, denied his Lord on the same night in which Judas betrayed him; Peter stood there by the fire that night and was ashamed, while Christ was standing before the high priest. Peter was the fearful one of little faith who sank into the sea. He was the disciple to whom Jesus said, "Get behind me, Satan!" [Matt. 16:23]. Even after that, he was the one who kept faltering, kept denying and falling down, a weak vacillator, subject to the whim of the moment. The church of Peter is the church that shares his weakness, the church that also keeps denying Christ and falling down, being disloyal, of little faith, fearful, a church that again and again looks away from its mission and toward the world and its opinions. The church of Peter is the church of all those who are ashamed of their Lord, at the very moment when they should be standing up for him. . . .

But Peter is also the one of whom it is said that he went out and wept bitterly. Of Judas, who also betrayed his Lord, it is said that he went out and took his own life. That is the difference. Peter went out and wept bitterly [Matt. 26:75]. The church of Peter is the church that can not only confess, not only deny; it is the church that can also weep. By the rivers of Babylon—there we sat down and there we wept when we remembered Zion [Psalm 137]. That is being church, for what does this weeping mean, if not that we have found the way back, that we are on our way home, that we are the prodigal son who falls weeping on his knees before his father [Luke 15]. The church of Peter is the church of divine sorrow, which leads to joy.

It's really shaky ground, isn't it? But it is still the rock, this ground; for this Peter, this reed bending in the wind, is called by God, taken prisoner by God, held fast by God. "You are Peter . . ." We are all Peter; not the pope, as the Catholics say, not this person or that person, but all of us who are just living by our confession of Christ, as fearful, disloyal persons of little faith, but who are held fast by God.

Yet it is not we who are to build, but God. No human being builds the church, but Christ alone. Anyone who proposes to build the church is certainly already on the way to destroying it, because it will turn out to be a temple of idolatry, though the builder does not intend that or know it. We are to confess, while God builds. We are to preach, while God builds. We are to pray to God, while God builds. We do not know God's plan. We cannot see whether God is building up or taking down. It could be that the times that human beings judge to be times for knocking down structures would be, for God, times to do a lot of building, or that the great moments of the church from a human viewpoint are, for God, times for pulling it down. It is a great comfort that Christ gives to the church: You confess, preach, bear witness to me, but I alone will do the building, wherever I am pleased to do so. Don't interfere with my orders. Church, if you do your own part right, then that is enough. But make sure you do it right. Don't look for anyone's opinion; don't ask them what they think. Don't keep calculating; don't look around for support from others. Not only must church remain church, but you, my church, confess, confess, confess. . . . Christ alone is your Lord; by his grace alone you live, just as you are. Christ is building.

And the gates of hell shall not prevail against you. Death is the great inheritor of everything that exists. This is as far as death goes. Right by the abyss of the valley of death is the foundation of the church, the church that confesses Christ as its life. The church has eternal life precisely there where death is reaching out for it, and death is reaching out for it precisely because it has eternal life. The church that confesses is the eternal church, for Christ is its protector. Its eternity is not visible to this world. It is not subject to challenge by the world, though the waves wash up over it and sometimes it looks completely covered over and lost. But victory belongs to the church, because Christ its Lord is with it and has overcome the world of death. Don't ask whether you can see victory but believe in the victory, for it is yours.

Our text is written in huge letters around the cupola of the great church of St. Peter, the church of the pope, in Rome. Proudly this church points to its eternity, its visible victory over the world through all the centuries. Such glory, which our Lord did not desire for himself or put on, is not allowed us. But we may be certain that a glory immeasurably greater than this worldly glory is our destiny. Whether the people gathered is great or small, lowly or highly placed, weak or strong, if they confess Christ, the victory is theirs for eternity. Fear not, little flock, for it is your Father's good pleasure to give you the kingdom [Luke 12:32]. For where two or three are gathered in my name, there am I in the midst of them [Matt. 18:20]. The city of God stands on a firm foundation. Amen.

# Ambassadors for Christ

## London, Nineteenth Sunday after Trinity, October 22, 1933

———— »«◐»« ————

In the summer of 1933, Bonhoeffer exchanged letters with the retiring pastor of St. Paul's and Sydenham Churches, both congregations for German-speaking people in London, and made a quick trip there to preach his candidate sermon. In October, in haste amid many other decisions that needed to be made and commitments fulfilled, he moved into two rooms in a building that housed a German school, which served as the parsonage. Bonhoeffer looked forward greatly to this chance to work full-time as a pastor, but he also felt torn about leaving behind the struggle going on in his home church over its true confessional identity. Many good friends were involved in the struggle, including Martin Niemöller and Karl Barth.

Now the day had come for him to stand in each of the two pulpits, face-to-face with the people whose lives he would share for the next year and a half. Could he help these two small churches to be what the church is called to be?

He must certainly give them "bread instead of stones" (a potent biblical image, more so in the Mediterranean world, where a worn, rounded stone may look remarkably like a hand-shaped loaf of bread). He must certainly proclaim the gospel. (Woe to the preacher who does not!) And so he began, reaching out to them with yearning words.

---

2 Corinthians 5:20: *So we are ambassadors for Christ, since God is making his appeal through us; we entreat you on behalf of Christ, be reconciled to God.*

---

Every change of pastors in a congregation is bound up with all sorts of human emotions. If all is well and as it should be in the congregation, it is painful to see the pastor leave who has served there faithfully. There are so many things that bind a good congregation and a good pastor. How could it be otherwise, when he has spoken with his congregation Sunday after Sunday about the ultimate matters of life and death? When he has celebrated the Lord's Supper with the believers, with those who mourn, the poor in spirit, those who hunger and thirst, the peacemakers, and the long-suffering? [Matt. 5:1–11]. When he has searched day by day in the homes of his parishioners, to find one soul that longs for love, for strength, justice, peace, and freedom, and when he then is able to speak not only about people searching for their God but also about God's seeking out human beings in the midst of their uncertainty, their questions and hesitations and the burdens they carry, in the midst of their loneliness—and when, there in the stillness, such a soul opens and reveals itself to the neighbor soul and to God? How near the pastor comes to his congregation at such times, at least to the part of the congregation that is alive! How much he knows about their hardships and difficulties that no one else will ever know; how much he carries, silently and humbly, with his congregation, and brings it before God in prayer, as the faithful shepherd of his flock.

Yes, when all is well between pastor and congregation, then it is very understandable to be overcome by human sadness when the time comes to part. The church members look toward the future with some reservations and somewhat worriedly, somewhat fearfully. How is it going to be with the new one? Will things feel the same with this new person? Will he or she have the same understanding of ministry or perhaps an entirely different one? For both pastors, of course, the same sort of thoughts and questions arise. So a moment like this is brimming and loaded with feelings of the most personal sort: pain, joy, worry, confidence.

So it would be good if, at a moment like this, we let ourselves be lifted up above the very personal level and take a broader, larger-scale view of things. A change of pastors is a situation in which we get stuck in our very personal feelings, but we should be encouraged to see something much larger, which does not concern persons at all, neither the old one nor the new one, but rather concerns the mission that is entrusted to both of them, no matter who they are. What matters is the one who gives the orders, not the one who carries them out, only the master, rather than the servant. The one thing that is really necessary is that this master's mission be carried out, whether it causes pastors to break down or not; or whether they are often rather strange people, perhaps because they know more than others about the strange things in life; whether they can win people over easily, or whether they have a hard time with themselves and others. If only the mission is carried out, in preaching and in life, if only the pastor's sole concern is to devote his or her life to this master and this commission.

For the congregation, however, this means that at this point everything depends on its being led to let go of the issue of the person and to look instead to the Lord of the church; to pay attention to the preaching rather than the preacher; and to have only one question: Is this truly the Gospel of our God that we are hearing? Or is it the kind of arbitrary thinking that human beings invent, which blossoms today and withers away tomorrow like the grass of the field? [Matt. 6:30 (Isa. 40:7)]. There is really only one question for a congregation to ask of its pastor: Are you offering us the eternal word of God, the word of life, wherever you can, in the pulpit and in daily life? Or are you giving us stones instead of bread? Are you giving us placebos that are perhaps more pleasant to take but do not satisfy our souls? Give us bread that fills our hungry souls! This should be the daily plea with which the congregation stands before its pastor, just as the pastor should stand before God and pray for this gift for the congregation, as their pastor, their shepherd.

Between you and your pastor there should be only Christ. The one important matter between you and your pastor, wherever we meet, whether in serious or joyful moments, is always Christ.

So then, we are ambassadors for Christ. . . . That means that we do not work under our own authority. We do not send ourselves on mission. Nor are we ourselves the guarantors of what we have to say, for Christ alone guarantees the truth of the Gospel. We preach because we are called and sent by Christ; it is Christ who gives us the mission of delivering his message. And all our words serve but to keep our eyes on one goal, and to point toward it: toward Christ, toward the Lord, toward the Word of God, which is beyond all our words, which God speaks at any time and in any place, touches and enters human hearts and brings fear and comfort to them, whenever and wherever God wants. Not our word, but God's Word: yet even so, God's Word speaking through ours.

This is what makes a sermon something unique in all the world, so completely different from any other kind of speech. When a preacher opens the Bible and interprets the word of God, a mystery takes place, a miracle: the grace of God, who comes down from heaven into our midst and speaks to us, knocks on our door, asks questions, warns us, puts pressure on us, alarms us, threatens us, and makes us joyful again and free and sure. When the Holy Scriptures are brought to life in a church, the Holy Spirit comes down from the eternal throne, into our hearts, while the busy world outside sees nothing and knows nothing about it—that God could actually be found here. Out there they are all running after the latest sensations, the excitements of evening in the big city, never knowing that the real sensation, something infinitely more exciting, is happening in here: here, where eternity and time meet, where the immortal God receives mortal human beings, through the holy Word, and cares for them, where human souls can taste the starkest terrors of despair and the ultimate depths of God's eternity.

Why do they not know this? How is it possible that thousands upon thousands of people are bored with the church and pass it by? Why did it come about that the cinema really is often more interesting, more exciting, more human and gripping than the church? Can that really be only the fault of others and not ours as well? The church was different once. It used to be that the questions of life and death were resolved and decided here. Why is this no longer so?

It is because we ourselves have made the church, and keep on making it, into something which it is not. It is because we talk too much about false, trivial human things and ideas in the church and too little about God. It is because we make the church into a playground for all sorts of feelings of ours, instead of a place where God's word is obediently received and believed. It is because we prefer quiet and edification to the holy restlessness of the powerful Lord God, because we keep thinking we have God in our power instead of allowing God to have power over us, instead of recognizing that God is truth and that over against God the whole world is in the wrong. It is because we like too much to talk and think about a cozy, comfortable God instead of letting ourselves be disturbed and disquieted by the presence of God—because in the end we ourselves do not want to believe that God is really here among us, right now, demanding that we hand ourselves over, in life and death, in heart and soul and body. And finally, it is because we pastors keep talking too much about passing things, perhaps about whatever we ourselves have thought out or experienced, instead of knowing that we are no more than the messengers of the great truth of the eternal Christ.

Every empire in this world sends out its ambassadors. Their job is to give visible expression throughout the world to the will and the might of their empire. They are not meant to be anything other than representatives, in this way, of their home empire and their ruler. The German ambassador or the French ambassador is supposed to be the quintessential German or French person. This has nothing to do with him or her as a person, but concerns only the person's mission. And in order to carry out their mission, ambassadors are vested with all the authority of their empire. They speak and act on behalf of their ruler.

And so the unseen Lord of the eternal kingdom and of the church sends out ambassadors into this world, giving them a mission that is greater than that of any other, just as heaven is greater than earth, and eternity is greater than time. And the authority that this Lord gives these ambassadors is that much greater than all the authorities in this world. God's eternal Word, God's eternal judgment, God's justice and God's grace, God's anger and God's mercy, salvation and damnation, reconciliation through Christ— these words are placed in the hands of the ambassadors of Christ as the most sacred and precious of goods, which they are called to administer through the grace of God. They will be required to give a full account to Christ their Lord, the Shepherd of shepherds, for every word they have spoken in his name in his church; as the shepherds of the flock, they will have to carry the blame and the responsibility. This is the ultimate meaning of the pastoral ministry!

But, we ask, what human being can do this? Who can fulfill this commission? Who can carry this burden without breaking down under it? No human being can, not even the most devout. Nobody would presume to demand such a commission. But because it is a commission, because Christ must be preached, and woe to us if we do not preach his Gospel [1 Cor. 9:16], we are carried by this obligation, this commission. We cannot do otherwise, even when we do it badly and not as we should, even when we keep breaking down under this burden and making mistakes. But then we need to know that the congregation is shouldering the burden with us, helping us, standing by us, pointing out our mistakes and praying for us, and forgiving us our sins. No pastor can do such a job properly if it is not given to him or her to know this. Many a pastor has failed because he or she wanted to carry the congregation, but the congregation did not carry the pastor. A congregation that does not pray for the ministry of its pastor is no longer a congregation. A pastor who does not pray daily for the congregation is no longer a pastor.

Our text sums up in one brief sentence the message that we are to convey: "We entreat you on behalf of Christ, be reconciled to God." What that means we cannot describe fully today. For every sermon is basically an interpretation of that sentence. That one short sentence will only be revealed in its full meaning when the end of the world is near and the last sermons are being preached, and when Christ himself comes to lead us into all truth.

"We entreat you on behalf of Christ." Christ asks through us. He does not bark orders at us, he who is the Lord of all the world. He who has all power and authority does not force us. Christ, who could make anyone do anything, comes to us as one who asks, as a poor beggar, as if he needed something from us. That he comes to us in this way is the sign of his love. He does not want to make us contrary, but rather wants to open our hearts so that he can enter. It is a strange glory, the glory of this God who comes to us as one who is poor, in order to win our hearts.

And what Christ asks of us, too, is so strange that we cannot get over our astonishment: "Be reconciled to God." This means nothing less than let a king give you his kingdom, take heaven as a gift. Let the Lord of lords of all the world give you his love, and be his friends, his children, those whom he protects. Come, surrender yourselves to him and to his will, and you will be free from every evil, from all guilt, and from all bondage. You will be free from your own selves, you will have found your way home, you will be at home with your Father.

We are unreconciled persons—that is our secret, which only Christ knows. We are persons who are not reconciled, which is why we are so worried, self-centered, unfriendly, distrustful, why we are untruthful and cowardly, why we are lonely, and why we are guilty. Be reconciled to God— give God the right to rule over you, and in finding God you will also find your brother and sister and neighbor again; be reconciled to God, and you will also be reconciled with each of them. Look into the abyss of your soul. Let Christ ask you whether you are reconciled with God or whether you have fallen away and are not at peace with God, and then look up, see and return to your God. Give God your unreconciled and irreconcilable heart. And God will give you a new heart.

O Lord, give all of us new hearts, open and obedient to you: hearts that love our neighbor and pray to you for our church. Lord, give us a good beginning; open your fatherly heart to us and lead us, one day, home to your kingdom of eternal reconciliation, through Christ the Lord! Amen.

# Turning Back

## London, Repentance Day, November 19, 1933

<hr />

Some European churches observe a Day of Repentance and Prayer in the autumn, near the end of the church year. The day was a national holiday in Germany in Bonhoeffer's time (it isn't any longer) and was of such importance that it was observed even by the German-speaking congregations in London Bonhoeffer was serving in 1933. He may have preached this sermon at a special evening service.

On the first page of his manuscript, Bonhoeffer noted the hymns to be sung during the service. The last one, "Wake, Awake, for Night Is Flying," looks forward to Advent, the season of light. Light is a theme throughout this sermon, beginning with a proverb from the Grimms' fairy tale "The Bright Sun Brings It to Light," in which a crime is revealed many years after the death of the victim. Every secret will be revealed to God, Bonhoeffer says. But Jesus Christ is the light that uncovers what is hidden in our lives, and in him we have the promise of God's grace. He echoes this understanding in a letter he wrote from prison on August 23, 1944, to his friend Eberhard Bethge: "My past life is brim-full of God's goodness, and my sins are covered by the forgiving love of Christ crucified."

2 Corinthians 5:10: *For all of us must appear before the judgment seat of Christ, so that each may receive recompense for what has been done in the body, whether good or evil.*

Nothing can remain a secret, nothing stays hidden. As a German proverb says, "No story is so cleverly made but the sun will bring it to light one day." That means this sun of ours, which is always bringing out into the light things that have taken place in the darkness—quite suddenly, to the great surprise and horror of everyone concerned. We clap our hands to our foreheads and say, how could such a thing be possible, and are terribly disappointed and strike terribly moralistic attitudes, while in the quiet of our hearts we ourselves are afraid of what the sun may find out. Sometimes it only takes a moment for a person's entire life and fate and secret to be laid bare. All it takes is for some strong hand unwittingly to pick up some old stone and to see underneath it a swarm of filthy vermin and creatures of the dark that had hidden themselves here from the sunlight, and are now exposed in all their frightening ugliness and trying to scurry away.

Such stones can lie around unnoticed for years until some clumsy foot knocks them aside. And such stones, under which no one expects to find anything, are quickly and easily seized upon as hiding places by these dark creatures of our hearts. But the dark things are still afraid; they tremble at every approaching step for fear of being exposed. Afraid of what actually? Other people—who most probably are in the same boat, all condemned together, but nonetheless pointing their long fingers at one another until their own secrets come to light.

Yet the course of this world often seems unjust, to the extent that not everything comes to light—only something here and something there, which allows everyone else to be so terribly morally outraged, as long as they have a shred of hope that it won't happen to them—certainly not because they have nothing to hide. So the proverb is not entirely right after all. And because it is not, all humanity can be divided into those whose secrets have come to light and those whose secrets have not. The latter are counted as moral and decent, while the former are considered immoral and despicable.

However, it is possible to live more or less discreetly. To be more discreet in this sense means to know how to stay in the shadows, to keep those things hidden in thoughts and feelings that someone else makes visible through actions. And the state of affairs in this world is that the sun can bring deeds to light, but not thoughts.

But how terribly mistaken we would be if we were satisfied simply to have realized this and therefore just went on living quietly, discreetly—but rotten in our innermost core.

The Day of Repentance and our text have more to say than the proverb. This text would not make a proverb. Proverbs must be moralistic and show at least one group of people that they are in the right. Our text does not do that; it doesn't say anyone is in the right. It is not moralistic at all, but rather thoroughly realistic. This text sheds light on the Day of Repentance, such a bright, glaring, dazzling light that it frightens us out of our wits. The Day of Repentance is not really a dark day, but rather a day of alarming brightness and transparency, uncontrollably lightfilled. In nature there are sometimes such days, when the air is so incredibly transparent that we can make out details that are usually shrouded in haze and distance. The Day of Repentance is this sort of day. Let us talk about this bright Day of Repentance. There is a sun here that has something to bring to light, but this sun, this light that reaches unsparingly into every corner and uncovers what is hidden, is Jesus Christ. And that changes everything.

The Day of Repentance is the day on which we are reminded in a truly unspectacular way—by a word from the Bible—that at the end of our existence, all our life will be uncovered and laid bare. "All of us must appear before the judgment seat of Christ."

We are people of today. Our way of living and thinking is not the Christian way; thus we have settled for a double self-deception about our lives that allows us to live in a certain degree of peace. One deception is in thinking that what has happened, what we have done in the past, has sunk into the dark depths of oblivion—that as long as we and others have more or less forgotten about it, it will stay forgotten. In other words, we live in the belief that forgetting is the ultimate and strongest power. Eternity means oblivion! The other deception under which we live is that we think we can decide between what is hidden and what is revealed, between what is secret and what is public. Each of us lives a public, visible life revealed to all, and in a completely separate compartment each of us has a hidden, secret life of thoughts, feelings, and hopes that no other person ever knows. We would be paralyzed with fear at the idea that all the thoughts and feelings we have had in just one day might suddenly lie open to the eyes of the world. We live under the very natural assumption that what is hidden stays hidden.

Yet here we see our lifelong comfortable assumptions unmasked, revealed as completely unjustified illusions. Eternity is not oblivion, but rather memory—eternal memory. Whatever happens in time, happens in this world, is preserved for all eternity. It leaves unavoidably immortal footprints. This is why our forebears left us the image of the Book of Life [Rev. 20:12], in which our lives are recorded. The blank page has been written on. Nothing has been forgotten. For everything we do is done in the sight of the everlasting God; this is why it is preserved for all eternity. It makes no difference whether we have forgotten or not. God does not forget.

And another thing: for God there is no difference between what is hidden and what is secret. To God, everything is as transparent as light. "For darkness is as light to you," says the psalm [130:3]. Because God is light [1 John 1:5], because God is openly revealed, then we must also be in the light and stand revealed before God. That is why, before God, there are no secrets. That is why every secret will be revealed to God; that is why the end of all things means the revelation of all mysteries, the mysteries of God and those of humankind.

"For all of us must appear before the judgment seat of Christ, so that each may receive recompense for what has been done in the body, whether good or evil." That goes against our innermost human nature. We all have things to hide; we have lifelong secrets, worries, ideas, hopes, desires, passions—about which no one else in the whole world knows. There is nothing we are more sensitive about than people touching on such areas with their questions. And here it says in the Bible, against everything we think of as fair play, that one day at the end we will have to stand revealed before Christ, with all that we are and have been, and not only before Christ but also before all the other people standing there with us. And all of us know that we may be able to stand trial in many a human court, but not in that of Christ. "Lord, who could stand? . . ." [Ps. 130:3]

Christ will judge. His spirit will distinguish between the spirits. He who was poor and powerless when he lived among us will in the end pass judgment on the whole world. For each person, therefore, there is only one essential question in life: what position do you take toward this Spirit—how do you stand toward this man Jesus Christ? Toward any other spirit, toward any other person, there are several possible positions to take. The ultimate decision does not depend on these. Toward Jesus Christ, there can only be an absolute Yes or an absolute No. For Christ is the Spirit against which every human spirit will be tested. Christ alone is the one whom no one can avoid, no one can pass by—even when we think we can stand on our own and be our own judge. No person is his or her own judge. Christ alone is the judge of humankind. No person is the judge over anybody else—Christ alone is the judge of us all, whose judgment is everlasting. And whoever has tried to pass him by here on earth without clearly saying Yes or No, will at the hour of death, at the moment when our lives are weighed for all eternity, have to stand face to face with Christ, to look into his eyes. His question will then be: have you lived in love toward God and your neighbor, or have you lived for yourself? Here there will be no escape, no excuses, no talking yourself out of it . . . here your whole life lies open to the light of Christ, "so that each may receive recompense for what has been done in the body, whether good or evil."

What a fearful moment that is to think about, when the book of our whole lives is opened, when we come face to face with what we have said and done against God's commandments, when we stand face to face with Christ and cannot defend ourselves. Lord, who could stand?

But the Bible is never intended to terrify us. God does not want human beings to be afraid, not even of the Last Judgment. We are to know about all this so that we can understand about life and its meaning. God lets people know about it now, today, so that today we can lead our lives in the open awareness and the light of the Last Judgment. We are to know for only one reason—so that we human beings will find the way to Jesus Christ, so that we will turn from our evil ways, turn back and seek to encounter Jesus Christ. God does not want to frighten people but sends us the word about the judgment only so that we will reach out more passionately, more hungrily for the promise of God's grace. It is so we will recognize that by ourselves we do not have the strength to stand before God, that before God we must certainly pass away, but that in spite of everything God does not want us to die, but rather wants us to live.

Christ sits in judgment. That is truly a serious matter. Yet Christ sits in judgment, which also means that we are judged by the Merciful One who lived among tax collectors and sinners, who was tempted as we are [Heb. 4:15], who carried and endured our sorrows, our fears, and our desires in his own body, who knows us and calls us by our names [Isa. 43:1]. Christ sits in judgment, which means that grace is the judge, and forgiveness, and love—whoever clings to them has already been acquitted. Those, of course, who want to be judged by their own works, Christ will judge and pass sentence based on those works. But we should be joyful when we think about that day. We need not tremble and hold back, but give ourselves gladly into his hands. Luther dared even to speak of it as that dear day of judgment. So as we leave worship on the Day of Repentance, let us be not downcast but joyful and confident. Come, Judgment Day, we look forward to you with joy, for then we shall see our merciful Lord and clasp his hand, and he will receive us with open arms.

What about the "good and evil" about which Christ will ask us on that final day? The good is nothing other than our asking for and receiving his grace. The evil is only fear and wanting to stand before God on our own and justify ourselves. To repent, therefore, means to be in this process of turning around, turning away from our own accomplishments and receiving God's mercy. Turn back, turn back! the whole Bible calls to us joyfully. Turn back—where? To the everlasting mercy of the God who never leaves us, whose heart breaks because of us, the God who created us and loves us beyond all measure. God will be merciful—so come then, Judgment Day. Lord Jesus, make us ready. We await you with joy. Amen.

# As a Mother Comforts
# Her Child

## London, Remembrance Sunday,
## November 26, 1933

A day dedicated to remembrance of those who have died in the past
year and in years long past is observed by Christians in many different
cultures. In Germany, this "Day of the Dead" comes in late autumn, on
the Sunday after the Day of Repentance and Prayer.

In his sermon on Remembrance Day 1933, Bonhoeffer spoke at
length about the experience of death—he still carried the vivid childhood memory of his brother's death—but also of the hope and comfort
offered by the church. His text comes from the Apocrypha, several books
between the Old and New Testaments that many Protestant churches do
not include in their Bibles. Reading from a book called the Wisdom of
Solomon, Bonhoeffer offered assurance that these people whom we love
are at peace with God. They live now in the "tabernacle of joy" (from a
poem by Johann Rist). He also quoted from two familiar hymns by Paul
Gerhardt, including a stanza of "I Am a Visitor on Earth" (translated by

Catherine Winkworth) and, earlier, from "The Golden Sun," describing how those who have died now know "joy in fullness and blessed stillness."

Here Bonhoeffer looks ahead to Advent and Christmas. It was an old German custom during Advent to keep closed one room in which Christmas preparations were made. On Christmas Eve the door was opened, and there were all the gifts and the tree aglow with candles. Likewise, many Christian accounts of death mention the joy of the dying person, who exclaims, "God, that's beautiful!" when suddenly heaven is opened wide to him or her. Bonhoeffer's friend, Franz Hildebrandt, who heard this sermon in person, recalled this passage when he spoke at Bonhoeffer's memorial service in London in 1945.

Wisdom of Solomon 3:3: . . . *but they are at peace.*

Two questions have brought us to church today, questions about which we human beings are never satisfied. They drive us from one place to another and burn continually within our souls, so that we never find rest on this earth. And now here in church they are seeking the answer, the truth, the solution to the riddle: Where have our dead gone? Where shall we be after our own death?

The church claims to have the answer to this final, most impossible question that people have. Indeed, the only reason the church exists is that it knows the answer to this ultimate question. If it did not know how to speak with all humility, but also with all conviction in this matter, then it would be nothing more than a pathetic society of the hopeless and the desperate, trying to interest one another in their sufferings and being a burden to one another. But that is just what Christ's church is not. We are here to talk not about our sufferings but about our salvation—not about our skepticism but about our confident hope. Skepticism is of no interest to us—it is never what people do not believe that is interesting, but rather that people do believe and hope, and what they believe—that alone is the important part. Church is the place of unshakeable hope.

Where have our dead gone? Here we are today, remembering their death; in memory we see them again before us—those whom we loved—as we saw them that last time. That image has stayed with us like no other. We can feel again the way in which, at that sight, we totally forgot our own selves, how infinitely vain and empty our own lives appeared to us in that hour; how our gaze was fixed as if spellbound on that dear person, so inexplicably still, who could only remain silent about the mystery that he or she had now discovered. The person has gone over, has set out on the road from which no one comes back, and is now in a hallowed state of knowing and seeing that is given to no living person. He or she has become an earth dweller as never before, sleeping quietly in the earth—but is also so far away from the earth, and marked by another world, as he or she never was in life. Today perhaps we must think of long, tormented hours, of illness and struggle and agitation—until death came, and all was very still and quiet. We remember how we sat dazed and stupefied by the bed, not yet understanding what had really happened, only needing to ask the same question over and over in the same tone: What happened? Where are you? And perhaps we were still asking the same question as we carried the dead person to the grave, and perhaps today it is still the same question that we call after him or her: Where are you? Where are you?

Perhaps we have long since resigned ourselves to the fact that it is all over for these persons, that they have sunk back into the nothingness from which they once came. But still our love cannot stop looking for them, from asking everywhere if anyone knows where our dear one has gone. A cry of pain rises from the depths and echoes through the world: the mother calling her child, the child her mother, the husband his wife; friend calls to friend, brother to brother, love weeps for its lost beloved: Where are you? Where are you, our dead whom we love?

In silence you went away from us, left us alone, and went into a strange land that no one knows. Why don't you speak to us? Where are you? Do you have to wander now, eternally, from one life to another? Are you all alone in the cold night of the grave, or are you forced to wander about in torment, finding no rest? Are you close by, around us? Do you have to suffer as we do, or perhaps much more dreadfully than we do? Are you longing for home, for warmth, for love, for us? Or is death like sleep for you, eternally dreaming and dozing, a weary sleep? Speak to us, why are you so far away?

But they do not speak. And when people think they have been able to call up the spirits of the dead in occult seances, there may well be all sorts of things going on between heaven and earth that we cannot know or comprehend, but one thing is certain: it is not our dead who appear here. They have been taken away from us—they are in the hand of God, and no torment will ever touch them [Wisdom 3:1]. We cannot torment them with our tears and pleas and conjuring. They do not speak. They are forever silent.

But who will answer our question? Who has an answer to love's questioning? Not even the church can make the dead speak or can call up their spirits. But what is the church to say to the mother who comes to it for refuge, asking about her child? What can it tell the child about his or her mother? What does it tell the wife, or the dear friend? It does not point to where the dead are, it does not say this or that about them. It does not point toward the world of the occult or show us the way into the world of the dead. It points only toward God. The world of the occult is still a human world that we can reach; it is accessible through all sorts of magic. But the realm of God is beyond all human worlds. No one can tell us about it but God and the one whom God sent, Christ. This is the world in which we must look for our dead.

So when someone comes to the church with the burning question, where are my loved ones who have died? he or she is told first of all to turn to God. There is no way to know anything about the dead without believing in God. God is the Lord of the dead; their fate is in God's hands. Only those who know about God will know anything about their dead loved ones. But this then also means that questions about the dead should not be asked selfishly. It is not we who are the lords of the dead. Whoever wants to ask about them and really get an answer, whoever is not to be satisfied with small comfort, must dare to approach God and ask directly. And God will answer. For it is God's will to be revealed to human beings who come and ask, who are longing for the word, the answer, the truth of God, who believe it when they receive it. To them, God will speak of this mystery.

Now, today, the God of peace and everlasting love is telling this mystery anew to the congregation that is God's own, and only to the congregation. It is for those who believe in God, and God tells it to the congregation as an ultimate certainty: Those whom you seek are with me, and they are at peace. The realm of God is peace, the final peace after the final struggle. God's peace means rest for those whom life has made weary; it means safety and security for those who have wandered without anyone to care for and watch over them; home for the homeless, calm for those who are worn out with struggling, relief for tormented and wounded hearts, consolation for those who are distressed and weeping, the chance to sleep for those trembling with exhaustion . . . God's peace is like a mother's hand consolingly stroking the forehead of her sobbing child. As a mother comforts her child, so I will comfort you [Isa. 66:13]. Your dead are comforted with God's own comfort: it is God who has wiped away their tears and put an end to their restless pursuits—they are at peace.

Above the beds of the dying, where strong and restless lives are fighting fearfully toward death, until with a heavy sigh it is all over . . . the word is clearly heard: "But they are at peace."

At the last moments of those who have sinned greatly, for whom death seems to hold the awful horrors of damnation, who are in despair with remorse and repentance, Christ himself appears and closes their eyes as they die, and says: "But they are at peace."

Over the coffins of children and the elderly, over the coffins of the devout, who in simple faith in their last hour placed their hope only in Christ, the angels sing: "But they are at peace."

While we who are left behind see only suffering and fear and anguish and self-reproach and remorse, where we see only hopelessness and nothingness, God says: "But they are at peace."

God's "But . . ." is set over against all our thinking and seeking. It is God's "But . . ." that does not leave the dead to die but awakens them and draws them close. It is God's "But . . ." that makes death into a sleep from which we awaken into a new world. It is God's "But . . ." that brings the dead into paradise. "Truly, I tell you, today you will be with me in Paradise," says Christ to the thief who hangs next to him on the cross and repents [Luke 23:43]. "But" they are at peace—this truly means, not something that is self-evident, but rather something completely new, the ultimate of ultimates, and it is God who makes it happen. Not our peace, but God's peace.

Let it be said again: there is no room here for selfish questioning. All our knowledge and all our hope come only from looking to God, whom we trust to do everything and whose word we believe: I am the resurrection and the life [John 11:25]. Because I live, you also will live. And we can never hear about this realm of God, which is not our world, about this kingdom of peace into which our loved ones who have died have gone ahead of us, without an immeasurable longing that steals over us, an indescribable homesickness for that world, like children waiting to go into the room where the Christmas tree is—where there will be joy in fullness and blessed stillness. No one has yet believed in God and the kingdom of God, no one has yet heard about the realm of the resurrected, and not been homesick from that hour, waiting and looking forward joyfully to being released from bodily existence.

Whether we are young or old makes no difference. What are twenty or thirty or fifty years in the sight of God? And which of us knows how near he or she may already be to the goal? That life only really begins when it ends here on earth, that all that is here is only the prologue before the curtain goes up—that is for young and old alike to think about. Why are we so afraid when we think about death? Why are we so anxious when we imagine lying on our deathbed? Death is only dreadful for those who live in dread and fear of it. Death is not wild and terrible, if only we can be still and hold fast to God's Word. Death is not bitter, if we have not become bitter ourselves. Death is grace, the greatest gift of grace that God gives to people who believe. Death is mild, death is sweet and gentle; it beckons to us with heavenly power, if only we realize that it is the gateway to our homeland, the tabernacle of joy, the everlasting kingdom of peace.

Perhaps we say, I am not afraid of death, but I am afraid of dying. How do we know that dying is so dreadful? Who knows whether, in our human fear and anguish, we are only shivering and shuddering at the most glorious, heavenly, blessed event in the world? Whether we are only like a newborn baby, wailing as it first sees the light of this world? What about all the strange things we experience at the bedsides of dying persons—are they not evidence of this? What does it mean when such a person, after long struggling and wrestling and being afraid, at the last moment suddenly opens his or her eyes wide, as if seeing something glorious, and cries out, God, that's beautiful! We ask, what does this mean?

Yes, death is indeed frightening, bony old Death with his scythe, inviting one person after another to the dance of death, ready or not—if a person does not have faith, if he or she is not among the righteous of whom our Scripture says: But they are at peace.

Death is hell and night and cold, if it is not transformed by our faith. But that is just what is so marvelous, that we can transform death. When the fierce apparition of the death's head, which frightens us so, is touched by our faith in God, it becomes our friend, God's messenger; death becomes Christ himself. Yes, these are great mysteries. But we are allowed to know about them, and our life depends on them. Those who believe in God will have peace, death will not frighten them; it can no longer touch them, for they are in the hand of God, and no torment will ever touch them.

Many are those who have tried to make a friend of death; but at the last hour it proved disloyal to them, it became their enemy. There is only one way to have death as a friend, and that is the way of faith. And then, then death becomes our best friend. Then one day, as we lie dying, we will hear the word of God ring out: "They are at peace." And our eyes will overflow with joy when we see the kingdom and its peace.

Perhaps it sounds childish to you that we speak this way. But in the face of such things as these, can we do otherwise than talk like children? In the face of these things can we be anything other than children, who really have no idea what it is about? And would we really want it otherwise? Would we want to be otherwise when we come into God's kingdom and are allowed to share in that day of joy? Look at children when they are full of joy and decide for yourself if you want to be better than that, and whether we should be ashamed to be so. "As a mother comforts her child, so I will comfort you."

Jesus has called us children of the resurrection [Luke 20:36]. Homesick children, that is what we are when all is as it should be with us.

> Then through this life of dangers
> I onward take my way;
> But in this land of strangers
> I do not think to stay.
> Still forward on the road I fare
> That leads me to my home.
> My Father's comfort waits me there,
> When I have overcome.

Amen.

# Come, O Rescuer

## London, First Sunday in Advent, December 3, 1933

⸻ ⸨◉⸩ ⸻

As Bonhoeffer stood up to preach on Advent Sunday 1933, people in churches throughout England were grieving a disaster. The *News Chronicle* had been reporting daily on a gas explosion and roof collapse at a mine in Derbyshire, on November 19: "Bands of rescuers in gas masks descended the pit immediately, some in their 'Sunday' clothes, and worked three hours with pick and shovel before the first body was reached." In all, fourteen men, imprisoned a mile underground, died waiting to be freed.

Ten years later, Bonhoeffer wrote from Tegel Prison to his friend Eberhard Bethge: "Life in a prison cell may well be compared to Advent; one waits, hopes . . . the door is shut, and can be opened only *from the outside*." Thus Bonhoeffer's theme this Advent Sunday: "Look up and wait. Be strong and without fear!—for Christ is coming."

Luke 21:28 RSV: *Now when these things begin to take place, look up and raise your heads, because your redemption is drawing near.*

You all know about accidents in mines. In the last few weeks we have had to read over and over in the papers about such an accident. The men who have to go down every day into the mine shafts, deep into the earth, to do their work are constantly in danger that some day one of the tunnels will collapse or that they will be buried alive by an underground explosion. Then they are down there in the earth, where it is dark as night, left all alone. Their fate has caught up with them.

This is the moment that even the bravest miner has dreaded all his life. Shouting can do no good, no more than raving and running head-on into the wall. Neither will it help to exhaust his strength in efforts to get out. But the more a human being realizes that he is totally helpless, the more he rages, while around him all remains silent. He knows that up above people have come running, that women and children are crying—but the way is blocked; he cannot reach them. Nothing is left for him but his final moments. He knows that people are working feverishly up there. His mates are digging with dogged energy through the rock toward the ones who are trapped. Perhaps here and there some will still be found and rescued, but down here in the depths of the farthest shaft there is no hope anymore. All that remains now is torment, waiting for death.

But then, suppose he should suddenly hear a faint sound, as if of knocking, of hammering, of rocks breaking, and then of faraway voices calling, calling into the emptiness and darkness; and this banging and digging gradually gets louder, until suddenly, with a mighty blow, the hammering comes close by, echoing back, and at last a friend's deep voice, one of his mates, shouts his name: "Where are you? Help is coming!"

Then all at once the despairing man leaps up, his heart almost bursting with excitement and waiting, and screams with all his might: "I'm here, here, help me!—I can't get through, I can't help, but I'm waiting, I'm waiting, I can hold on till you come. Just come soon . . ." And he listens, beside himself with concentration, as each blow comes nearer. Each passing second seems like an hour. He can't see anything at all, but he can hear the voices of his helpers. Then a last, wild, desperate hammer blow rings in his ear. Rescue is at hand, only one more step and he will be free . . .

You know, don't you, why I am talking about this on this first of Advent? What we have been talking about here is Advent itself. This is the way it is; this is God coming near to humankind, the coming of salvation, the arrival of Christ . . . look up and raise your heads, because your redemption is drawing near.

To whom might these words be spoken? Who would be interested in hearing them? Who would get excited on hearing something like this? *Think of a prison.* For many years, the prisoners have borne the humiliation and punishment of being in prison. They have endured the misery of heavy forced labor, until they have become a burden to themselves. Often one or another of them has tried to escape, but was either caught and dragged back again, and then it was even harder, or was hunted down and shot. The rest bear their fate and their chains with sighing and tears. Then suddenly a message penetrates into the prison: Very soon you will all be free, your chains will be taken away, and those who have enslaved you will be bound in chains while you are redeemed. Then all the prisoners look up, in chorus, with a heartbreaking cry: Yes, come, O Savior!

*Think of the sick.* Think of someone who is tormented by an incurable disease, dying slowly, slowly in unspeakable pain, longing only for the end of this misery. And then comes the day when the doctor can say to him or her, quietly and firmly: "Today you will be released." Then the mortally ill person lifts his or her head joyfully, looking toward this release.

*And now think of the people who are oppressed,* not by outward imprisonment or physical disease, but by a heaviness in their souls. Think of the people with secrets, of whom we were speaking on Repentance Day, people living with guilt that has never been forgiven, for whom the meaning of life has been lost and with it all the joy of life. Think of us ourselves, trying to live in obedience to Christ and failing again and again. Think of the son who can no longer look his father in the eye, the husband who cannot face his wife; think of the deep brokenness and hopelessness that grows out of all these situations. Then let us hear the words again: Look up and raise your heads, because your redemption is drawing near. You shall be free from all that, the anguish and fear in your souls will come to an end. Salvation is near. (As a father says to his child: Look up here, not down at the ground; look at me, I'm your father . . . this is what it says in the Gospel: look up and raise your heads, because your redemption is drawing near.)

So then, whom is this text actually addressing? People who know that they are unredeemed people, that they are in bondage and in chains, that they are in the power of a slave driver, so that they have to work without wages—people like the man trapped underground, like the prisoners, who are still watching and waiting for freedom, for true redemption—those people who would like to be redeemed people. Those to whom it is *not* addressed are all those who have become so used to their condition that they no longer even notice that they are prisoners, who, for so many practical reasons, have settled for being unredeemed—who have become so indifferent and dull that they don't even react if someone calls to them: Your salvation is near!

It is not for the well-satisfied with their full stomachs, this word of Advent, but rather for the hungry and the thirsty. *It knocks at their door*, powerfully and insistently. And we hear it, just as the miner trapped in the mine heard and followed with all the energy he had left, every hammer blow, every new stage as the rescuer approached. Is it even imaginable that he would have paid attention to anything else, from the moment when he heard the first knocking—anything except his approaching liberation? What the first of Advent says is no different: Your redemption is near! It is knocking at your door now; can you hear it? It wants to make its way through all the rubble and hard stone of your life and of your heart. That will not happen very fast. But he is coming, Christ is clearing his way toward you, toward your heart. He wants to take our hearts, which have become so hard, and soften them in obedience to him. He keeps calling to us during these very weeks of waiting, waiting for Christmas, to tell us that he is coming, that he alone will rescue us from the prison of our existence, out of our fear, our guilt, and our loneliness.

Do you want to be redeemed? That is the one great, decisive question that Advent puts to us. Is there any remnant burning in us of longing, of recognition of what redemption could mean? If not, then what do we want from Advent? What do we want from Christmas? . . . a little sentimentality, a little inward uplifting . . . a nice atmosphere? But if there is something in us that wants to know, that is set on fire by these words, something in us that believes these words—if we feel that once more, once more in our lives, there could be a complete turning to God, to Christ—then why not just be obedient and listen and hear the word that is offered us, called out to us, shouted in our ears? Redemption is near, don't you hear? Wait, wait just a moment longer, and you will hear the knocking grow louder and more insistent, from hour to hour and from day to day. Then Christmas will come, and we will be ready. God is coming to us, to you and me— Christ the Savior is born.

Perhaps you will say yes, this is what you have always heard in church, and nothing ever really happened. Why didn't anything happen? Because we didn't want it to happen, we didn't want to hear or to believe; because we said: it may be that one or another of those who were trapped are saved, but as for us, so deeply buried, so distant, so out of the habit of these things, surely the Savior will never reach us. We aren't really devout; we don't have any gift for religious belief—we'd like to, but this just doesn't speak to us.

But with all that we are only talking ourselves out of it. How can we tell, if we haven't ever tried it? If only we really wanted to—if it weren't all just talk and trying to get out of it—then we would finally, finally begin praying and pray that this Advent would come into our hearts too. Let us not deceive ourselves. Redemption is near, whether we know it or not. The question is only: will we let it come in to us too, or will we refuse it entry? Will we let ourselves be caught up in this movement, which is coming down to earth from heaven, or will we close ourselves off from it? Christmas is coming, with or without us—it is up to each of us to decide.

That such a genuine Advent produces something quite different from a fearful, petty, downtrodden, weak sort of Christianity, such as we often see, and which often tempts us to be scornful of Christianity itself, that is made clear by the two powerful challenges that introduce our text. Look up, lift your heads! Advent makes people human, new human beings. We, too, can become new human beings at Advent time.

Look up, you there who are staring emptily down at the earth, who are transfixed by the little events and changes taking place on the surface of this earth. Look up at these words, you who have turned away from heaven in disappointment. Look up, you whose eyes are heavy with tears, with weeping for that which this world has mercilessly snatched away from us. Look up, you who feel so loaded down with guilt that you cannot raise your eyes—look up, your redemption is drawing near. Something different is happening from what you see every day, something much more important, infinitely greater and mightier—if only you would take it in, be on the watch for it, wait just a moment longer, wait, and something completely new will break into your lives. God will come to you, Jesus is coming to take you for his own, and you will be redeemed people. Look up, be on the watch, keep your eyes open, watch, and wait for your redemption, which is drawing near.

Lift up your heads, the host of you who are bowed down, humiliated, despondent, like a beaten army with heads hanging. The battle is not lost—raise your heads, the victory is yours! Take courage, fear not, do not be worried or anxious. Be of good cheer, be assured of the victory, be strong, be valiant. This is no time to shake your head, to doubt and look away—freedom, salvation, redemption is coming. Look up and wait! Raise your heads! Be strong and without fear!—for Christ is coming.

Again let us ask: Can we hear it now, the knocking, the driving, the struggling forward? Can we feel something in us that wants to leap up, to free itself and open up to the coming of Christ? Do we sense that we are not just talking in images here, but that something is really happening, that human souls are being raised up, shaken, broken open, and healed? That heaven is bending near the earth, that the earth is trembling and people are desperate with fear and apprehension and hope and joy? That God is bending down to humankind, coming to us where we live? Can the trapped miner pay attention to anything but the hammering and knocking of his rescuers? Can anything be as important to us as paying attention to this same hammering and knocking of Jesus Christ in our lives? Can we do anything, amid whatever is happening, other than to stop and listen, to tremble and reach out to him? Something is at work, within us too. So let us not block the way but rather open up to him who wants to come in. Once when Luther was preaching on our text during Advent, in the middle of winter, he announced: "Summer is near, the trees want to burst forth in blossom. It is springtime." Whoever has ears to hear will hear [Matt. 13:43]. Amen.

# My Spirit Rejoices

## London, Third Sunday in Advent, December 17, 1933

—————⸺«(●)»⸺—————

The verses just before the text for this Sunday in Advent describe the visit between Mary, with Jesus in her womb, and Elizabeth, her aged cousin, who also is pregnant with the one who is to be John the Baptist. Elizabeth tells Mary that on hearing her greeting, "The child in my womb leapt for joy" (Luke 1:44). Mary responds by bursting forth with a song of praise. These two women of strong faith, neither of whom was normally expected to be pregnant, were quite ready to accept the miracle and lift up their voices joyfully. Bonhoeffer points out what many women in oppressed countries, like Palestine in Mary's time and in our time, have noticed how revolutionary Mary's words are, describing how society as we know it will be turned upside down and the oppressed will be liberated. She echoes prophetic women of the Old Testament: Deborah (Judges 4 and 5), Judith, who took a murder upon herself to liberate her people, (Judith 8–16 in the Apocrypha), and Miriam (Exodus 15:20–21). But for Bonhoeffer, the revolution could begin anytime, in the way we celebrate Christmas, if we are willing to see as God sees.

Luke 1:46–55: *And Mary said,*
*"My soul magnifies the Lord,*
    *and my spirit rejoices in God my Savior,*
*for he has looked with favor on the lowliness of his servant.*
    *Surely, from now on all generations will call me blessed;*
*for the Mighty One has done great things for me,*
    *and holy is his name.*
*His mercy is for those who fear him*
    *from generation to generation.*
*He has shown strength with his arm,*
    *he has scattered the proud in the thoughts of their hearts.*
*He has brought down the powerful from their thrones,*
    *and lifted up the lowly;*
*he has filled the hungry with good things,*
    *and sent the rich away empty.*
*He has helped his servant Israel,*
    *in remembrance of his mercy,*
*according to the promise he made to our ancestors,*
    *to Abraham and to his descendants forever."*

The song of Mary is the oldest Advent hymn. It is also the most passionate, the wildest, and one might almost say the most revolutionary Advent hymn that has ever been sung. This is not the gentle, tender, dreamy Mary as we often see her portrayed in paintings. The Mary who is speaking here is passionate, carried away, proud, enthusiastic. There is none of the sweet, wistful, or even playful tone of many of our Christmas carols, but instead a hard, strong, relentless hymn about the toppling of the thrones and the humiliation of the lords of this world, about the power of God and the powerlessness of humankind. This is the sound of the prophetic women of the Old Testament—Deborah, Judith, Miriam—coming to life in the mouth of Mary. Mary, who was seized by the power of the Holy Spirit, who humbly and obediently lets it be done unto her as the Spirit commands her, who lets the Spirit blow where it wills [John 3:8]—she speaks, by the power of this Spirit, about God's coming into the world, about the Advent of Jesus Christ.

She, of course, knows better than anyone else what it means to wait for Christ's coming. Her waiting is different from that of any other human being. She expects him as his mother. He is closer to her than to anyone else. She knows the secret of his coming, knows about the Spirit, who has a part in it, about the Almighty God, who has performed this miracle. In her own body she is experiencing the wonderful ways of God with human-kind: that God does not arrange matters to suit our opinions and views, does not follow the path that humans would like to prescribe. God's path is free and original beyond all our ability to understand or to prove.

There, where our understanding is outraged, where our nature rebels, where our piety anxiously keeps its distance—that is exactly where God loves to be. There, though it confounds the understanding of sensible people, though it irritates our nature and our piety, God wills to be, and none of us can forbid it. Only the humble believe and rejoice that God is so gloriously free, performing miracles where humanity despairs and glo-rifying that which is lowly and of no account. For just this is the miracle of all miracles, that God loves the lowly. God "has looked with favor on the lowliness of his servant." God in the midst of lowliness—that is the revolutionary, passionate word of Advent.

It begins with Mary herself, the carpenter's wife: as we would say, a poor working man's wife, unknown, not highly regarded by others; yet now, just as she is, unremarkable and lowly in the eyes of others, regarded by God and chosen to be mother of the Savior of the world. She was not chosen because of any human merit, not even for being, as she undoubt-edly was, deeply devout, nor even for her humility or any other virtue, but entirely and uniquely because it is God's gracious will to love, to choose, to make great what is lowly, unremarkable, considered to be of little value. Mary, the tough, devout, ordinary working man's wife, living in her Old Testament faith and hoping in her Redeemer, becomes the mother of God. Christ, the poor son of a laborer from the East End of London, Christ is laid in a manger. . . .

God is not ashamed of human lowliness but goes right into the mid-dle of it, chooses someone as instrument, and performs the miracles right there where they are least expected. God draws near to the lowly, loving the lost, the unnoticed, the unremarkable, the excluded, the powerless, and the broken. What people say is lost, God says is found; what people say is "condemned," God says is "saved." Where people say No! God says Yes! Where people turn their eyes away in indifference or arrogance, God gazes with a love that glows warmer there than anywhere else. Where people say something is despicable, God calls it blessed. When we come to a point in our lives where we are completely ashamed of ourselves and before God; when we believe that God especially must now be ashamed of us, and when we feel as far away from God as ever in all our lives—that is the moment in which God is closer to us than ever, wanting to break into our lives, wanting us to feel the presence of the holy and to grasp the miracle of God's love, God's nearness and grace.

"Surely, from now on all generations will call me blessed!" sings Mary joyfully. What does it mean to call her blessed, Mary, the lowly maidservant? It can only mean that we worship in amazement the miracle that has been performed in her, that we see in her how God regards and raises up the lowly; that in coming into this world, God seeks out not the heights but rather the depths, and that we see the glory and power of God by seeing made great what was small. To call Mary blessed does not mean to build altars to her, but rather means to worship with her the God who regards and chooses the lowly, who "has done great things for me, and holy is his name." To call Mary blessed means to know with her that God's "mercy is for those who fear him from generation to generation," who are amazed as we reflect on the ways of God, who let the Spirit blow where it wills, who obey it and say humbly, together with Mary: Let it be with me according to your word [Luke 1:38].

When God chooses Mary as the instrument, when God decides to come in person into this world, in the manger in Bethlehem, this is not an idyllic family occasion but rather the beginning of a complete reversal, a new ordering of all things on this earth. If we want to be part of this event of Advent and Christmas, we cannot just sit there like a theater audience and enjoy all the lovely pictures. We ourselves will be caught up in this action, this reversal of all things; we will become actors on this stage. For this is a play in which each spectator has a part to play, and we cannot hold back. What will our role be? Worshipful shepherds bending the knee, or kings bringing gifts? What story is being enacted when Mary becomes the mother of God, when God comes into the world in a lowly manger?

The judgment and redemption of the world—that is what is happening here. For it is the Christ Child in the manger himself who will bring that judgment and redemption. It is he who pushes away the great and mighty of this world, who topples the thrones of the powerful, who humbles the haughty, whose arm exercises power against all who are highly placed and strong, and whose mercy lifts up what was lowly and makes it great and glorious. So we cannot come to this manger in the same way as we would approach the cradle of any other child. Something will happen to each of us who decides to come to Christ's manger. Each of us will have been judged or redeemed before we go away. Each of us will either break down or come to know that God's mercy is turned toward us.

What does this mean? Is it not just a figure of speech, the way pastors exaggerate a beautiful, pious legend? What does it mean to say such things about the Christ Child? If you want to see it as just a way of speaking, well, then go ahead and celebrate Advent and Christmas in the same pagan way you always have, as an onlooker. For us it is not just a figure of speech. It is what we have said: that it is God, the Lord and Creator of all things, who becomes so small here, comes to us in a little corner of the world, unremarkable and hidden away, and wants to meet us and be among us as a helpless, defenseless child—not as a game or to charm us, because we find this so touching, but to show us where and who God really is, and from this standpoint to judge all human desire for greatness, to devalue it and pull it down from its throne.

The throne of God in the world is set not on the thrones of humankind but in humanity's deepest abyss, in the manger. There are no flattering courtiers standing around his throne, just some rather dark, unknown, dubious-looking figures, who cannot get enough of looking at this miracle and are quite prepared to live entirely on the mercy of God.

For those who are great and powerful in this world, there are two places where their courage fails them, which terrify them to the very depths of their souls, and which they dearly avoid. These are the manger and the cross of Jesus Christ. No one who holds power dares to come near the manger; King Herod also did not dare. For here thrones begin to sway, the powerful fall down, and those who are high are brought low, because God is here with the lowly. Here the rich come to naught, because God is here with the poor and those who hunger. God gives the hungry plenty to eat, but sends the rich and well-satisfied away empty. Before the maidservant Mary, before Christ's manger, before God among the lowly, the strong find themselves falling; here they have no rights, no hope, but instead find judgment.

And even if today they think nothing will happen to them, it will come tomorrow or the next day. God puts down the tyrants from their thrones; God raises up the lowly. For this Jesus Christ came into the world as the child in the manger, as the son of Mary.

In eight days we will celebrate Christmas, for once really as the festival of Jesus Christ in our world. Before that, there is something we must clear up, something very important in our lives. We need to make clear to ourselves how, from now on, in the light of the manger, we are going to think about what is high and what is low in human life. Not that any of us are powerful persons, even if we would perhaps like to be and don't like to have that said to us. There are never more than a few very powerful people. But there are many more people with small amounts of power, petty power, who put it into play wherever they can and whose one thought is: keep climbing higher! God, however, thinks differently, namely, keep climbing down lower, down among the lowly and the inconspicuous, in self-forgetfulness, in not seeking to be looked at or well regarded or to be the highest. If we go this way, there we will meet God himself. Each of us lives among persons who are the so-called higher-ups and others who are the so-called lowly. Each of us knows someone who is lower in the order of things than we ourselves. Might this Christmas help us learn to see this point in a radically different way, to rethink it entirely, to know that if we want to find the way to God, we have to go, not up to the heights, but really down to the depths among the least of all, and that every life that only wants to stay up high will come to a fearful end?

God is not mocked [Gal. 6:7]. It does not escape God's notice that we celebrate Christmas from year to year without taking it seriously. And we can count on God's word. At Christmas, when the Holy One, full of power and glory, lies in the manger, the mighty will be brought down from their thrones if they do not at last turn again and repent.

It is an important matter for a Christian congregation to come to an understanding of this point, and having realized it, to draw the consequences for its members' life together. There is reason enough here to reconsider a number of things in our own congregation in this light.

Who among us will celebrate Christmas rightly? Who will finally lay down at the manger all power and honor, all high regard, vanity, arrogance, and self-will? Who will take their place among the lowly and let God alone be high? Who will see the glory of God in the lowliness of the child in the manger? Who will say with Mary: The Lord has looked with favor on my lowliness. My soul magnifies the Lord, and my spirit rejoices in God my Savior. Amen.

# Beginning with Christ

## London, New Year's Day, January 1, 1934

———— ((◉)) ————

This short meditation was published in the January 7, 1934, issue of the Newsletter for German-Speaking Congregations in Great Britain. Later, when writing his book *Discipleship* (first published in English as *The Cost of Discipleship*) during the Finkenwalde years, Bonhoeffer referred back to it and developed an interpretation of the text from Luke on which this meditation is based (DBWE 4:59–61, 115). So it is possible that it not only served to inspire his colleagues who were pastors of other German congregations in Britain, but also was discussed in the course of his teaching in the Finkenwalde seminary.

———— ((◉)) ————

Luke 9:57–62: *As they were going along the road, someone said to him, "I will follow you wherever you go." And Jesus said to him, "Foxes have holes, and the birds of the air have nests; but the Son of Man has nowhere to lay his head." To another he said, "Follow me." But he said, "Lord, first let me go and bury my father." But Jesus said to him,*

*"Let the dead bury their own dead; but as for you, go and proclaim the kingdom of God." Another said, "I will follow you, Lord; but let me first say farewell to those at my home." Jesus said to him, "No one who puts a hand to the plow and looks back is fit for the kingdom of God."*

---

"The road to hell is paved with good intentions"—this saying is found in many different countries. But it is not the worldly wise, impertinent statement of someone who refuses to do better. No, it rather reveals a profound Christian insight. Anyone who knows nothing better to do on New Year's Day than to make a list of bad things he or she has done, and then decide from now on—how many such "from now ons" have we heard before!—to start off with better intentions, is still far from being a Christian.

*First* of all, such a person thinks that a good intention is enough for a new beginning. That is, he or she supposes that one can make a new start entirely on one's own, whenever one wants to. This is an evil illusion. It is God alone who makes a new beginning with a person, when God is pleased to do so, and not the human being who undertakes to do it with God. So a new beginning is not something one can do for oneself. One can only pray for it to happen. As long as people rely only on themselves and try to live that way, that is still the old way, the same way as in the past. Only with God is there a new way, a new beginning. And we cannot command God to do anything; all we can do is pray. But we can pray only when we have realized that there is something we cannot do for ourselves, that we have reached our limit, that someone else must be the one to begin.

*Second*, if you are relying entirely on your own good intentions, you have no idea where they come from. You had better take another look. Our so-called good intentions are nothing other than the products of a weak and fearful heart, which is afraid of bad deeds and sins and is arming itself with all too human weapons to fight these powers. But anyone who is afraid of sin is already fully caught up in it. Fear is the net spread by the Evil One, in which we can easily become entangled and brought to a fall. If we are afraid, we have already fallen in, just as someone who is overcome by fear during a difficult mountain climb is sure to stumble.

So nothing comes of making good resolutions out of fear or anxiety. They will not bring us to a new beginning. The road to hell is paved with good intentions.

How do we find our way to a new beginning? Our text tells us about a young man who is obviously very taken with Jesus, who perhaps has been waiting a long time for a chance to express his enthusiasm. Now here comes Jesus into the town, and the enthusiast runs to meet him, stands in front of him, and says: I will follow you wherever you go. He wants to make the first move himself: with glowing devotion he offers himself, thinking he will be able to do everything asked of him and to leave everything behind, for this man. But Jesus demurs, suspicious of this enthusiasm. Do you know what you are doing? Do you know who I am, and where following me is going to lead you? Do you know that I need not someone who throws himself at me with enthusiasm, but rather someone with a firm, unshakeable faith based only on my having called you? Have I called you? Are you coming simply and only in answer to my call? You are enthusiastic; you want to make a new beginning: think about what you are doing and whom you are daring to approach and remember that enthusiasm is only one step away from embarrassment!

Jesus himself calls to the second person in the story. This is someone living in the past, hanging onto some significant grief that he cannot forget. This person no longer looks forward to the future but would rather fade away into the past and into the world of the dead. Jesus' call is to step forward, out of all that. The person hesitates, wants to go back once more. No, "Let the dead bury their dead"—leave the past behind, free yourself—now or never. Christ calls you to a new beginning—take your chance, just because it is he! Now, today, because Christ is moving on—go with him, answer his call, now!

The third person surely would like to go with Christ. This is someone who takes it seriously and therefore surely can be allowed to attach a small condition to the offer to come and follow Jesus. "Please let me first . . ." Certainly I want to come, but surely you understand, Lord, I just need to do this and that "first." No, Christ doesn't understand, doesn't want to understand. "No one who puts his hand to the plow . . ." A man guiding a plow does not look back, but he also doesn't look way ahead into the unpredictable distance—only as far as the next step he has to take. Looking back is not the Christian thing to do. Leave your fear, worry, and guilt behind. Look up at the one who has given you a new beginning. Through him you will forget everything else.

The coming year will have its share of fear, guilt, and hardship. But let it be, in all our fear, guilt, and hardship, a year spent with Christ. Let our new beginning with Christ be followed by a story of going with Christ. What that means is beginning each day with him. That is what matters.

# Repent and Do Not Judge

## London, Sixth Sunday after Trinity, July 8, 1934

═══»«◆»═══

The first incident to which this passage in Luke refers was very much the news of the day, in the context of revolutionary activity in Palestine during Jesus' ministry. Pilate particularly feared Galileans as the worst rebels and, on this occasion, had slaughtered a group of them who had come to worship in the temple in Jerusalem. Those who died at Siloam belonged to another rebel group, perhaps Zealots. Bonhoeffer preached this sermon only a week after news from Germany that spread shock and horror in Britain: Hitler's powerful SS troops, claiming that a *Putsch* (coup) was imminent, had massacred many of Hitler's rivals in the Nazi party. Bonhoeffer's brother-in-law Hans von Dohnanyi reported that more than two hundred people had been killed.

In the face of this horror, Bonhoeffer surprised his hearers by urging them not to judge but to repent, saying with Jesus (see Matt. 7:1), that we all share in the guilt of those responsible. As he later wrote to his friend Erwin Sutz, "*We* are the ones to be converted, not Hitler."

The "great man" whom he quotes is Gandhi. Bonhoeffer hoped at the time to visit Gandhi's ashram in India and did indeed receive a personal invitation, but instead he had to return urgently to Germany in 1935 to help train pastors for the Confessing Church.

---

Luke 13:1–5: *At that very time there were some present who told him about the Galileans whose blood Pilate had mingled with their sacrifices. He asked them, "Do you think that because these Galileans suffered in this way they were worse sinners than all other Galileans? No, I tell you; but unless you repent, you will all perish as they did. Or those eighteen who were killed when the tower of Siloam fell on them— do you think that they were worse offenders than all the others living in Jerusalem? No, I tell you; but unless you repent, you will all perish just as they did."*

---

Perhaps this text frightens you, and you think it sounds only too much like the news of the day—too dangerous for a worship service. In church we would rather get completely away from the world of the newspapers and the latest sensations. That's right, that is what we are doing here, really getting away from this world. But we want to do it in such a way that it cannot jump on us again almost as soon as we are out the church door and take us captive and oppress us; instead, we want to leave the worship service having *overcome* it.

So it cannot really be our purpose to "get away" from these things by closing our eyes to them or forgetting them as quickly as possible, even for a little while; but rather to know the position we should take on them *as Christians*. What matters is not *that* we get away from these things but rather *how* we get away from them.

There are people who cannot bear to go to a funeral—or rather, do not want to go. Why not? Because they are afraid of the shock of being that close to a dead person. They don't want to see this side of human life, and they think that if they don't look at it, they have managed to get rid of the thing itself altogether.

There are even people who think themselves particularly *devout* if they do not see the dark side of life, if they close themselves off from the catastrophes of this world and just lead their own tranquil, pious lives in peaceful optimism.

But it can never do any good to fool oneself into ignoring the truth, for in deceiving oneself about the truth of one's own life, one is certainly deceiving oneself about God's truth as well. And it is certainly never pious to close the eyes that God gave us to see our neighbor and his or her need, simply to avoid seeing whatever is sad or dreadful. So it can certainly never be the right way to try to get rid of the things that frighten and depress us.

There is also another way, a much more human and serious way of dealing with these things—but that also turns out to be a very unchristian way. Let us take a simple example: suppose we see an accident happen in the street. We see someone get run over. We are unspeakably shocked and stand there stunned for a moment. But then our first thought is: *Whose fault is it?* This is an everyday example of a very common attitude. When something terrible happens to us personally or to our family or our nation, our first question when we have recovered from the shock is: *Whose fault is it?* And now we cannot rest, our thoughts go back and forth, in our mind's eye we see all the people who are in any way involved with this accident, and we keep examining them more closely and insistently, asking in a more and more embittered way, Whose fault is it? Who is right? Who is wrong? Human beings are moralists through and through. They want to accuse one person and exonerate the other. They want to be the judges of what happens. And *this is their way of dealing with a terrible disaster—by saying that one person is right and the other wrong.* Whether we are thinking of small happenings in our lives or great catastrophes like wars and revolutions, it is the same everywhere. What people want is to be the judge.— Now let us just stop here for a moment.

It is immeasurably valuable for us that Luke—alone among the gospel writers—has preserved for us the report of how Jesus reacted to such news of a catastrophe that had hit his country, a sensation for the newspapers, we might say, and what he had to say about it.

Jesus was told by eyewitnesses that Pilate had ordered the execution of several Galileans, that is, compatriots of Jesus, apparently as rabble-rousers and enemies of the state. The executions had taken place under circumstances that made the blood of devout Jews boil: the condemned persons were said to have been seized while making their sacrifices in the temple in Jerusalem and thus to have been killed within the temple domain. Truly a report guaranteed to make feelings run high, if anything would, to stir up judgment and counter-judgment and start an energetic political discussion. It must have gone back and forth: Pilate was right—Pilate was wrong; the Galileans were victims of a tyrant—the Galileans got the punishment they deserved. But the prevailing view seems to have been that the Galileans would not have met such a terrible fate, such a fearsome death, if they had not been guilty. Some serious transgression must have been involved, for otherwise God would not have allowed such a dreadful thing to happen. This was the interpretation of serious and pious persons; they believed that even this event could not be separated from the fact that a God exists, from whom all things come, for good or evil, and whose judgments are just. All one could now do was to turn away with a shudder from these punished sinners, who had become the target of God's wrath. This was how people dealt with this event.

This was the official view, we would say, of the daily press. And now Jesus begins by joining them in the idea that in any case one cannot separate God from this terrible event; that ultimately it is not Pilate who is at work here, but rather that God alone is at work in this world, in both good and evil. But this very thought, that the hand of God is in this, means for Jesus something entirely different from what it means for public opinion.

Not a word does he say about Pilate, whether he was right or wrong; not a word about the Galileans, not a word of political judgment, not a word of moralistic judgment. This is very clear: Jesus does not judge! Jesus does not say which side is right, especially not to the pious, who have interpreted this event so earnestly and moralistically. *Jesus says "No" to them.*

"Do you think that because these Galileans suffered in this way they were worse sinners than all other Galileans? *No, I tell you.*" Jesus says No to the devout, he says No to their attempt to deal with this dreadful event by judging. Jesus says *No*—meaning, first of all, *stop* all your advice and interpretations, your know-all judgments. . . . Stop trying to put these things behind you in all these ways—*stop*—for these things are too enormous; God is at work here . . . I tell you *No* . . . that means that this is *God's holy mystery*, and human beings are not meant to presume upon it. So away with all your judgments and saying who is right, one side or the other, be still and silent. . . . Here is God's holy mystery.

And after Jesus has commanded them to be silent and reverent, after God has become visible behind his stern "No," he then proceeds to attack those who have immediately rushed to judgment. "Do you think . . . No; but unless you repent you will all likewise perish . . . Siloam . . ."

What is Jesus doing here? On the occasion of this report Jesus is doing one and the same thing he did throughout his life: calling people to repentance. Here is God—therefore repent. For Jesus, then, this shocking newspaper report about the terrible things that happened in the temple is nothing other than a renewed call from God to all who can hear, in unmistakable terms, to repent and to turn back. It is for him a palpable, living illustration for his preaching that human beings must humble themselves before the mystery and power of God, and repent and submit themselves to God's justice.

Now we are on dangerous ground. Now we are no longer bystanders, onlookers, judges of these events, but we ourselves are being addressed; we are affected. This has happened for us, God is speaking to us, this is all about us.

*And therefore, first of all:* Do not judge, so that you may not be judged! Do not set yourselves up as being better than those Galileans or that Pilate. In the face of such terrible acts of God, do not say with pride, "God, I thank you that I am not like other people. . . ." Instead, pray silently within yourselves, "God, be merciful to me, a sinner" [Luke 18:9–14].

Jesus too raises the question of guilt. But he answers it differently. It is not Pilate or the Galileans who are meant here, but we, we ourselves. In the face of terrible human catastrophes, Christians are not to assume the arrogant, know-all attitude of looking on and judging, but rather are to recognize: this is my world in which this has happened. This is the world in which I live, in which I sin by sowing hate and lovelessness day by day. This is the fruit of what I and my brothers and sisters have sown—and these people here, these Galileans and Pilate, are my brothers and sisters, in sin, in hate and evil and lovelessness, my brothers and sisters in guilt. Whatever happens to them is meant for me too; they are only showing me God's finger pointed in anger, pointed at me as well. So let us repent and realize *our* guilt and not judge.

It is hard to think like this, and it is even harder to believe—as we must believe—that it is this attitude alone which can overcome the world, that only through repentance can the world be renewed. So isn't it fruitless to think this way? Does it make anything better? Yes, it does; it makes *everything* better. How so? Because through our repentance, God's grace can find its way back to us; because in our repentance no human being can be in the right, but rather God alone is right in all God's ways, whether in making us know fear or in showing us mercy.

A great man of our time—who is not a Christian, but it is tempting to call him a heathen Christian—tells a story, in his autobiography, which took place when he was director of a school. He was doing everything in his power for these young people, and one day within this school community an injustice was done, which shook him to the core. However, he took this not as an occasion that called for him to judge or to punish anyone but only as a call to repentance. So he went and spent long days in repentance, with fasting and all kinds of self-denial. What did this mean? It meant first of all that in the guilt of his pupils he saw his own guilt, his lack of love, patience, and truthfulness. Then, it meant that he knew there could be room for the Spirit of God only in the spirit of humble realization of guilt. Finally, it meant the recognition that faith and love and hope could be found only in repentance. We have not yet believed enough; we have not yet loved enough—can we be judges? Jesus speaks: *I tell you, No.*

It is a quiet journey, a strange and slow-moving journey, which leads through repentance to newness of life. But it is the only way that is God's way. And if we have realized this and go home with it from church and are serious about it, only then have we overcome the world we find in the newspapers, the world of terror and the world of judgment.

Lord, lead your people to repentance, beginning with us! Amen.

# Come unto Me

## London, late September 1934

＝＝＝＞«(●)»＜＝＝＝

We can only guess when this undated sermon might have been given from its mention of Bonhoeffer's visit to his friend Jean Lasserre. The two had met in 1930 while both were on scholarships at Union Seminary in New York and had shared deep theological discussions. Lasserre was pastor of a poor working-class congregation in Bruay-en-Artois, northern France, an area that had suffered greatly during and after World War I. He also engaged in street evangelism, in which Bonhoeffer had participated with him during his three-day visit.

Bonhoeffer refers in this sermon to a famous etching by Rembrandt titled "Christ Healing the Sick" (1642–1645) and to a poem by Friedrich Rückert that became the text for Franz Schubert's song "My Sweet Repose" (*Du bist die Ruh*). The four lines of verse at the end are the epitaph of Danish theologian Søren Kierkegaard (1813–1855); this English translation was made from the somewhat free German version quoted by Bonhoeffer.

＝＝＞«(●)»＜＝＝

Matthew 11:28–30: *Come to me, all you that are weary and are carrying heavy burdens, and I will give you rest. Take my yoke upon you, and learn from me; for I am gentle and humble in heart, and you will find rest for your souls. For my yoke is easy, and my burden is light.*

---

Since the day when Jesus spoke these words, there should no longer be anyone on earth who is so forsaken and alone as to say of himself or herself: Nobody has ever asked about me; nobody has ever wanted me or offered to help me. Whoever has heard these words of Jesus even once in his or her life and still talks that way is lying, is showing contempt and scorn for Jesus Christ and not taking his words seriously. For Christ was calling *everyone* who labors and is heavy-laden. His was not a narrow circle; it was no intellectual or spiritual-religious aristocracy that he gathered around him. Instead, he made his circle as wide as possible, so wide that no single person could say with a good conscience that he or she wasn't being addressed, wasn't among those who labored and were heavy-laden. This is just what is so amazing about this call: it really puts every human being in the embarrassing situation of admitting that they too are called and are meant, indeed, perhaps they in particular.

Those who labor and are heavy-laden—who are they? Jesus intentionally says nothing here that sets any limit. People are laboring and heavy-laden if they feel that way—in truth, including those who do not feel that way because they do not want to feel it. Laboring and heavy-laden certainly describes those men and women and children who outwardly have a hard lot in life and heavy work to do, those who, we might say, have been placed by chance into the dark side of life, into servitude and into outward and moral misery. I have seldom felt so strongly that I was among those who labor and are heavy-laden as in the mining town in northern France where I have just been on holiday. It is a joyless, driven, humiliated, abused, and soiled existence, which is inherited and passed on from fathers and mothers to children and children's children. Wherever people experience their work as God's curse on humanity [see Gen. 13:17–19]—there you will find those who labor and are heavy-laden.

But it is all too easy for us to see such people only among those who are outwardly poor. Jesus certainly searched for and found those who were struggling hardest and carrying the heaviest burdens, not among the poor but among the so-called rich. Think of the rich young man whom, it is said, Jesus loved, who "went away sorrowful" because he was not strong enough to follow Jesus [see Matt. 19:16–22]. There is hardly a more depressing realization for a person than to see that, while outwardly having everything one could want, inwardly one can be hollow and empty and superficial; that all our possessions will not buy us the most important things in this earthly life: inner peace, joy of spirit, a loving marriage, and family life. How much unspeakable inner suffering, lives weighed down by the heavy debts that wealth brings, is found in the homes of those who seem so fortunate!

No, those who labor and are heavy-laden do not all look the way Rembrandt drew them in his "Hundred Guilder" picture—poverty-stricken, miserable, sick, leprous, ragged, with worn, furrowed faces. They are also found concealed behind happy-looking, youthful faces and brilliantly successful lives. There are people who feel utterly forsaken in the midst of high society, to whom everything in their lives seems stale and empty to the point of nausea, because they can sense that underneath it all, their souls are decaying and rotting away. There is no loneliness like that of the fortunate.

But even those who are so intoxicated with their busy lives that they do not seem to feel how alone they are, who do not think about whether they are laboring and heavy-laden, are actually so. It has the opposite effect for them, because at the bottom of their hearts they know or suspect that this is also their condition, but they are afraid to admit it. So they throw themselves even more madly into their supposedly happy lives and keep running away from every word that might speak the truth to them. They do not want to be considered as those who labor and are heavy-laden, but in Jesus' eyes they are doubly so.

*Everyone, all of you,* is what it means. Come to me, *all* who labor and are heavy-laden. The latter words are meant, *not as a limitation* on who is included in "all," but as a *statement* about them. Who would want to say, when Jesus calls, that this has nothing to do with them? Who would want to say they know nothing about the state of laboring and being heavy-laden?

When people come to the end of their inner strength and have become a burden to themselves, when they do not want to go another step, are afraid of the next hill looming ahead, are weighed to the ground by some kind of guilt, and feel betrayed and deceived by the whole world—then no words, no ideals or dreams one builds for the future will help. These people need only one thing: a human being who can be trusted completely, unconditionally; someone who understands everything, listens to everything, bears with everything, who believes, who hopes, who forgives all things [1 Cor. 13:7]—someone to whom one can say, "You *are* sweet rest and gentle peace, my longing, yes, and my heart's ease"—someone in whose presence our sorrows are dispelled, our hearts open in love without words; someone who quietly takes away our burden and all the strain and anxiety and thus redeems our souls from their bondage in this world.

But who has someone like that? Where can such a person be found? This is the miracle above all miracles, that everyone has and can find such a person, that this person himself is calling us to come to him, inviting us, and offering himself. This person who is our rest, our peace, who refreshes and redeems us, is Jesus Christ alone. He alone is fully human, and in being truly human is also God, and Redeemer, and peace and rest. Come to me, all who labor and are heavy-laden, and *I* will give you rest. Everything depends on this "I"—not as an idea, not as a word, not as a preacher, but *I*, Jesus the human being, who knows each one of us, who has suffered and struggled though everything that we have to suffer, the human person Jesus, our Redeemer.

There are two possible ways to help someone who is bowed down under a burden. One can either remove the entire weight of it, so that from now on the person has nothing to carry anymore, or one can help carry it, so that it becomes lighter and easier to carry. Jesus does not go the first way. Our burden is not taken away. Jesus, who himself carried his cross, knows it is part of being human to carry our cross, to shoulder our burden, and that only with our burden and not without it will we be sanctified. The burden that God has laid on someone's shoulders, Jesus will not take away. But he lightens our load by showing us how better to carry it.

"Take my yoke upon you, and learn from me . . ." A yoke is itself a burden, a burden added to the weight of the other burden, but it has the peculiarity of being able to lighten the load. A burden that would otherwise crush a person down to the ground can be made bearable by using a yoke. We know this from pictures of people carrying water with a yoke over their shoulders, and of draught animals with a yoke that makes it possible for them to pull heavy loads without experiencing pain and torment and without injuring themselves. Jesus wants to put us human beings under such a yoke, so that our burdens will not be too heavy. "My yoke," he calls it—for it is the yoke under which he learned to carry his burden, his load, which is a thousand times heavier than any of ours, because it is all our burdens together that he is carrying. "Take my yoke upon you" means "come with me under my yoke"—yoked together with him, so that we can no longer pull away, and with all those who want to be yoked together with Jesus—yoked together until the day when the yoke will be lifted entirely from our shoulders.

"Learn from me . . ." see how I carry this yoke, and do it the same way. "Learn from me; *for I am gentle and humble in heart.*" This then is the yoke he carries, *his gentleness and lowliness,* and it is the yoke that we are to take upon ourselves, which Jesus knows will help to make our burdens light. To be "gentle" means not to kick against the goads, not to rebel against the burden, not to bump against it and rub ourselves sore, but to be quiet and patient and carry the load that has been put on us, knowing that it is God who lays the burden on us and will help us to go on. ". . . *gentle and humble in heart.*" To be humble means to give up one's own will entirely, not to try to get one's own way, but to be happier when the other's will is done than when mine is done. To be humble means to know that we are servants of God, and that it is the servants' job to carry the load—but it is also to know that we have a good master, who will some day lift the load from our shoulders, after this burden has sanctified and humbled and purified us.

Whoever will bear this yoke, and learn from it, receives a great promise: ". . . *and you will find rest for your souls.*" This is the end, this peace is the last, although we experience it already here under the yoke of Jesus, yoked together with him in gentleness and lowliness. But only at the end, when every burden falls away, will we experience the longed-for perfect rest.

As we look ahead to that blessedness, as we hope for our release from toil and guilt, we can already hear Jesus saying, today, ". . . For my yoke is easy, and my burden is light . . ." Woe to anyone who plays games with these words, making it seem that Christ's cause is an easy one. The person who really understands what it is about is the one who shrinks back in horror from the seriousness and the dreadfulness of the cause of Christ, who does not dare to approach it for fear of what it means for our real lives. But once someone has grasped the meaning of Jesus Christ and his will for us, then we must certainly say to that person, go now to Jesus himself, take his yoke upon you, and you will see that everything, everything changes, that all your fear and horror disappears, and that all at once, for the person who is with Jesus, it is true: "my yoke is easy . . ."

In conclusion, there is still one question remaining between us, which we have to call by its name so that it will not confuse us. Some say: Jesus is dead . . . how shall we go to him . . . how will he comfort us, how will he help us? What else can we answer but this: No, Jesus is living, living here in our midst. Look for him, here or at home, call to him, ask him, beg him, and suddenly he will be there with you, and you will know that he lives. You cannot see him, touch him, or hear him, but you will know that he is there, helping and comforting you, and only he. And you will take his yoke upon you and be joyful and wait with longing for the final rest in him.

> A short while yet, and it is won.
> Of painful strife there will be none.
> Refreshed by life-streams, thirsting never,
> I'll talk with Jesus, forever and ever.

# . . . and Have Not Love

## London, Twentieth Sunday after Trinity, October 14, 1934

⟫⟨●⟩⟪

In the autumn of 1934, Bonhoeffer preached a sermon series on 1 Corinthians 13. In this sermon, the first in the series, he gives three reasons for preaching on the apostle Paul's famous "love chapter." With the second reason, he was thinking of those in Germany who were struggling for a church that truly confessed Christ. He mentions the temptation for them to forget that they must also live the meaning of the statements they made in words.

This sermon is just one example of the high standard for the Christian life that Bonhoeffer consistently upheld, for himself first, and for those whose education in the faith was entrusted to him. He encountered some resistance to such a demanding concept of Christianity, both from people in his London congregations and later from seminary students who were soon to be pastors. But many kept throughout their lives the memory of the example he set and the vision of a God who really expects more from us than moral conduct, good deeds, and pious words, but who also forgives us when we fall short.

First Corinthians 13:1–3 is quoted here from the Revised Standard Version (1946), which preserves the older reading of verse 3 in the Luther Bible, which Bonhoeffer used: "and if I deliver my body to be burned." Here, Paul is evoking a religious custom in the ancient world of giving one's body as a burnt-offering of ultimate devotion.

---

1 Corinthians 13:1–3 RSV: *If I speak in the tongues of men and of angels, but have not love, I am a noisy gong or a clanging cymbal. And if I have prophetic powers, and understand all mysteries and all knowledge, and if I have all faith, so as to remove mountains, but have not love, I am nothing. If I give away all I have, and if I deliver my body to be burned, but have not love, I gain nothing.*

---

The reasons that have moved me to preach this series of sermons on the thirteenth chapter of the first letter to the Corinthians are these: First, this chapter is one that we need in our congregation, just as it was needed by the church in Corinth. What does it mean, after all, to be a Christian church-community, if in all the fine things that happen here, one thing is not completely clear, indeed self-evident—that the members of a church-community are to love one another? What image is the congregation offering, to itself and to the world, if not even this first obligation is being taken seriously? If there was one human thing about the first Christians that pagans found convincing, it was quite simply that they could physically see with their own eyes that two neighbors, or a master and his slave, or estranged brothers or sisters suddenly were no longer against each other but rather with and for each other. So it really made a difference, outwardly and visibly, that they had become Christians. But do we think this means that, since we are already Christians, nothing more needs to change? Wouldn't it be better to say that if we too were to become Christians, many things in our own lives would suddenly change? Would not these words of judgment also apply to a congregation . . . and if everything happened just so in our congregation, if we all came to church and did all sorts of good deeds—"but had not love, we would be nothing"?

The second reason I had for choosing this text is the particular situation of our German churches. Whether or not we want to see it, whether or not we think it is right, the churches are caught up in a struggle for their faith such as we have not seen for hundreds of years. This is a struggle—whether or not we agree—over our confession of Jesus Christ alone as Lord and Redeemer of this world. But anyone who inwardly and outwardly joins in this struggle for this confession knows that such a struggle for faith carries a great temptation with it—the temptation of being too sure of oneself, of self-righteousness and dogmatism, which also means the temptation to be unloving towards one's opponent. And yet this opponent can never truly be overcome if not through love, since no opponent is ever overcome, except by love. Father, forgive them; for they do not know what they are doing [Luke 23:34]—how many people have truly been overcome by these words of Jesus! Even of the most passionate battle for the faith it could well be said: ". . . *but had it not love, it would be nothing.*"

This brings us to the third reason: the Protestant church has been able to proclaim, with unparalleled confidence, the victory and the power of faith in the Lord Jesus Christ alone and thus has caused the world to hear again the message of the Bible in its purity. But who still hears this word of faith the way it is meant to be heard?—that what it really means is that God is to be *loved* above all? To love God does not just mean that when things are going badly for us, we say: God will help us again! That truly amounts to a feeble and puny faith. To love God means to rejoice in God, to think and pray gladly to God, to love being alone in God's presence, to wait impatiently for God, for every word and every request; it means not causing God sorrow but rejoicing simply that there is God, that we can know and have and speak with and live with God. To love God—and for love of God, to love our neighbors as well—in our disillusioned Protestant church, do we still understand this? Can we hear it without saying that it is simply pietism—and what if it were? Is not this the declaration upon which we stand as the Protestant church, which preaches "by faith alone": ". . . but had it not love, it would be nothing"?

In everything I am now going to say, let us keep one thing in mind: that we are not going to look at other people but rather look within *ourselves* and ask whether *we* have love. Who knows—maybe that neighbor of ours who seems such a lone wolf, so odd, self-centered, not friendly at all, might turn out to be full of longing to love greatly—only it takes a long, long time for the ice to break and set his or her heart free. And who knows whether all our efforts to be friendly, and what we say to others about this person, only do all the more to prevent the true breakthrough to great love for God and for others. So let us look only at ourselves and hear what is said as being meant just for us.

In the first place it is very simple, what is being said here—that a human life is only meaningful and worthwhile to the extent that it has love in it, and that a life is nothing, is meaningless and worthless, when it is without love. A life is worth as much as the love in it. Everything else is nothing at all, a matter of indifference, unimportant. All the good and bad, big and little things are unimportant. Only one thing is asked of us— whether or not we have love.

We have all had the experience of standing at the grave of someone about whom we could think of absolutely nothing to say, where we simply felt terribly depressed: how unspeakably poor this person's life was, how meaningless, how much time and effort was lost here. For this person had no one to love and was not loved by anyone. We watch dully, without pain or tears, as this life is finally laid to rest, as it may perhaps have longed to be. This was a skinflint, a jealous, tyrannical person who only knew and wanted and looked out for himself, who hated other people and thought they got in the way of the happiness that she never actually found. This was someone who remained alone and lonely—one cannot but wonder if he or she must remain alone for all eternity. These are the graves that perhaps distress us the most, for they preach to us in the most simple and vivid way the meaning of the words ". . . but have not love, I am nothing."

And then there are the graves where a mother, a faithful father, a happy child passes before our eyes, and standing all around are those who have known this person's love. There are an enormous number of them, including many whom the others do not know, but they themselves know why they are there. And our voices are lifted up and will not be silent, in praise of the love that was glorified in this human life.

These are very simple experiences in life, from which we begin to have an idea why Paul sings the praises of love so exclusively. Any life without love is really nothing, not worth living, but where love is, the meaning of life is fulfilled. Compared with love, the rest really does not matter: good luck or bad luck, poverty or riches, honor or shame, being at home or far away, life or death—what meaning do they have for people who dwell in love? They do not know, it makes no difference to them; all they know is that good luck or bad, poverty or wealth, honor or shame, home and foreign lands, life and death are all given so that they can love all the more strongly, purely, and fully. Love is the one thing that is beyond all differences, comes before all differences, and remains within all differences. Love is strong as death [Song of Sol. 8:6]. Love makes everything else petty; whatever seems great is really pitiful and crumbles to nothing, a picture of misery. What is the value of a life of pleasure, honor, fame, and brilliance compared to a life lived in love? But we must not stop even there, for this question is amazingly powerful and insists on continuing: what is, furthermore, the value of a pious and moral life, a disciplined life of sacrifice and self-denial, if it is not a life lived in love?

As we read this text, images arise before us of people who are so serious and able, so dedicated and zealous in their life of faith that humankind can be proud, we can be proud of them, and we imagine that the Creator too must be proud. We look up to these people in awe and admiration; we bow completely before them and would never venture a word of criticism of them, since they seem beyond our common humanity, alone in their exalted greatness. And then comes the terrible spectacle in which these mighty ones, whose seriousness and devoutness we can never match, are seized and brought down by one little word—"and had not love." They who seemed everything to us are made as nothing before God, whose light of truth streams over them and from whom they cannot hide the truth that, despite all their exalted power, the hearts within them were stony and cold.

"And if I speak in the tongues of mortals and of angels . . ." About what? About that which is sacred to me in life, and important and serious.—To whom? Indeed, to those to whom I want to make these things real, those whom I want to win over to this sacred cause. Let us suppose, then, that we can do this, speak of the greatest and holiest things in such a way that we forget everything else and are carried away by enthusiasm. Suppose, too, that we have a unique gift for expressing our feelings in words, feelings that others can only carry silently inside them. Suppose we

speak thus with one another in complete honesty and devotion. Yet still—
"If I speak in the tongues of mortals and of angels, and do not have love, I
am nothing, a noisy gong or a clanging cymbal."

That devastates and paralyzes us like a bolt of lightning. That is the
possibility we hadn't foreseen, that even our holiest words could become
unholy, godless, and mean, if there is no heart in them, if they are without love. So it is possible for that which is given to us human beings in
order that we may create the most intimate communion among ourselves,
the power of the *Word*, to become unholy if the love is torn out of it and
it becomes self-serving and self-absorbed. A noisy gong, a clanging cymbal—a hollow roar, empty chatter, without heart or soul—that is what can
become of our words. That is what they do become, for the other person—
even our most sacred, solemn, truthful assertions, even our declarations of
love, if they are not spoken in love. So this is the first thing: the one who
speaks solemn, pious words, if he or she does not pass the test of love, turns
out to be a noisy gong or a clanging cymbal, a nothing; while the one who
is perhaps slow of tongue, with stuttering speech, like Moses [Exod. 4:10],
or whose mouth may be closed and dumb, can be saved by his or her love.
The word without love—that is the first point.

But deeper than the word lies insight, knowledge of the mysteries of
this world and the one beyond, devoted and prayerful thinking on God,
contemplation of things past and present, and illumination of things to
come. Are these not also forms of the devout life, awe-inspiring for us?
How much sacrifice and self-denial are demanded of us to arrive at truth
and insight—"and if I have prophetic powers, and understand all mysteries and all knowledge. . . ." When we hear these words, are we not seized
by a great longing—if I only had these, then my thirst would be satisfied;
if I knew why I must go this way and why another must go that way, if I
could discover, here and now, the hidden ways of God—wouldn't that be
blessedness? Then it says again, "but have not love, I am nothing." Insight,
knowledge, truth without love is nothing—it is not even truth, for truth is
God, and God is love. So truth without love is a lie; it is nothing. "*Speaking the truth in love*," says Paul in another letter [Eph. 4:15]. Truth just for
oneself, truth spoken in enmity and hate is not truth but a lie, for truth
brings us into God's presence, and God is love. Truth is either the clarity
of love, or it is nothing.

But we have left out a little phrase in between, one that opens up a terrible riddle to us: "and *if I have all faith*, so as to remove mountains . . . but have not love, I am nothing." "If I have all faith . . ." What does that mean, what chord does that strike within us? All faith, all confidence, certitude that I am with God and God is with me in all the sorrows and anxieties of my life—all faith, so that I no longer have to be afraid of what tomorrow may bring—is this not what we pray for every day? That would be enough for us, that we could hold onto until the end of our lives. And yet here it comes again, *but have not love, I am nothing*. What a baffling thing—imagine a person who had all faith and still did not love, did not love God and his or her brother or sister! What a dark abyss we are looking into now—a faith that is self-glorifying and self-centered in its very foundations, in which I am only looking out for myself; a godless faith—believing, not for the sake of God, but for my own sake. God, keep us from such an abyss, such superstition, which fools us into thinking that we are with you—when we are really far away from you, God. Who will help us escape such danger?

Now there is no holding back—it keeps getting worse, to our despair. Not only is there faith without God and without love, but also good deeds that look like works of love but have nothing to do with love. If I give everything I have to the poor—if I deny myself and make sacrifices as only love can do and still "have not love" but rather make the sacrifices out of a heart full of vanity and selfishness, *thinking that such sacrifices would fool God and my neighbor about what kind of heart I have*—I gain nothing.

So what can the devout person give, in the end, beyond his or her naked life itself as a sacrifice for God and for Christ, as a martyr? If I give my body to be burned, if I give proof of how seriously devout I am and seal it with my death, if I become a martyr for God's cause—God, what grace it would be to die for you!—but have not love, I truly gain nothing. If I appear to love God to the extent of sacrificing my life, but still do not really love God, but only myself and my dream of martyrdom and the fame it will bring. . . . The judgment applies even to the martyr—the lack of love plunges him or her into nothingness.

Who can understand this? We might indeed say, who doesn't understand it? Which of us does not see that, in all these instances, we are the ones who talk big and have knowledge and faith and do good deeds and sacrifice ourselves only for our own sake, without love, without God? Which of us does not see that God must condemn such doings—because God is love and wants only our whole, undivided love—and nothing more?

What then is love, this love of God and the other person? It is not words, or knowledge or faith, not deeds of love or the sacrifice of our lives, in the way we think of it. Do we have love? Has judgment already been passed on us too? Let us call upon love, that it may come from God's very self and snatch us from the pit of destruction. O God of all love, come into our confused hearts and save us, because you love us, through love. Amen.

# What Love Wants

———— )((◉)) ————

Traditionally the Lutheran Church has required men and women studying to be pastors to learn Hebrew and Greek, the original languages of
the Old and New Testaments. At school, Bonhoeffer had been taught the
classical Greek of Plato and Aristotle. As part of his theological training,
he also learned Koine Greek, the language of the New Testament. Greek
was the common language spoken throughout the Roman Empire in Jesus'
time, when there were many local languages as well, including Aramaic,
which Jesus spoke. The apostle Paul, a Jewish Roman citizen, spoke Greek
and could communicate with the Corinthians and other Christian com-
munities in Greece in their own tongue.

In 1 Corinthians 13, Paul uses the word *agape*, which we translate as
"love." Another Greek word, *eros*, also means "love," and both are used in
English to help us distinguish erotic and possessive love from the kind of
which Paul is speaking here. In English, agape may be a name for a Christian celebration, a "love feast," but it also has a far deeper meaning. This
sermon, the second in a series that Bonhoeffer preached on 1 Corinthians

13, helps to define this unconditional love. Psychology since his time has convinced us that some self-love is healthy, but such love must be as much in the image of *agape* as of *eros*—self-forgiving, self-accepting.

———

1 Corinthians 13:4–7: *Love is patient; love is kind; love is not envious or boastful or arrogant or rude. It does not insist on its own way; it is not irritable or resentful; it does not rejoice in wrongdoing, but rejoices in the truth. It bears all things, believes all things, hopes all things, endures all things.*

———

Last Sunday we learned that despite all our ideals, our seriousness, our knowledge, and our faith, even our good deeds and sacrifice, our lives are worth *nothing* if we do not have that one thing that Paul calls love. So it could be that our whole life is meaningless, even if we do our full duty, earnestly and with all our might—because it is done not out of love but out of pride or fear or the vanity of our hearts. And that all our piety is not worth a penny either, if people say of it that it "has not love." But if all human life and activity amount to nothing without love, we are confronted with the question: What *is* this love on which everything depends? What is this love, without which all of us are *nothing?*

It is true that no one lives entirely without love. Every person has love within him or her and knows its power and passion. Each of us knows, furthermore, that it is this love that makes our whole life meaningful; that without this love that we know and have, we could just throw away all our lives—they would no longer be worth living. However, this love, with its power and passion and meaning, which everyone knows, *is self-love—our love for our own selves.* This is what fulfills us and gives us energy to be active and inventive; it is that without which life would not be worth living. So we do know love, but only in a fiendishly distorted way, as in a mirror—as self-love. But this self-love is love that has gone wrong, that has fallen away from its origin. It is self-satisfied and is therefore condemned never to bear fruit—a love that is really hatred of God and my brother and sister, because they could only disturb me within the tight little circle I have drawn around myself. It has all the same power, the same passion, the same exclusiveness as real love—here or there. What is totally different is its goal—myself, rather than God and my neighbor.

But self-love is also clever. It knows that it is only a distorted likeness of love's original image. So it pretends, veils itself, and dresses itself up in a thousand different forms, trying to look like real love—and it succeeds so well that human eyes can hardly tell the difference between the real thing and the fake. Self-love disguises itself as love of our neighbor or our country, as public charity, as love of humankind, trying not to be recognized for what it really is. Yet Paul cuts through all of self-love's attempts to cloud the issue and to deceive and compels it to face its proper responsibility by drawing for it, for us, his picture of what God considers real love.

Each of the characteristics listed here can be interpreted somewhat differently on its own. But taken all together, there is no doubt that they break the spell of self-love and let the love of God and one's neighbor become a reality. But where is this taking place? It doesn't say *a loving person* does this or that, but rather says *love* does this or that. Who is this love? Whom are we talking about? How do we know it?

Before we answer that, let us listen to what is being said. "*Love is patient and kind. . . .*" That means love can wait a long, long time, till the very end. It doesn't become impatient, doesn't try to hurry things or force them to happen. It expects to wait a good long time. It is confident only of being able finally, finally to overcome the other's resistance. Being patient and waiting, continuing to be kind and loving, even if it doesn't seem to serve any purpose, is the only way to overcome a human being. That is the only way to loosen the chains that bind every person, the chains of fear of the other, of the fear of a radical change, of a new life. Friendliness often seems totally inappropriate, but *love is patient and kind*—it waits, the way one waits for someone who has lost the way, waits and rejoices whenever he or she finally gets there.

*For that reason love is not jealous*—but self-love is jealous. It wants something for itself, it wants to win over and possess the other person for itself, *it* wants something from that person. But *love* doesn't want anything *from* the other person—what it wants is everything *for* that person. It doesn't want to possess the other person, especially not to have him or her jealously all to itself. It only wants to love the other person, because it cannot do otherwise; it only wants the person for his or her own sake.

It wants nothing from other people but desires everything for them. Jealousy, which supposedly enhances and safeguards love, actually destroys love, soils and desecrates it.

Because love is not jealous, because it seeks nothing for itself, it therefore doesn't try to make anything of itself—it would rather be wholly inconspicuous or not really be seen at all. It does not call attention to itself, or put on airs, or try to be anything special—it is not boastful; it is not arrogant or rude. We do everything to point out what is special about our love; we play the roles of the saint, the innocent, the fool, or even the martyr with our love. We try to make the other afraid that we might suddenly withdraw our love; that is, we play games with our love, we use it to treat others any way we like. We are ready and able to break the rules of decency and custom, modesty and reserve, in order to get attention for our love. *But love is not rude*—it does *not* do all those things that we do in the guise of love. It does not do them, because *it does not insist on its own way.* It wants nothing for itself, really and truly—it forgets itself and does not see itself, any more than our eyes can see themselves.

What love might want, if it tried to get its own way—at least what in any case we are looking for when we love someone—is at least to be loved back, or some degree of gratitude for our love. But even what we might think belongs to love, what it deserves, *it does not insist on* having for itself. For it is just when it does not so insist—not even surreptitiously and secretly—that perhaps it will find what it seeks. Love is happy and grateful when others find what they are looking for; and it looks on without envy when the other person loves someone else, the way a good mother rejoices when her child finds someone to love with his or her whole heart, even when the mother herself has to stand back.

Even when the other person turns out to be sinful and spiteful, love does not become bitter, because it is not looking to receive kindness. It is thinking not of itself at all but only of the other. It grieves over the other's nastiness, is saddened by it, and loves him or her all the more, but does not become bitter. When our whole life seems bitter because we are not loved in return, love says to us: you haven't yet really loved someone if you let his or her hate or inattentiveness destroy your love; otherwise you would be free of bitterness. You allow yourself to become bitter, but love never does. *It doesn't let the bad things count.* Wherever we think that justice demands that we keep count of good and bad and determine it—there, love is blind, knowingly blind; it sees the bad, but doesn't count it, rather forgives—and only love can forgive. It forgets, instead of bearing grudges. If we could only understand that one thing: love does not bear grudges. It meets the other person each day anew, with new love. It forgets what went on yesterday—it is even willing for others to be scornful and think it is being foolish. It never loses faith but simply goes on loving.

So don't right and wrong make any difference to love? No, love does *not* rejoice at injustice, but it does rejoice in the truth. It wants to see things as they are. It would rather see clearly the hate and injustice and lies that are there than all sorts of charming masks that only serve to cover up the hate and make it even uglier. Love wants to create and to see clear relationships. It rejoices in the truth—for only truth enables love to love again, anew.

Now comes the great summing-up, which we hardly dare to expound, because it is so immensely deep and vast and serious. *Love bears all things, believes all things, hopes all things, endures all things.* The focus here is on *all things*—there is no compromising here; it really means *anything*. Perhaps once, in a great moment of our lives, we might say to someone, I'd do anything for you, I'd give up anything for you, I'd bear anything, together with you. But even as we say it, we are silently setting the one great condition: As long as you will do the same for me. For love, no such condition exists. Love's "anything" is not subject to any circumstances—it is, unconditionally, *all things*.

*Love bears all things*—that means it cannot be frightened by any evil. It can look upon and take in all the horror of human sin. It doesn't look away from what is unbearable; it can stand the sight of blood. Love can stand anything. No guilt, no crime, no vice, no disaster is so heavy that love cannot look at it and take it upon itself, for it knows: love is still greater than the greatest guilt.

*Love believes all things*—and because of that *it can be fooled but is still in the right*. Because of that, one can betray love and lie to it, but still it stands. But who would be foolish enough to believe everything? Isn't that just asking others to take me for a fool? Yes, it would be foolish if I had in mind getting anything for myself with my love. But if I really and truly do not want anything out of it for myself, just to love unconditionally, boundlessly, without prejudice—then it is not foolish at all. Then it is *the* way to overcome other persons, the way to make them begin to wonder, until they turn around and come back. Love believes *all things*, because it cannot do otherwise than believe that in the end the very final word will be that everyone, yes, everyone, is called to be overcome by love.

Has it ever happened to you that you were talking with someone who was considered really bad, someone who nobody expected ever to do anything right or honest, but you listened to him or her and believed in what he or she was saying? And then the person simply broke down, just from being believed, and said to you, "You are the first one who has believed me in a long time." And that then that person really took heart from your belief in him or her—even if he or she had just been lying to us. On the other hand, can you remember the despair of someone whom we didn't trust, but who we found out later had been telling us the truth, and who, because of our mistrust, had come to doubt his or her entire faith? After these experiences, one understands why love does not make any distinctions, but with open eyes believes all things—or with blind eyes, sees the true future.

*Love hopes all things.* It never gives up on anyone, knowing the day will come when the lost one will turn back, will have to return to the love he or she has denied, broken up, shaken off, forgotten, when the sickness finally yields and the person stands erect, healed. Love is like the doctor at the bedside who "doesn't give up hope" for the patient, and this hope makes the patient take heart. And because love has no other desire than that the patient take heart, it will *never* give up on him or her but will keep hoping all things—not just for individual persons, but for a whole people and for a church. If one has not love, then to hope for all things is crazy recklessness and over-optimism. But to hope for all things out of love is the power that a people and a church need in order to stand upright again. This is what we are called to do—to hope so unconditionally that our loving hope can empower others.

Anyone who believes and hopes all things for the sake of love, for the sake of helping people stand tall again, must be patient and suffer. The world will take him or her for a fool, and perhaps a dangerous fool, because this foolishness challenges the malicious forces and brings them out. Yet the malicious can only be fully loved when they come out into the light. *Therefore: love endures all things*—and is blessed in its endurance, for this endurance makes it grow ever greater and ever more irresistible. Love that only has to endure a little will stay weak. Love that endures all things will gain the victory.

Who is this love—if it is not he who bore all things, believed all things, hoped all things—and indeed, had to endure all things, all the way to the cross? Who was never looking for his own gain, never became bitter, and never kept count of the evil done to him—and thus was overpowered by evil? Who even prayed for his enemies on the cross [Luke 23:34] and thereby totally overcame evil? Who is this love, which Paul was talking about, other than Jesus Christ himself? Who else could it be, if not he? What better symbol could there be, standing over this entire passage, than the cross?

# Must I Be Perfect?

## London, Twenty-Second Sunday after Trinity, October 28, 1934

In this sermon, the third in a series on 1 Corinthians 13, Bonhoeffer speaks of knowledge, of the search for understanding that he assumed was in some way a goal in every person's life. Having an older brother, Karl Friedrich Bonhoeffer, who was a physical chemist, Dietrich Bonhoeffer was well aware of the achievements of physical science and of the recent shake-up in scientific understanding regarding the theories of quantum mechanics and relativity. His correspondence with his brother, who later struggled mightily to go on doing his research during the war, shows how he longed for Karl Friedrich to realize that his, Dietrich's, goal was also plausible. Though their paths toward understanding were different, each of the two brothers remained respectful of the other's beliefs.

1 Corinthians 13:8–12 RSV: *Love never ends; as for prophecies, they will pass away; as for tongues, they will cease; as for knowledge, it*

*will pass away. For our knowledge is imperfect and our prophecy is imperfect; but when the perfect comes, the imperfect will pass away. When I was a child, I spoke like a child, I thought like a child, I reasoned like a child; when I became a man, I gave up childish ways. For now we see in a mirror dimly, but then face to face. Now I know in part; then I shall understand fully, even as I have been fully understood.*

In troubled times, if we stop to ask ourselves what will really come of all our agitation, when our thoughts go back and forth from one idea to another; what will come of all our worries and fears, all our wishes and hopes, in the end—and if we are willing to have an answer from the Bible—what we will hear is: There will be just one thing in the end, and that is the love that was in our thoughts, worries, wishes, and hopes. Everything else ends and passes away—everything we did not think, and long for, out of love. All thoughts, all knowledge, all talk that has not love comes to an end—*only love never ends.*

Now if we are aware that something will come to an end, then it is probably not even worth starting. Life is too short and too serious for us to have time to waste, to spend on things that will only come to an end. Now and then we realize this for ourselves with shattering clarity. On New Year's or on our birthday, when we look back at what we have done during the past year or in the period of our lives just past, we are sometimes horrified to see that we have done nothing of lasting value. All our worries and efforts, all the things we have thought and said, have long since died away to nothing. Nothing is left—except perhaps an act of love, a loving thought, a hope for someone else, which may have occurred almost by chance, perhaps without our even being aware of it.

Where this is leading is clear: everything, all our knowledge, insight, thinking, and talking should in the end move toward and turn into love. For only what we think because of love, and in love, will remain, will never end.

Why must everything else come to an end, and why does only love never end? Because only in love does a person let go of himself or herself and give up his or her will, for the other person's benefit. Because love alone comes not from my own self but from another self, from God's self. Because it is through love alone that God acts through us—whereas in everything else it is we ourselves who are at work; it is *our thoughts, our speaking, our knowledge*—but it is God's love. And what is ours comes to an end, all of it—but what is of God remains. Because love is God's very self and God's will; that is why it never ends, it never doubts, it stays its course. It pursues its way with sure steps, like a sleepwalker, straight through the midst of all the dark places and perplexities of this world. It goes down into the depths of human misery and up to the heights of human splendor. It goes out to enemies as well as to friends, and it never abandons anyone, even when it is abandoned by everyone. Love follows after its beloved through guilt and disgrace and loneliness, all of which are no part of it; it is simply there and never ends. And it blesses every place it enters. Everywhere it goes, it finds imperfection and bears witness to perfection.

Love desires to enter into the world of our thoughts and our understanding. Understanding is the most like love. This is because its object is the other; it goes toward the other. Knowledge wants to grasp and understand and explain the world and other people and the mysteries of God. There is no human being who does not take part in the search for understanding. Human beings are fundamentally creatures who seek to understand, who must try to understand, even against their own will, even when thinking is not their calling and not their personal goal. There are great questions on which each person tries out his or her capacity to understand and comes to understand the limits of our understanding. These questions are: What is a person's own path that he or she should follow through life? What is the other person's path? What is the path of God, which underlies all our human paths? There is no one who is not familiar with these questions and does not have to keep asking them, but there is no human person who would be able to answer them on the strength of his or her own ability to understand.

All the solutions that people in this world have tried, which we try every day, are imperfect; they will all pass away. No one knows this better than someone who has done a lot of thinking and knows a great deal. Today there is no one who knows it better than those who, not so long ago, were so proud and confident in their success—physicists and other scientists. And this truth was recognized by one of the greatest thinkers of all time [Socrates] as the end and the beginning of all wisdom, when he said: *I know that I know nothing.* That was indeed the end; that was his final certainty.

But beyond this certainty, Paul recognized an infinitely greater certainty: Our knowledge is imperfect—but when that which is perfect comes, the imperfect will end. That which is perfect is love. Understanding and love are the imperfect and the perfect. And the more longing for perfection there is in the person who seeks knowledge, the more loving he or she will be. *Perfect understanding is perfect love.* This is a strange but very profound and true statement by Paul.

Perhaps someone will ask: But what does understanding have to do with love in the first place? Knowledge means precisely the objective, factual kind of knowing, without any personal opinion entering into it. Certainly that is true. But in order even to be able to see something, we need to love it. If we are indifferent toward a person or a thing, *we will never understand it.* We will always misunderstand a thing or a person we hate. Only a person whom we love *can we fully know.* We will know only as much about a person as we love in him or her.

The so-called worldly wise person, who is reckoned to be a good judge of people, actually knows and understands nothing about them. He or she has a trick of knowing about people's evil inclinations and being especially wary of them—but must do this precisely because of not really understanding people. Imagine that someone whom we do not find likable has done something to us that surprises us, and then that someone whom we love very much has done something that we simply cannot understand. In the first case we will immediately have all sorts of explanations for the bad motives that led that person to such an action; while, on the other hand, we will endlessly search and ask, and indeed invent excuses, in an effort to understand why the person we love acted the way he or she did. We will certainly finish by knowing this second person better than we know the first.

All real understanding is a piece of love, even if it is a love that is still all wrapped up in vanity and self-centeredness and thirst for fame. But it has within it a longing for the perfection that will come when the imperfect has passed away, when perfect truth, knowledge, and love will dawn on us.

*"But when the perfect comes,* the imperfect will *pass away"*—it doesn't happen gradually, as if the imperfect could grow up into the perfect. Instead, the perfect, which the imperfect can never achieve, simply *comes*

by itself. It will come, in complete freedom, in the perfection of its power, and the imperfect will stop, will break up, as a reflected image breaks up when one sees the reality.

It is a surprising image that we have here, in which childhood is compared to imperfect knowledge and mature adulthood to the perfection of love. *"When I was a child,* I spoke like a child, I thought like a child, I reasoned like a child. . . ."* Knowing without loving is childish, childish reasoning, a childish attempt to become master of the world in a sneaking way. Proud knowledge without love is like the bragging of a stupid youngster who does not deserve to be taken seriously, at which a mature adult can only smile. "When I became a man, I gave up childish ways." We would have said it exactly the other way around—childishness is knowledge with love in it, and maturity is realistic knowledge without love. But Paul says that love is the thing that shows mature insight, true knowledge, adulthood. The way of love is the way an adult acts. This makes the distinction clear between this sort of love and any sort of passion, weakness, or sentimentality. Love means truth in the eyes of God; it means perfect knowledge in the eyes of God.

Then another image: "For now we see in a mirror. . . ." The thoughts of God are only seen in the world as if reflected in a mirror. We see them only as if in mirror writing. And God's mirror writing is hard to read. It says that the great is small and the small is great, that right is wrong and wrong is right, that a promise awaits the hopeless while judgment awaits those who are full of hope; it says that the cross signifies victory and death signifies life. We can read God's mirror writing in Jesus Christ, in his life and sayings and dying.

"For now we see in a mirror *dimly.* . . ."—seeing the cross dimly, in God's mirror writing, makes it really hard to recognize and to understand. That is the way we see now, certainly—*"but then* face to face." *"But then,"* when the perfect comes breaking in, when the mirror of this world is shattered and the glorious light of God surrounds us. *"But then,"* at the end, at our end, in the hour of our dying and ceasing and departure. *"But then,"* face to face. . . . Then all will be clear, and perfect love will be with us. *"Face to face"*—to see God as God truly is; not only to believe in love but to see it and feel it, touch it and experience it, to live in its blessedness. *"Blessed are* the pure in heart, for they will *see God"* [Matt. 5:8]—then, face to face.

"Now I know in part; then I shall understand fully, even as I have been fully understood." The answer is in that last phrase, "even as I have been fully understood." That is the only reason why I may hope to understand fully and to experience perfection—that I am understood by God, by love, by that which is perfect. God's light seeks out my eyes; God's love seeks my heart. God has long since known me and loved me—that is why I am so irresistibly drawn to God, to know God and to love God in return. That is why I press on so urgently toward God, toward perfection, even though I know only in part. I could never know God if God had not first known me. God and the human creature recognize each other. They see each other face to face, they know about each other, they know about their love for each other; they know that they cannot and should not be without each other. And now they are with each other and in each other, they are one in knowledge, one in the blessed mystery of their love. The human creature sinks down to the ground and stretches out his or her hands, and is no longer his or her self, but is in God. That is perfection. Amen.

# A Church That Believes, Hopes, and Loves

## London, Reformation Sunday, November 4, 1934

><<<•>>>

Since the Reformation of Luther began in Germany, the observance of Reformation Sunday was and continues to be very important for the German church. German Protestants living in London who grew up in Germany might remember nostalgically the splendid worship services on dark November Reformation Sundays, with the music of brass choirs. For Bonhoeffer, the final verse from 1 Corinthians 13 provided the occasion, at this dark time in the history of the German Protestant church, for him to lift up his vision of what the churches that were heirs of the Reformation might become.

In his sermon, Bonhoeffer calls on Scripture, including Jesus' Sermon on the Mount, which for him was essential for the Christian life, and on Luther to show that the church must do more than believe. It must be the church of faith, hope, and above all, love. The quote from Luther has not been verified. In Germany, many favorite Luther "sayings" have long since lost any reference to their sources in his writings. The quote from Goethe's poem "Symbolum," "We bid you be of hope!" is given here in the English of Thomas Carlyle.

---

1 Corinthians 13:13: *And now faith, hope, and love abide, these three; and the greatest of these is love.*

---

This series of sermons was very intentionally planned so that this text would fall on Reformation Sunday. With this we wish to say that the church that has spoken, as probably no other has done, about the power and the salvation and the victory of faith in Jesus Christ alone, the church that is so great in its faith, must be even greater in its love. On the one hand, then, we want to look back to the original Reformation; on the other, we want to respond actively to a danger and degeneration that has threatened Protestantism since its beginnings. For the message of the faith that alone saves and redeems has become hardened, a dead letter, because it has not been kept alive by love. A church may have great faith—the most orthodox beliefs, the firmest loyalty to its confession—but if it is not even more a church of pure and all-embracing love, it is good for nothing.

What does it mean to believe in Christ, who was himself love, if I still hate? What does it mean to confess Christ as my Lord in faith if I do not do his will? Such a faith is not faith but hypocrisy. It does nobody any good to protest that he or she is a believer in Christ without first going and being reconciled with his or her brother or sister—even if this means someone who is a nonbeliever, of another race, marginalized, or outcast. And the church that calls a people to belief in Christ must itself be, in the midst of that people, the burning fire of love, the nucleus of reconciliation, the source of the fire in which all hate is smothered and proud, hateful people are transformed into loving people. Our churches of the Reformation have done many mighty deeds, but it seems to me that they have not yet succeeded in this greatest deed, and it is more necessary today than ever.

"And now faith, hope, and love abide, these three . . ." "Faith"—that certainly means that no person and no church can live by the greatness of their own deeds, but rather they live by the mighty deeds of God alone, past and present, and (this is the decisive thing) that God's great works remain hidden, unseen in the world. It is just not the same for the church as it is in the world and the history of the peoples. In the world it is important to be able to point to the great things one has done, but the church that did that would be showing that it has become enslaved to the laws and the powers of this world. *The church of success* is truly far from being *the church of faith*.

The deed that God has done in this world, the source of life for all the world ever since, is the cross of Golgotha. This is what God's "success" looks like, and this is what the successes of the church and of individual Christians will look like, if they are acts of faith. That faith abides—this means that it remains true that *humankind must live by that which is unseen*, that we do not live by our own visible work, but rather by the invisible act of God. The believer sees error and believes in truth, sees guilt and believes in forgiveness, sees death and believes in eternal life, or sees nothing—and yet believes in the work and the grace of God. "My grace is sufficient for you, for power is made perfect in weakness" [2 Cor. 12:9].

So it is with the church of the Reformation. It can never live by its own actions, not even those performed in love. Instead, it lives by that which it has not seen, yet believes [John 20:29]. It sees doom, yet believes in salvation; it sees false teaching, yet believes in God's truth; it sees betrayal of the gospel, yet believes in God's faithfulness. The church of the Reformation is never the visible communion of saints but rather the church of sinners, which believes, against all appearances, in grace and lives only by that grace. "If you want to be a saint, get out of the church," Luther once exclaimed. Church of sinners—church of grace—church of faith—that's what it is. "So faith abides"—because it lives before God and only from God. There is only one sin, and that is to live without faith.

But a faith that bravely clings to the unseen and lives by it, as if it were already here and now, hopes at the same time for the age of fulfillment and of seeing and having. It hopes with the certainty of a hungry child whose father has promised him or her bread, who can wait for awhile, but in the end really wants to have that bread; or like someone listening to music, who is willing to stay with it through a dark tangle of dissonances, but in the certainty that dissonance will resolve into harmony; or like a patient who takes a bitter drug so that it will finally take away the pain. Faith that has no hope is sick. It is like a hungry child who will not eat or a tired person who will not go to sleep. As surely as a person believes, surely he or she will also hope.

And hope is nothing to be ashamed of, hope beyond all bounds. Who would want to talk about God, without hope—the hope of seeing God someday? Who would want to talk about peace and love among human-kind without wanting to experience them someday, for all eternity? Who would want to talk about a new world and a new humanity without the hope of sharing in them oneself? And why should we be ashamed of our hope? It is not our hopes of which we will one day have to be ashamed, but our puny and fearful lack of hope, which doesn't trust God in anything, which in false humility fails to reach out for God's promises when they are given, which is resigned to this life and cannot rejoice in God's eternal power and glory. "We bid you be of hope!" "Hope does not disappoint us" [Rom. 5:5]. The more a person dares to hope, the greater he or she will become in his or her hope. Through hope, people grow—if it is hope in God alone and in God's power alone. So hope abides.

"And now faith, hope, and love abide, these three; and the greatest of these is love."

Again we hear the echo of the first verses of this chapter: . . . and if I have all faith, so as to remove mountains . . .—and we can add: and if I have all hope but have not love, I am nothing. For the greatest of these is love.

What can be greater than to live in faith *before* God? What can be greater than to live one's life *toward* God? What is greater is the love that lives *in* God. "Walk before me!" [Gen. 17:1]. "Those who abide in love, abide *in* God" [1 John 4:16]. What is greater than the humility of faith, which never forgets how infinitely far the Creator is from the creature; what is greater than the confidence of hope, which longs for the coming of God and the moment of seeing God's reality? What is greater is the love that here and now is sure of God's presence and nearness everywhere, that clings to God's love and knows that God's love desires nothing other than our love. What is greater than faith, which hopes for and holds fast to its salvation in Christ and will be justified by him? What is greater than hope, which is prepared at any moment for the blessedness of death and of going home? What is greater is the love that serves, forgetting everything for the sake of the other, and even gives up its own salvation in order to bring it to brothers and sisters—for those who lose their love for my sake will find it [see Matt. 10:39].

Faith and hope abide. Let no one think it possible to have love without faith and without hope! Love without faith would be a stream without a source. That would mean that one could have love without Christ. *Through faith alone we are justified* before God, through hope we are prepared for our end, and through love we are made perfect.

Through faith alone we are justified—our Protestant church is built on this sentence. To the human question, how can I stand before God? Luther found the one answer in the Bible: if you believe in God's grace and mercy through Jesus Christ. To the question of how human beings can be justified before God, the answer is through grace alone, through faith alone. We would be entirely right if, here at the end, we turned the first sentence of the chapter around and said, *and if I have all love, so as to accomplish all good works*, but have not *faith*, I am nothing. Faith alone justifies—but love makes perfect.

Faith and hope enter into eternity transformed into the shape of love. In the end everything must become love. Perfection's name is love. But the sign of perfect love in this world bears the name cross. That is the way that perfect love must go in this world, must go over and over again. That shows us first of all that this world is ripe, even overripe, for its destruction; only God's indescribable patience can wait for the end time. Second, it shows us that the church in this world remains the church under the sign of the cross. In particular, the church that wants to become the church of God's visible glory, here and now, has denied its Lord on the cross. Faith, hope, and love together lead us through the cross to perfection.

When we go out the doors of this church now, we enter into a world that is longing for the things we have spoken of here—not simply for the words, of course, but for the reality. Humanity, betrayed and disappointed a thousand times over, needs faith; humanity, wounded and suffering, needs hope; humanity, fallen into discord and mistrust, needs love. Even if we no longer have any compassion for our own poor souls, which are truly in need of all three, do at least have compassion for your poor fellow human beings. They want to learn from us how to believe again, to hope, to love again; do not deny them. On this Reformation Sunday, let us hear the call—believe, hope, and above all, love—and you will overcome the world. Amen.

# My Strength Is Made Perfect in Weakness

## London, Evening Worship, 1934, undated

I n this sermon, Bonhoeffer reflects on questions that had occupied him since his stay at Bethel, a church center and care facility for persons with mental and physical disabilities near Bielefeld, Germany. He and other theologians had been there in August 1933 to work on a new confession for the German Protestant church, explaining the errors of the "German Christians," which helped to prepare for drafting the Barmen Declaration. Bonhoeffer attended church services at Bethel along with the patients being cared for there. He wrote to his grandmother that he was struck by their "situation of being truly defenseless, [which] perhaps gives these people a much clearer insight into certain realities of human existence, the fact that we are indeed basically defenseless, than can be possible for healthy persons."

But Bethel patients were also vulnerable to Hitler's aim of eliminating the sick and weak from the German population. In the end, Bethel was spared, but hundreds of thousands of other vulnerable people, including persons with epilepsy, which could not be treated as successfully then as today, were forcibly sterilized and murdered by the Nazis. In July 1934 (perhaps the time of this sermon), Bonhoeffer arranged for a donation from his London congregations, St. Paul's and Sydenham, to the work at Bethel and other nearby institutions. Ten years later, he wrote from prison, "The Bible directs us to God's powerlessness and suffering; only the suffering God can help."

This sermon was preached in English; Bonhoeffer's errors have been corrected. St. Paul's Church held evening services in English once a month, as not all the parishioners, particularly younger ones, were fluent in German.

2 Corinthians 12:9 KJV: ". . . *my strength is made perfect in weakness.*"

All philosophy of life has to give an answer to the question which presents itself everywhere in the world: what is the meaning of weakness in this world, what is the meaning of physical or mental or moral weakness? Have we ever thought about it at all? Have we ever realized that ultimately our whole attitude toward life, toward humanity and God depends on the answer to this problem? Even if we have never faced this question intellectually, do we know that actually we are bound to take an attitude towards it every day? What has remained unconscious with us becomes conscious now, conscious in the light of the word of God. There is a certain inclination in human nature to keep away from all problems that might make us feel uncomfortable in our own situation. We like to leave these questions in the darkness of subconscious action, rather than see them in the light of a clear and responsible intellectual attitude. We are all dealing with the problem of weakness every day, but we feel it is somewhat dangerous to give an account of our fundamental attitude. But God does not want us to put our heads into the sand like ostriches; instead, God commands us to face reality as it is and to take a truthful and definite decision.

Someone might ask: why is this problem of weakness so all-important? We answer: have you ever seen a greater mystery in this world than poor people, ill people, insane people—people who cannot help themselves but who have to rely on other people for help, for love, for care? Have you ever thought what outlook on life a cripple, a hopelessly ill person, a socially exploited person, a coloured person in a white country, an untouchable— may have? And if so, did you not feel that here life means something totally different from what it means to you, and that on the other hand you are inseparably bound together with such unfortunate people, just because you are human like them, just because you are not weak but strong, and just because in all your strength you will feel their weakness? Have we not felt that we shall never be happy in our life as long as this world of weakness from which we are perhaps spared—but who knows for how long—is foreign and strange and far removed from us, as long as we keep away from it consciously or subconsciously?

Let us be truthful and not unrealistic; let us ask the question: What is the meaning of weakness in this world? We all know that Christianity has been blamed ever since its early days for its message to the weak. Christianity is a "religion of slaves" [Friedrich Nietzsche], of people with inferiority complexes; it owes its success only to the masses of miserable people whose weakness and misery Christianity has "glorified." It was the attitude towards the problem of weakness in the world which made everybody followers or enemies of Christianity. Against the new meaning which Christianity gave to the weak, against this glorification of weakness, there has always been the strong and indignant protest of an aristocratic philosophy of life which glorified strength and power and violence as the ultimate ideals of humanity. We have observed this very fight going on up to our present day. Christianity stands or falls by its revolutionary protest against violence, arbitrariness and pride of power, and by its apologia for the weak.—I feel that Christianity is doing too little in making these points rather than doing too much. Christianity has adjusted itself much too easily to the worship of power. It should give much more offence, more shock to the world, than it is doing. Christianity should take a much more definite stand for the weak than for the potential moral right of the strong.

In between the Christian and the aristocratic view there is a great variety of attempts to mediate between them. The most dangerous of these positions is the very common attitude of benevolence and beneficence. There the seriousness of the problem is not recognized at all.

In these views, weakness is nothing but imperfection. This includes, of course, the belief that the higher value in itself is strength and power. Strength and weakness are considered as the perfect in proportion to the imperfect. Here Christianity must protest. With all due respect for the real sacrifices that have been made out of such a benevolent attitude, it must be said frankly that this approach is wholly wrong and unchristian, for it means condescension instead of humility. Christian love and help for the weak means humiliation of the strong before the weak, of the healthy in the face of suffering, of the mighty over against the exploited. The Christian relation between the strong and the weak is that the strong has to look *up* to the weak and never to look down. Weakness is holy, therefore we devote ourselves to the weak. Weakness in the eyes of Christ is not the imperfect over against the perfect; instead, strength is the imperfect and weakness the perfect. It is not the weak that has to serve the strong, but the strong has to serve the weak, and not through benevolence but with care and reverence. Not the powerful is in the right, but ultimately the weak is always in the right. So Christianity means a devaluation of all human values and the establishment of a new order of values in the sight of Christ.

Here we have arrived at the last question: What is the reason for this new conception of the meaning of weakness in the world? Why is suffering holy? Because Christ suffered in the world at the hands of humankind, and has to suffer at our hands again wherever he comes. God suffered on the cross. That is why all human suffering and weakness shares in God's own suffering and weakness in the world. We suffer: God suffers much more. Our God is a suffering God. Suffering conforms humanity to God. The suffering person is in the likeness of God. "My strength is made perfect in weakness" says God. Wherever one of us, in physical or social or moral or religious weakness, is aware of our existence and likeness to God, there we are sharing God's life, there we feel God being with us, there we are open for God's strength, that is God's grace, God's love, God's comfort, which passeth all understanding [see Phil. 4:7 (KJV)] and all human values. God is glorified in the weak as God in Christ was glorified on the cross. God is mighty where humanity is nothing.

# Lord, Help My Unbelief

## London or Berlin, date unknown

———⪻⟨⟨◇⟩⟩⪼———

This undated sermon may have been given in London or Berlin at an evening service. Bonhoeffer mentions having seen a play about St. Francis; such a play, in its third edition, by Otto Bruder is known to have been published at that time by Christian Kaiser Verlag in Germany.

———⪻◇⪼———

Mark 9:23–24: *If you are able!—All things can be done for the one who believes. . . . I believe; help my unbelief!*

———⪻◇⪼———

To a person who is in what appears, to human eyes, to be a hopeless situation, Jesus says this: if you could believe. Then everything in your life would be different. Then you wouldn't be standing here so timidly, so desperately, because then you would know that nothing is impossible for you. These words are spoken to a father whose child, in human terms, is incurably ill, who would do anything to help his son and yet must look on helplessly while the child is destroyed. The father has tried everything he can think of and finally has come to Jesus' disciples; and now only one way is left, one that he treads in fear and trembling, the way that causes everyone to tremble, the first time we walk it—the *way to Jesus*.

Why would we rather take any other way than the way to Christ himself when something goes wrong in our lives? Why do we avoid really choosing this way? Why do we shudder and turn away? Because we know that we will have to answer a mighty question, and this question is: Can you believe? Can you believe in such a way that your whole life becomes, or will become, one great act of trust in God, of daring to believe in God? Can you so believe that you never look to left or right but do what you have to do for God's sake? Can you so believe that you obey God? Can you believe? If you could believe, then yes, help would be at hand. Then nothing would be impossible for you any longer.

How often we are terrified by our own lack of faith. Oh, if only I *could* believe! At the bedsides of those who are sick and dying, at the edge of despair over myself and others, this is the cry that rises up in me: oh, if only I *could* believe! Yet when we have the chance to observe the life of someone who lived and died in faith, as I did a few weeks ago when I saw a moving play about the life of St. Francis, then we are totally convinced that this is the only way that is worthwhile—just to live the way Christ wants us to, without worrying about what is going to happen to us personally. Then it takes hold of us irresistibly: if only I could believe, yes, then my whole life really would be different. Then I would be free, perhaps even somehow happy, because nothing would be impossible for me anymore. "I can do all things through him who strengthens me, Jesus Christ" [Phil. 4:13].

We do believe in all sorts of things, far too many things in fact. We believe in power, we believe in ourselves and in other people, we believe in humankind. We believe in our own nation and in our religious community, we believe in new ideas—but in the midst of all those things, we do not believe in the One—in God. And believing in God would take away our faith in all the other powers, make it impossible to believe in them. If you believe in God, you don't believe in anything else in this world, because you know it will all break down and pass away. But you don't need to believe in anything "else," because then you have the One who is the source of all things, in whose hands everything comes to rest.

We know the victories that can be won by a person who truly believes in himself or herself, or who believes in any power or idea in this world to the point of total self-surrender to it and living it out. Such a person can accomplish superhuman things, impossible things. How much greater will be the victory of the person whose faith is not in some subjective illusion but in the living God! The miracles of Jesus, the effect that he had on people, were nothing other than his faith! *We* should be the ones to live by such faith. How ashamed we must be when we look at our lives, even compared to the accomplishments of people who had faith in the things of this world. Oh, if only we could believe!

Why can we not believe? What are the obstacles to our faith? There are as many answers to that as there are unbelieving people. One would cite intellectual difficulties, another would plead not having a "gift for religion," for another it would be a hard experience of life, a generally pessimistic outlook, and so on. There is no lack of reasons that we can put forward to excuse ourselves. No human being ever lacks these, even when everything else is lacking. But the *one* honest answer to this question is that we basically do not *want* to believe. I know we feel offended if someone says that. We say we must have tried a hundred times over in our lives to believe, and even now we still want to, but it is just that way for us in particular—we really, even with the best will in the world, just simply *cannot* believe. This is not true; it is all a sham, even though we may not be consciously aware of it. What is true is that in all these despairing and strained efforts to believe, what we really wanted was not to believe. That is, we didn't want that which is the first requirement of faith, namely, to surrender ourselves totally, not to think of ourselves anymore, to extinguish completely our need for recognition and recognize God alone, to put our trust and dare to believe in God alone. We would surrender what was uncomfortable to us, but not that which we cared about! To have faith means to trust and to dare *unconditionally*, and that we didn't want; we wanted to set conditions, and thereby we missed the whole point, and our whole effort was not genuine. *We did not want to believe.*

If someone comes with pious arguments proving that the Bible says there are people whom God has predestined not to be able to have faith but rather to be objects of wrath that are made for destruction [see Rom. 9:19–26], our answer is, That may be true, but how do you know that you are one of them? Who told you that? How do you know that it is not actually your fault that you refuse to believe, when God has never stopped calling you? You want to have faith—all right, isn't that enough to show that God is calling you, that you are supposed to have faith and that you can believe if you will only trust in him? *We do not want to believe.*

But Jesus says: if you could believe. There is longing and infinite compassion in these words. If only you would decide to take this step that you have wanted all your life to take and never did, to believe. If only you would give yourself up, quite simply and in everything that is most personal and specific to you, and let Jesus be your Lord.

All things are possible for the one who believes. Here we are talking about an incurable illness, which is really supposed to be broken through faith in the power of God and in fact is broken. We stand amazed; we look for excuses, ways it could have happened: suggestive influences or unconscious psychotherapy. Christ says no, none of that; it was faith, it was God.

All things. People who study the human mind know that the thing that seems least possible is to break through a mental pattern or mental compulsion that has a person in its grip, to turn the person in a different direction. Jesus says, *All things.* People who live lives of religious devotion know that we have no hope of combating our sins, our selfishness, our weaknesses, as long as we rely on ourselves alone, that nothing is more desperate than a human being's struggle against sin. Jesus says, all things are possible for those who believe. The most hardened and stubborn sinner becomes a new being, free from all fear, all compulsiveness, all evil habits, if he or she will only believe—that is, will dare to put his or her trust in God. The most melancholy person becomes joyful, the most timid soul becomes outgoing, the most diffident and lukewarm character is suddenly glowing with new life—"if only you could believe."

All things are possible—We can think of so many times when we turned to God wanting to believe, when we prayed and called to God to help us, "if it be thy will"—and we did not receive the help, at least not in the way we asked for it. All things—is it really true?

Doesn't that almost mean that faith can *compel* God? Yes, that is indeed what it means! But that is just what is so incredible, that God *wants* to be compelled by our faith—not by our complaining and lamenting and worrying and sighing, but by our faith. That almost sounds blasphemous—but could it be true? Isn't *God's will*, after all, the place where every true faith must meet its limit? What does it mean, to believe in God, if not to make room for God's will, what God wills for us, for the world? Can there then be anything at all that is not possible, if it is God's will? And don't we know very well what God's will is for our lives? Don't we know very well what God's will is for our nation and for our church? Shall we not dare at last, in faith, to let God's will for us be done?

You answer: Lord, I believe; help my unbelief! The promise that Jesus has given to the one who believes draws this father out beyond his own limitations, compels him to believe. Jesus himself compels the man to have faith, so that he says, Lord, I believe—I believe what you say, I believe that your word and your promise are true. I believe, *when I am looking at you*, when I hear the words, when I see. But *when I am looking at myself*, then, dear Lord, *help my unbelief.* When I am besieged, when everything in me resists such a promise—reason, history, the world, my experience—help my unbelief.

*We are being asked whether we believe.* We are being called upon—oh, if only you could believe! To us the promise is given: all things are possible. *Looking at these words*, is there any answer we can make, other than: Lord, I believe—and looking at our own nature, is there any prayer we can make, other than: Lord, help my unbelief. No one can escape this paradox. Do you believe? I believe—help my unbelief, which is there anew every day. Who is ready to say, I believe, in the face of the temptations we experience every hour? Lord, we want to dare it, at your word—but our faith cannot make it happen; only you can. Not we ourselves, not even our faith, but you alone—for you, nothing is impossible. Lord, help my unbelief! Amen.

# Forgiveness

## Finkenwalde, Next-to-Last Sunday
## of the Church Year, November 17, 1935

―――――=》《◉》《=―――――

Finkenwalde, the country estate where Bonhoeffer trained pastors for the Confessing Church from 1935 to 1937, had previously housed a school. In what had been the gym, the seminarians created a simple chapel, large enough to invite their neighbors to join them for Sunday morning worship. Usually, the preacher on Sunday mornings was a seminarian, gaining experience, while Bonhoeffer himself preached for vespers on Saturday evenings and at Communion services. However, when he had an urgent theme to emphasize, Bonhoeffer occasionally took the pulpit on a Sunday. That was the case for this sermon. For Bonhoeffer, forgiveness was absolutely central to the community life of Christians. We can see this in his book *Life Together*, which describes life in the Finkenwalde community. The last paragraph of the sermon refers to the practice he promoted of turning to a peer, a fellow seminarian, to hear one's confession of sin and assure liberating forgiveness in God's name.

Matthew 18:21–35: *Then Peter came and said to him, "Lord, if another member of the church sins against me, how often should I forgive? As many as seven times?" Jesus said to him, "Not seven times, but, I tell you, seventy-seven times. For this reason the kingdom of heaven may be compared to a king who wished to settle accounts with his slaves. When he began the reckoning, one who owed him ten thousand talents was brought to him; and, as he could not pay, his lord ordered him to be sold, together with his wife and children and all his possessions, and payment to be made. So the slave fell on his knees before him, saying, 'Have patience with me, and I will pay you everything.' And out of pity for him, the lord of that slave released him and forgave him the debt. But that same slave, as he went out, came upon one of his fellow slaves who owed him a hundred denarii; and seizing him by the throat, he said, 'Pay what you owe.' Then his fellow slave fell down and pleaded with him, 'Have patience with me, and I will pay you.' But he refused; then he went and threw him into prison until he would pay the debt. When his fellow slaves saw what had happened, they were greatly distressed, and they went and reported to their lord all that had taken place. Then his lord summoned him and said to him. 'You wicked slave! I forgave you all that debt because you pleaded with me. Should you not have had mercy on your fellow slave, as I had mercy on you?' And in anger his lord handed him over to be tortured until he would pay his entire debt. So my heavenly Father will also do to every one of you, if you do not forgive your brother or sister from your heart."*

Right here at the beginning of this sermon, let us quietly and honestly ask whether we know anyone from our own circle of friends and family whom we have not forgiven for some wrong that person might have done us; a person from whom we once separated ourselves in anger—perhaps not even in open anger, but in quiet bitterness, thinking: I cannot stand it any longer, I can no longer associate with this person.

Or are we really so inattentive that we say we do not know anyone like this? Are we so indifferent to other people that we do not even know whether we are living in peace or at odds with them? Whether one after another may not someday stand up and accuse us, saying: "You separated yourself from me in discord—you could not tolerate me—you broke off fellowship with me—you found me unsympathetic and turned away from me—I once did you wrong, and you left me alone—I once wounded your honor, and you broke with me—and I could not find you again—I often looked for you, but you avoided me—and we never spoke frankly with each other again, but I wanted nothing more from you than your forgiveness, and yet you were never able to forgive me. Here I am now, and I am accusing you—do you still even know me?"—Whether or not in that particular hour names will come back to us that we hardly recognize anymore—many, many wounded, rejected, poor souls whose sin we did not forgive. And among these people perhaps even a good friend, a brother or sister, one of our parents?

And at that moment a single, great, threatening, terrible voice will speak against us: *You have been a hard person*—all your cordiality cannot help you; you were hard and proud and as cold as a stone; you did not concern yourself with any of us; you were indifferent to all of us and hated us, you never knew what forgiveness might accomplish; you never knew how it benefits the person who experiences it and how it liberates the person who forgives. You have always been a hard person.

We make it too easy for ourselves with other people. We completely blunt our sensibility, and then believe that not thinking ill of someone is the same as forgiving that person—yet in so doing we utterly fail to see that, as a matter of fact, we have no *positive* thoughts about the person— and to forgive would mean having nothing but good thoughts about the person and *supporting* that person whenever we can. But precisely that is what we avoid—we do not support such persons. Instead, we continue alongside them and grow accustomed to their silence; indeed, we do not take it seriously to begin with—and yet *the whole point is to support such persons*—to support them in all situations, with all their difficult and unpleasant sides, including any injustice and sin they may commit even against me—to be silent, to support, and to love without ceasing—that would come close to forgiveness!

Those who do indeed take this posture toward others, toward their parents, their friends, their wives, their husbands, but also toward strangers, in fact, toward all those whom we encounter in our lives—they know how difficult this really is. They know how often they want to say: I just cannot do it any longer; I just cannot stand this person any longer; I'm just worn out from it. One cannot always just keep on as before. "Lord, if another member of the church sins against me, how often should I forgive?" How long must I endure this person who acts so harshly toward me, hurting me, wounding me, who is so completely inconsiderate and insensitive and who has hurt me immeasurably—Lord, how often . . . ? At one point or another, it simply must end; wrong simply must be called for what it is; my own rights simply cannot continue to be violated on and on—"As many as seven times?" We probably will smile at Peter here, since seven times does not seem like all that much to us—how often have we already forgiven and overlooked? And yet we certainly should not smile, indeed, we have absolutely no reason to do so with regard to Peter here. To forgive seven times, genuinely to forgive, would mean making the best of the wrong that has been done to us, would mean repaying evil with good; it means accepting the other person as if that person had always been our dearest friend—no small feat. Indeed, it is what we tend to call forgiving and forgetting: Live and let live. But then genuinely forgiving, out of pure love, love that simply refuses to turn the other person loose and instead insists on continuing to support that person—that is certainly no small feat.

Such questions are a real torment. How can I deal with this person? How can I endure this person? Where do my own rights begin with regard to this person? When these questions arise, let us always go to Jesus, just as did Peter. For if we were to go to anyone else, or if we were simply to ask ourselves, we would only get insufficient help or no help at all. Jesus, however, will indeed offer help, albeit only in a quite peculiar fashion. Not seven times, Peter, but seventy-seven times, Jesus says, and he knows that only in this way can he help Peter. *Do not count*, Peter; instead, forgive without counting—do not torment yourself with the question of how long—endlessly, Peter, endlessly, that is what it means to forgive—and precisely that is what grace is for you, that alone will make you free.

When you count, once, twice, three times, the whole matter gets increasingly threatening—and your relationship with that person gets increasingly agonizing—but do you not notice that as long as you are still counting, for that long you are still reckoning that earlier sin against the person, for that long you still have not really forgiven that person, not even for the first time! Peter, free yourself from such counting—forgiving and pardoning know neither number nor end. You need not worry about your own rights, since they are already taken care of with God—you may forgive without end! Forgiving has neither beginning nor end; it takes place daily, unceasingly, for ultimately it comes from God. This is what liberates us from forced relationships with others, for here we are liberated from ourselves; here we may surrender our own rights merely in order to help and serve others.

Listen, there is no longer any need for us to be so sensitive—we gain nothing by it—no need for us to be so concerned about our own honor—no need to be indignant when others repeatedly wrong us—no need to continually judge those persons—we need only *accept them just as they are* and forgive them for everything, absolutely everything, without end, without qualification. Is it not truly an enormous grace that we can enjoy such peace with our neighbor,—that no one and nothing can ever disturb that peace? Here our friendships, our marriages, our brotherhood and sisterhood receive precisely what they need, namely firm, enduring peace through forgiveness.

When Jesus said this to Peter, he was telling and giving him something joyous, something wonderful, something that would free Peter from the agonizing opposition between people. You *may* forgive one another, Jesus says. This is truly good news.

What is unfortunate is that precisely when Jesus wants to give us such enormous help, something so truly great, we immediately say: Ah, but how difficult it is, what Jesus is putting on us here, how unbearably difficult. Rather than helping us, this merely burdens us further. For who is able to do this, to forgive brother or sister for everything and to bear it together with them? All our defiance reawakens: No, I do not want to do it and I cannot do it. Nor have the other persons really earned such forgiveness.

And behold, it is only when we start talking in this way that Jesus gets angry with us. We may ask him for help without end—but to resist his help, saying: That is not really help at all,—Jesus does not want to hear that from us. "You cannot forgive, you do not want to forgive, the other person does not deserve to be forgiven,—indeed, who do you think you are, talking like that?"

And now, with great anger, Jesus recounts the terrible story about the roguish slave, the slave who experienced mercy and yet remained a hard person, to whom all mercy was thus denied and who experienced God's terrible judgment. And by telling us this angry story, Jesus gives us the greatest help possible by showing us the *path* to true forgiveness. It is this path that we now want to understand.

Are we able to recall a moment in our own lives in which God called us to judgment, a moment in which we were lost ourselves, in which our own lives were at stake? God demanded that we render an account of ourselves, and yet we could show nothing but debts, immeasurably great debts. Our life was stained and impure and guilty before God, and we had nothing, absolutely nothing to show but debts and even more debts. Let us recall how we felt at that time, how we had nothing to hope for, how futile and meaningless everything seemed. We could no longer help ourselves; we stood there completely alone—facing nothing but punishment, righteous punishment. Before God we were utterly unable to stand up straight; and before God, before the Lord God, we fell down on our knees in despair and pleaded: Lord, have patience with me—and we came out with all sorts of prattle, just as does the roguish slave here: I promise to pay back everything and to make restitution—that sort of talk, even though we knew too well that we would never be able to pay it. And then suddenly everything changed; God's countenance was no longer filled with anger, but rather with enormous misery and pain because of us human beings. And so God remitted all our debt, and we were forgiven. We were free, and all anxiety departed from us, and we were once again joyous and were once again able to look God in the eye and to offer thanks.

Thus did we, too, once appear just like this roguish slave. But how forgetful we are! And now we go and seize someone who may have done us a slight wrong, who may have deceived us or slandered us, and we say to that person: Make good what you have done to me! I can never forgive what you have done! Can we not see that what we really ought to say is: Whatever that person has done to me is nothing, absolutely nothing compared to what I have done to God and to that other person? Who has called us to condemn that person when we ourselves are so much more culpable?

But, looking at verses 31-34, now we have forfeited grace; now all our earlier guilt emerges anew; now wrath rains down upon us—now we are lost people, lost because we have had contempt for grace. That is the whole lesson here: Though you certainly see the other person's sin, you do not see your own. Only by recognizing in penitence God's mercy for you will you yourself then also be capable of forgiveness.

How can we get to the point that we are able to forgive each other's sins, all of those sins, from the bottom of our hearts? My dear friends, those who have experienced what it means for God to lift us up out of a great sin and to forgive us, those to whom God has in such an hour sent another brother or sister to whom we might then confess our sin, whoever knows how a sinner resists such help because the sinner simply does not want to be helped, and whoever nonetheless has experienced how a brother or sister genuinely can release us from our sin in God's name and in prayer—that person will surely lose all inclination to judge or to hold grudges and will instead want but one thing: to help bear the distress of others, to serve, to help, to forgive,—without measure, without qualification, without end,—such a one can no longer hate sinful brothers and sisters, but will instead want only to love them all the more and to forgive them for everything, everything. Lord, our God, may we experience your mercy so that we, too, may practice mercy without end! Amen.

# The Betrayer

## Finkenwalde, Fifth Sunday in Lent
## [Judica Sunday], March 14, 1937

⟫⟨◆⟩⟪

The fifth Sunday in Lent, often called Passion Sunday, is called *Judica* in churches where worship services were once held in Latin. The name comes from Psalm 43, which is read for evening prayer on that day. The psalm begins, *"Judica me, Deus . . ."* ("Vindicate [or judge] me, O God, and defend my cause against an ungodly people.") In his book *Saved from Sacrifice*, theologian S. Mark Heim points out that many psalms, the laments of a victim being unjustly persecuted, foreshadow Jesus' passion. Jesus' cry on the cross, for example—"My God, my God, why have you forsaken me?"—echoes Psalm 22:1.

For the twenty or so seminarians who had become a close-knit group during the winter semester at the underground seminary in Finkenwalde, Jesus' betrayal by one of his own disciples must have felt particularly horrifying. Bonhoeffer calls a cloud of scriptural passages to witness to Judas's betrayal. Matthew 26:50 is translated differently in the NRSV ("Friend, do what you are here to do.") from Luther's Bible ("My friend, why have you come?") Stanzas from sixteenth- and seventeenth-century hymns by

Paul Gerhardt and Michael Weiss, long sung in German churches during Holy Week, and a line of song from medieval passion plays—"O, poor Judas, what have you done?"—remind us of the church's traditional Good Friday emphasis on our personal guilt and our redemption through Jesus' undeserved suffering. But Bonhoeffer also emphasizes Jesus' love, even for Judas.

---

Matthew 26:45b–50: *"See, the hour is at hand, and the Son of Man is betrayed into the hands of sinners. Get up, let us be going. See, my betrayer is at hand." While he was still speaking, Judas, one of the twelve, arrived; with him was a large crowd with swords and clubs, from the chief priests and the elders of the people. Now the betrayer had given them a sign, saying, "The one I will kiss is the man; arrest him." At once he came up to Jesus and said, "Greetings, Rabbi!" and kissed him. Jesus said to him, "My friend, why have you come?" Then they came and laid hands on Jesus and arrested him*

---

Jesus kept one secret concealed from his disciples up until the final Passover meal. He had indeed left no doubt about his own path of suffering and had attested to them three times [Mark 8:31–33, 9:30–32 and 10:32–34] that the Son of Man would be delivered into the hands of sinners. He had not, however, revealed to them his most profound secret. It was only in the final hour of fellowship with them, at the holy Passover meal, that he was able to tell them: the Son of Man will be delivered into the hands of sinners—through betrayal. One of you will betray me.

By themselves, his enemies can gain no power over him. For that they need one of Jesus' friends, a close friend who will give him away, a disciple who will betray him. This terrible thing comes about not from the outside, but from the inside. Jesus' path to Golgotha begins with a disciple's betrayal. While some of the disciples sleep that incomprehensible sleep in Gethsemane, one betrays him, and in the end "all the disciples deserted him and fled" [Matt. 26:56].

The night of Gethsemane comes to an end. *"See, the hour is at hand"*—the hour Jesus had predicted, the hour about which the disciples had long known and whose arrival made them tremble, the hour for which Jesus was so completely prepared and the disciples were so completely unprepared, the hour which now no earthly means could put off—"See, the hour is at hand, *and the Son of Man is betrayed into the hands of sinners.*"

"Betrayed," Jesus says. That is, it is not the world that gains power over him. Instead, Jesus is turned over, surrendered, given up by his own. All protection is denied him. They no longer want to be burdened with him: Leave him to the others. That is what happens. Jesus is thrown away. The protecting arms of his friends are lowered. Let the hands of sinners do with him what they will. Let them lay their hands upon him, those whose unholy hands were never permitted to touch him. Let them play with him, deride and strike him. We can change none of this now. Betraying Jesus means no longer intervening on his behalf, means surrendering him to the derision and power of the public, means allowing the world to do with him whatever it pleases, means no longer standing by him. Jesus' own followers deliver him over to the world. That is his death.

Jesus knows what is in store for him. Firmly and resolutely he summons his disciples: "*Get up, let us be going.*" His threatening enemies often had to give way before him; he passed freely through their midst; their hands sank [see Luke 4:28-30]. His hour had not yet come at that time. But now that hour has arrived. And now he freely meets it. And just so that there can be no more doubt, just so it is unequivocally clear that the hour has come in which he is to be betrayed, he says: "*See, my betrayer is at hand.*" Not once does he pay attention to the large crowd approaching, nor to the swords and clubs of the enemy. They would have no power! Jesus looks solely at the person who has brought about this hour of darkness. His disciples, too, are to know where the enemy is to be found. For a single moment, everything, the entirety of salvation and world history, is in the hands of that one person—the betrayer. See, my betrayer is at hand—and in that night the disciples shudder when they recognize him—Judas, the disciple, their brother, their friend. They shudder—for when earlier that evening Jesus had told them that one of them would betray him, none had dared accuse the other. No one could believe that one of the others might be capable of such an act. Hence each one had to ask: Surely not I, Lord? Surely not I, Lord? Each thought his own heart more capable of such a deed than that of the other, the brother.

"*While he was still speaking, Judas, one of the twelve, arrived; with him was a large crowd with swords and clubs.*" Now our attention focuses on only two people. The disciples and pursuers recede, both failing to do their own work well. Only two do their work properly, namely, Jesus and Judas. Who is Judas? That is the question. It is one of the most ancient and haunting questions of Christendom. Let us consider first only what the evangelist himself tells us: *Judas, one of the twelve.* We can still sense some of the horror the evangelist must have felt when he wrote these few words. Judas, one of the twelve—what more need be said? And did this not really say everything? Judas' entire, dark secret and at the same time the most profound horror at his deed. Judas, one of the twelve: that means it was impossible for such a thing to happen, it was completely impossible, and yet it did happen. No, nothing more needs to be explained or understood here. It is wholly and completely inexplicable, incomprehensible, and will always remain an utter riddle—and yet it did indeed happen. Judas, one of the twelve, someone who was with Jesus day and night, someone who had followed Jesus, someone who had paid a price, who had had to leave everything behind in order to be with Jesus—a brother, a friend, a confidant of Peter, of John, of the Lord himself.

Yet it also meant something even more incomprehensible: Jesus himself had called and chosen Judas! The real mystery is that Jesus had known from the outset who would betray him. To John, Jesus says: Did I not choose you, the twelve? [John 6:70] Yet one of you is a devil. Judas, one of the twelve—here the reader will look not only at Judas, but even more so and with enormous consternation at the Lord himself, who chose Judas. And those whom he chose he also loved. He allowed them to participate in all parts of his life, in the mystery of his person, sending them all out equally to preach the gospel. He gave them the power to exorcise devils and to heal—and Judas was one of them. Not even the smallest indication that Jesus might have secretly hated Judas. No, and indeed Judas seemed singled out from the others through his office of treasurer for the disciples. Although John does say once that Judas was a thief [John 12:6], should this remark not rather be understood as suggesting in a dark fashion that Judas was a thief with regard to Jesus, namely, that from Jesus he stole what was not his, handing it over to the world? And are the thirty pieces of silver not merely a symbol of how common and paltry the gift of the world is for those who know the gift of Jesus? And yet Jesus knew from the very outset who would betray him!

Indeed, John even recounts what is a wholly mysterious sign of intimacy between Jesus and Judas. On the night of the Passover meal, Jesus gives Judas the piece of bread he has dipped in the dish; and following this symbol of the most intimate community, Satan enters into Judas, whereupon Jesus speaks to Judas in the fashion half of a petition, half of a command: Do quickly what you are going to do. No one else understood what was going on here. Only Jesus and Judas knew.

Judas, one of the twelve, chosen by Jesus, granted community by Jesus, loved by Jesus—does all this mean that Jesus wants to show and prove all his love even to his betrayer? Does it mean that Judas should know that there is basically nothing in Jesus to betray? Does it also mean that Jesus profoundly loves God's will, even as that will comes to fulfillment in Jesus' own path of suffering, and that he also loves the person whose betrayal opens up that very path, and indeed, the person who for a brief moment holds Jesus' very fate in his hands? Does it mean that Jesus loves Judas as the one through whom the divine will comes about, and yet knows: Woe to the one through whom it happens? That is the great, unfathomable mystery—Judas, one of the twelve.

But all this is also a mystery from the perspective of Judas. What does Judas want from Jesus? It must be that evil cannot pull itself away from the innocent, from the pure. Judas hates Jesus; yet because he also cannot bring himself to leave him, he ends up loving him as well with precisely that dark, passionate love with which even evil, even the devil, is still aware of its own origin in God, in the pure. The one who is evil wants to be the disciple of the one who is good. The one who is evil is the most passionate disciple of the one who is good—until he betrays him. The one who is evil knows that he must serve God and thus loves God for the sake of God's power; although the one who is evil does not himself have that power, he still is driven by the one urge to gain power over God. Hence he is a disciple and yet must still betray his own Lord. Jesus chooses Judas, and Judas cannot tear himself away from Jesus. Jesus and Judas belong together from the outset. Neither lets go of the other.

And now we see this illustrated by the story itself: Jesus and Judas bound by a kiss. Just listen to the horrific story: *"Now the betrayer had given them a sign, saying 'The one I will kiss is the man; arrest him.' At once he came up to Jesus and said, 'Greetings, Rabbi!' and kissed him. Jesus said to him, 'My friend, why have you come?' Then they came and laid hands on Jesus and arrested him."* And: *"Judas, is it with a kiss that you are betraying the Son of Man?"* And once again we are seized by the question: Who is this Judas who betrays the Son of Man with a kiss? It is, of course, far too superficial merely to point out that the kiss was the customary form of greeting at the time. This kiss was far more than that! This kiss brought the path of Judas to its conclusion, and was the most profound expression of the fellowship and subsequent utter separation of Jesus and Judas.

*"My friend, why have you come?"* Do you hear how Jesus still loves Judas, how even at this hour he calls him his friend? Jesus does not yet want to let go of Judas. He allows Judas to kiss him. He does not turn him away. No, Judas must kiss him. His fellowship with Jesus must complete itself. Why have you come? Jesus knows full well why Judas came, and yet: Why have you come? And: Judas, is it with a kiss that you are betraying the Son of Man? One final expression of a disciple's love, united with betrayal. One final sign of passionate love, coupled with much more passionate hatred. One final enjoyment of a subordinating gesture, conscious of the superior power of the victory gained over Jesus. What a profoundly divided act, this kiss of Judas! *Not being able to pull himself away from Jesus, and yet surrendering him.* Judas, is it with a kiss that you are betraying the Son of Man?

Who is Judas? Should we not also consider here the name he bore? "Judas," does it not refer here to the profoundly divided people from whom Jesus himself came, to the chosen people that had received the promise of the Messiah and yet had also rejected him? To the people of Judah, who loved the Messiah and yet could not love him in that way? "Judas"—translated, his name means "gratitude." Was this kiss not the gratitude offered to Jesus by the disciple's divided people and yet at the same time the eternal rejection? Who is Judas, who is the betrayer? In view of this question, can we do anything other than speak with the disciples themselves: Surely not I, Lord? Surely not I?

*"Then they came and laid hands on Jesus and arrested him."* "I am the one, I should do penance on hands and knees, bound in hell. The scourge and bonds and all which you have endured is what my soul has earned."

Let us now consider the very end! At the very hour when Jesus Christ completes his redemptive suffering on the cross on Golgotha, Judas went and hanged himself, damning himself in futile remorse. A terrible fellowship!

Christendom has always seen in Judas the dark mystery of divine rejection and eternal damnation. With horror, it has recognized and testified to the seriousness and judgment of God with regard to the betrayer. For precisely that reason, however, it has never looked upon Judas with pride or arrogance; instead, it sings in trembling recognition of its own enormous sin: O, poor Judas, what have you done! Thus do we, too, say nothing more than this: O, poor Judas, what have you done! And we will seek refuge in the One who was hung on a cross for our sins, bringing about redemption for all of us. And we will pray:

Help, O Christ, God's Son
through your bitter suffering
that we, always obedient,
avoid all that is not virtuous.
That we consider with horror
your death and its cause,
and offer you thanksgiving
though paltry and weak. Amen.

# Loving Our Enemies

## Gross-Schlönwitz, Third Sunday
## after Epiphany, January 23, 1938

———— )«(●)»( ————

The northern edge of East Pomerania, formerly part of Germany but now in Poland, is a windswept plain along the Baltic coast where trees and wooden houses are bent by the wind and where winters are icy cold. In 1937, Bonhoeffer brought part of his pastoral training group to live in the parsonage in the little village of Gross-Schlönwitz. Here he hoped to provide them with a safe and quiet place for study and to teach them to help in ministry in the small parish. He preached this sermon on the third Sunday after Epiphany in the village church of Gross-Schlönwitz. Notes found on the last page of the manuscript indicate that he probably used the sermon as an example for discussion in a homiletics (preaching) class. The first line of the text for the sermon, "do not claim to be wise," is taken from the Luther Bible, which is the version that Bonhoeffer used.

---

Romans 12:16c–21: . . . *do not claim to be wise. Do not repay anyone evil for evil, but take thought for what is noble in the sight of all. If it is possible, so far as it depends on you, live peaceably with all. Beloved, never avenge yourselves, but leave room for the wrath of God; for it is written, "Vengeance is mine, I will repay, says the Lord." No, "if your enemies are hungry, feed them; if they are thirsty, give them something to drink; for by doing this you will heap burning coals on their heads." Do not be overcome by evil, but overcome evil with good.*

---

"Mercy has befallen me"—as we just sang. The same hymn is sung by the entire Christian church-community on each new day. "Mercy has befallen me"—when I still closed my heart before God, when I walked on the path of my own sin, when I loved my sin more than God, when through my sin I lived in pity and misery, when I had gone astray and could not find my way back—this was when God's word met me and I heard: God loves me. This was when Jesus found me. He was with me—he alone—he comforted me and forgave all my sins and did not count the evil against me [2 Cor. 5:19]. "Mercy has befallen me."

When I was hostile toward God because of God's commandments, God dealt with me as one would with a friend. When I committed evil against God, God did only good to me. God did not make an accounting of my evil, but looked for me tirelessly and without bitterness. Jesus suffered with me; he died for me. Nothing was too difficult for God, for my sake. This is when God overcame me, and had thus won over an enemy. The father had found his child again. Is that not what we mean when we sing this hymn? Even though I do not understand why God loves me so much, why I was so precious to the Almighty, even though I cannot grasp that Christ could and wanted to overcome my heart through his life, now I can say: "Mercy has befallen me . . ."

Yet precisely because I do not grasp and understand any of this, our text states: "Do not claim to be wise "—that is, you may be very smart and competent people in your business, at your work, but there is one thing that by nature you do not know anything about at all. There is one aspect where you are as unwise and as foolish as an underage child—namely, in the divine things of mercy or, much more, in how an enemy turns into a friend, how an enemy of God is overcome.

Our text for today speaks about the *behavior of Christians in relation to their enemies* or *how Christians "overcome" their enemies.* This question will always be of great importance for the life of the individual and of a Christian church-community. Yet we are so absolutely ignorant about this, and we have such completely wrong thoughts, that our text begins with: "Do not claim to be wise." First and foremost, this might be *a reminder of* how incomprehensible God's way with us was to our wisdom. Truly, it is foreign and inaccessible to our wisdom that God sought us, forgave us, that our Father sacrificed his Son for us, and thereby won over and converted our hearts. With that we are told: If you meet an enemy, think first about *your own enmity against God and about God's mercy toward you.*

"Do not claim to be wise"—this then is an important reminder about the beginning of our human race. The devil promised wisdom to Adam and Eve, offering to make them as wise as God, and they were to know what is good and evil [Gen. 3:4–5]. With that they were supposed to become judges over good and evil. Since the time when Adam accepted the devil's gift of wisdom, all human beings think that they know something about all divine things and have something to say about them. They imagined that they would now know how to deal with God and with humankind. With the aid of their wisdom, they would now certainly build a good world. But what happened? The first son of Adam and Eve was Cain, the murderer of his brother [Gen. 4:1–16]. The first human being born of humans on this earth was a murderer of his brother. This is when the seeds of evil sprouted. This was the fruit of the wisdom of the first human beings!

Does this give us something to think about? "Do not claim to be wise"—lest you become murderers of your kin. Do not believe that you know how to deal with human beings, with enemies, or that you know what is good or evil, or otherwise human beings will devour each other. "Do not claim to be wise", but focus on God's path to humankind, how God meets enemies, that path that Scripture itself calls foolish [1 Cor. 1:18], the path of God's love toward all enemies, the love that Christ extends to them all the way to the cross. It is wisdom at its best to recognize the cross of Christ as the invincible love of God for all humankind, for us as well as for our enemies.

Or do we think that God would love us more than our enemies? Do we think that we of all people are the favorite children of God? If we thought that way, then we would be deeply rooted in pharisaism, then we would have ceased being Christians. Does God love our enemies less, having come for them, suffered for them, died for them as well as for us? The cross is not the private property of any human being, but it belongs to all human beings; it is valid for all human beings. *God loves our enemies*—this is what the cross tells us. God suffers for their sake, experiences misery and pain for their sake; the Father has given his dear Son for them. Everything depends on this: that whenever we meet an enemy, we immediately think: this is someone whom God loves; God has given everything for this person. *Therefore, do not consider yourselves to be wise.* Concerning our attitude toward our enemies, this means first and foremost: Remember that *you as well were God's enemy* and *mercy* has happened *to you* without your merit or deserving. Second, that means: Remember that God also *went to the cross* for your enemy and *loves your enemy as dearly as you.*

Therefore, "do not repay anyone evil for evil, but take thought for what is noble in the sight of all. If it is possible, so far as it depends on you, live peaceably with all." Let's be very clear: there is a person, a neighbor, or someone else who continuously speaks ill of me, who vilifies me, who openly wrongs me, who plagues and tortures me at every opportunity. I only have to see this person, and my blood boils and I am filled by a terrible, threatening anger. The one who causes that within me is the enemy. But now I have to be careful. Now I need to remember quickly: *mercy has happened to me*, not by human doing, no, but *by God*, and *for this person* Jesus Christ *died*—and suddenly everything changes. Now we hear: *do not repay anyone evil* for evil. Do not lift your hand for a blow; do not open your mouth in anger but instead be quiet. What can the evildoer do against you? Evil done to you harms not you but the evildoer. Suffering injustice does not hurt any Christian. But the doing of injustice causes harm. The evil one wants to instill one thing in you, namely, that you will also become evil. But with that evil would surely win. Therefore, do not repay anyone evil for evil. You will harm not the other but yourself. You are not in danger when evil is done to you, but the other person is in danger, the one who perpetrates evil against you and will die in it unless you help. Therefore, for the sake of the other and for the sake of your responsibility for the other—do not repay anyone evil for evil. Has God ever repaid you in such a way?

"Take thought for what is noble in the sight of all . . . live peaceably with all." With *everybody*, with *all* people—there is no exception. Be worthy of respect, not only toward *the respectable,* but also toward those who are not respectable; be *peaceable* not only with *the peaceful,* but especially with those who do not want to let us live in peace. Heathens can do the opposite, as well as we can. But Jesus Christ did not die for the respectable and for the peaceable, but especially for sinners and enemies, for those who are not respectable, the haters, the killers. Our heart always yearns to dwell among friends, among the just and the respectable. But Jesus Christ was in the midst of his enemies. He wanted to be precisely there. This is where we also should be. This is what distinguishes us from all other sects and religions. Their devout members want to be among themselves. But Christ wishes us to be among our enemies as he was. Amid his enemies he died the death of God's love and prayed: Father forgive them, for they do not know what they are doing [Luke 23:34]. Christ wants to win his victory among our enemies.

Therefore, do not retreat, do not isolate yourselves, but "take thought for what is noble" for everybody, create peace with all people so far as it depends on you. "So far as it depends on you"—it is not in your hands if you are not left in peace, if you are vilified and persecuted. But "so far as it depends on you," that means that you shall never be the source of strife. Your heart should always be full of peace. Does that mean that we should also leave the word of God unspoken for the sake of peace? Never—for is there a more peaceful word and deed than preaching about the peace that God has made with the world, with the human beings God created? "So far as it depends on you"—: one thing does not depend on you, namely, to leave God's word unsaid, but it does depend on you to speak it for the purpose of peace, to speak it for the purpose of the peace of humankind with God, in the midst of a torn-apart and divided human world. Jesus made peace with us when we were enemies [Rom. 5:10]. He has also created peace with all our enemies, on the cross. Let us witness to this peace in front of everyone!

"Never avenge yourselves . . ." If I take revenge into my own hands, I am making myself the judge of the world and of humankind. The revenge I wanted to take will come upon my own head. In seeking revenge, I take the life of my enemy into my own hands and forget that God's hand already rests upon this person for whom Christ died on the cross. Whoever seeks revenge on a human being undoes the death of Christ and becomes guilty of denying the blood of reconciliation. Christ died for me and for my enemy, for the salvation of both of us. If I seek revenge, I disregard the salvation of the other. That might not harm the other person, but by that very act I would break with the deeds of Christ.

Christ demands a difficult sacrifice from us, namely, to let go of our revenge, perhaps the most difficult, for all of human nature screams for revenge against enemies. The lust for revenge is stronger in our human blood than any other addiction. But this we know: we cannot take revenge anymore. If my enemy stands before my eyes and the craving for revenge overcomes me, at once Jesus Christ stands behind my enemy and bids me: do not lift your hand, vengeance is mine, I will take it.

". . . Leave room for the wrath of God . . . I will repay, says the Lord." What terrible words. Can we hear them and know what it means that God will take revenge, without asking at once: "No, do not take revenge; no, I do not and cannot wish that even my enemy should fall into God's wrathful hands." But God says: "Vengeance is mine, I will repay"; God wants to and has to wreak vengeance upon the evil. But—miracle upon miracle—God has already wrought vengeance in an incomprehensible way, not upon us who were enemies and who still sin against God every day, and not upon our enemies, but instead upon God's own self, upon God's dear Son. Upon Jesus God visited all our sins and punished them. God cast him out into the hell of despair and of abandonment by God. And in the same hour, Jesus prayed: Father, forgive them . . . This is God's vengeance, namely, that of accepting self-inflicted pain and suffering while sparing and accepting us. This is God's vengeance, namely, that of carrying the suffering on God's own shoulders and forgiving all enemies. Does it not resonate in us: Do not consider yourselves to be wise! God's paths to you are too wonderful and too superior, too merciful and too loving.

It remains astonishing that this word about the vengeance of God is followed immediately by the statement: "If your enemies are hungry, feed them; if they are thirsty, give them something to drink. For by doing this you will heap burning coals upon their heads" [Prov. 25:21–22]. For the enemy, God gave up life, gave up everything; now you give your enemies what you have: bread if they are hungry, water if they are thirsty, help if they are weak, blessing, mercy, love of the enemy. Are they worth that? Yes. Who would be worthy of our love, who would need our love more than the one who hates? Who is poorer than such a person, who is more in need of help, who is more in need of love than your enemy? Have you ever looked at your enemy in this way, as the one who basically stands in front of you, poor as a beggar, and who asks you, without being able to say it himself or herself: help me, grant me the one thing that can still lift me out of my hate, grant me love, the love of God, the love of the crucified Savior. Indeed, all threats and all showing of fists stem from this poverty, and at its root is begging for the love of God, for peace, for neighborliness. You repudiate the poorest of the poor when you repudiate your enemy.

Burning coals. Coals burn and hurt when they touch us. Love can burn and hurt as well. It teaches us to realize that we are poor as beggars. It is the burning pain of repentance that appears in the one who finds love, nothing but love, despite hate and menace. God has taught us to know this pain. When we felt it, the hour of repentance had come.

Now you are at the goal: "Do not be overcome by evil, but *overcome evil with good.*" This is what Christ did for us. He did not become confused by our evil; he did not let himself be overcome by it. He *overcame our evil* with good. Let's repeat how that happens: not by feeding the other person's evil with our evil, the hatred of the other person with our hatred. Rather, it happens when the evil hits emptiness and finds nothing on which it can ignite. How do we overcome evil? By forgiving without end. How does that happen? By seeing the enemy as he or she truly is, the one for whom Christ died, the one whom Christ loved. How will the church-community win victory over its enemies? By letting the love of Christ win victory over our enemies. Amen.

# The Gift of Faith

## Confirmation, Kieckow, April 9, 1938

While directing the seminary at Finkenwalde, Bonhoeffer had become acquainted with Ruth von Kleist-Retzow and her family, members of the Pomeranian landed aristocracy, who attended the Sunday church services at the seminary. They became dear friends of Bonhoeffer's and important supporters of the seminary's work. Ruth von Kleist's home was from then on a congenial retreat where Bonhoeffer did much of his later theological work.

Mrs. Von Kleist often brought her grandchildren with her to church, and Bonhoeffer confirmed three of them. The confirmation service was held at the manor of her son Hans-Jürgen von Kleist-Retzow, for his son Hans-Friedrich and two cousins. One of the cousins, Max von Wedemeyer, had a sister, Maria, who was considered too young to join the confirmation class but later became Bonhoeffer's fiancée. She lost both her brother and her father, as well as her cousin Hans-Friedrich, in the war on the eastern front. In August 1941, Bonhoeffer conducted Hans-Friedrich's memorial service. He preached on Proverbs 23:26, the verse the boy had chosen for his confirmation.

The sentence, "I believe, dear Lord, help my unbelief," that Bonhoeffer includes several times in this sermon is the translation of Mark 9:24 from the Luther Bible.

———————◦◦◦———————

Mark 9:24: *I believe, dear Lord; help my unbelief!*

———————◦◦◦———————

Dear confirmation pupils! This is a very sober word. But it is good that from the very beginning we get used to not bragging about our faith. Faith is not like that. Precisely because all depends today on our *really* keeping the faith, all desire for great words fades away. Whether we believe or not will be evident every day; protests do not change a thing. You know from the Passion story that Peter says to Jesus: "Even though I must die with you, I will not deny you," and Jesus answers: "Before the cock crows, you will deny me three times" [Matt. 26, 34–35]. And the story ends: "And Peter went out and wept bitterly." [Matt. 26:75]. He had denied his Lord. Great assertions, even if they were said truthfully and were meant seriously, are always closest to denial. May God protect you and all of us from this.

This confirmation day is an important day for you and for us all. It is not an insignificant thing that you profess your Christian faith today before the all-knowing God and in the hearing of the Christian church-community. For the rest of your life, you shall think back on this day with joy. But for that very reason I admonish you to speak and act today in full Christian soberness. You shall not and may not say or do anything on this day that you will remember later with bitterness and remorse, having said and promised more in an hour of inner emotion than a human being can and may ever say. Your faith is still weak and untried and very much at its beginning. Therefore, when later on you speak the confession of your faith, do not rely on yourselves and on your good intentions and on the strength of your faith, but rely only on the one whom you confess, on God the Father, on Jesus Christ, and on the Holy Spirit. And pray in your hearts: I believe, dear Lord, help my unbelief. Who among us adults would not and should not pray the same with you?

Confirmation day is a serious day. But truly, you know that it is still easy enough to confess one's faith in the church, in the fellowship of Christians, your parents, siblings, and godparents, in the undisturbed celebration of a worship service. Let us be thankful that God grants us this hour of common confession in the church. But all of this will only become utterly serious, utterly real after confirmation, when daily life returns, our daily life with all its decisions. Then it will become evident whether even this day was serious. You do not have your faith once and for all. The faith that you will confess today with all your hearts needs to be regained tomorrow and the day after tomorrow, indeed, every day anew. We receive from God only as much faith as we need for the present day. Faith is the *daily* bread that God gives us. You know the story about manna [see Exodus 16]. This is what the children of Israel received daily in the desert. But when they tried to store it for the next day, it was rotten. This is how it is with all the gifts of God. This is how it is with faith as well. Either we receive it daily anew or it rots. One day is just long enough to preserve the faith. Every morning it is a new struggle to fight through all unbelief, faintheartedness, lack of clarity and confusion, anxiety and uncertainty, in order to arrive at faith and to wrest it from God. Every morning in your life the same prayer will be necessary: I believe, dear Lord, help my unbelief.

"I believe." Today, when the Christian congregation acknowledges you as autonomous members of the church, it expects you to begin to understand that your faith must be your very own individual decision. The "we believe" must now grow more and more into an "I believe."

Faith *is* a decision. We cannot avoid that. "You cannot serve two masters" [Matt. 6:24], from now on either you serve God alone or you do not serve God at all. Now you only have *one* Lord, who is the Lord of the world, who is the Savior of the world, who is the one who creates the world anew. To serve God is your highest honor. But to this Yes to God belongs an equally clear No. Your Yes to God demands your No to all injustice, to all evil, to all lies, to all oppression and violation of the weak and the poor, to all godlessness and mocking of the Holy. Your Yes to God demands a brave No to everything that will ever hinder you from serving God alone, whether it be your profession, your property, your house, your honor before the world. Faith means decision.

But it is *your* very own decision! No one can relieve you of it. It must arise from loneliness, from the solitude of the heart with God. It will be born out of the hot struggles against the enemy in your own heart. You are still surrounded by a church-community, by homes that carry you, by parents who pray for you, by people who help you wherever they can. Thanks be to God for this! But God will lead you more and more into loneliness. God wants to prepare you for the great hours and decisions of your life when no human being can stand by your side and when only one thing is true: I believe, yes, I myself, I cannot do otherwise; dear Lord, help my unbelief.

Dear confirmation pupils, the church therefore expects of you that you will come of age in your dealings with the Word of God and in prayer. Your faith today is a beginning, not a conclusion. First, you must dive into Scripture and into prayer, you alone, and you must learn to fight with the weapon of the Word of God wherever it is needed. Christian fellowship is one of the greatest gifts that God gives us. But God *can* also take this gift away from us as it pleases God, and has done so already to many of our brothers and sisters today. Then we stand and fall on our very own faith. Someday, however, each and every one of us will be placed in this solitude even if he or she has evaded it throughout life, namely, in the hour of death and the Last Judgment. Then God will not ask you, have your parents believed, but: have *you* believed? May God grant that in the loneliest hour of our life we can still pray: I believe, dear Lord, help my unbelief. Then we shall be blessed.

"I believe, *dear Lord* . . ." In life, it is not always easy to say, "Dear Lord." But faith must learn this. Who would not wish sometimes to say: I believe, harsh Lord, severe Lord, terrible Lord. I submit to you. I will be silent and obey. But to learn to say "dear Lord" is a new and difficult struggle. And yet we will have found God, the father of Jesus Christ, only when we have learned to speak that way.

Your faith will be led into difficult temptations. Jesus Christ was tempted as well, more than all of us. At first, temptations will come to you not to obey God's commandments any longer. They will assault you with great force. Satan, Lucifer, the bearer of light, will come to you, handsome and alluring, innocent and with the appearance of light. He will obscure God's law and call it into doubt. He will want to rob you of the joy you have in God's path. And once the evil one has caused us to waver, he will tear our entire faith out of our hearts, will trample it under foot and cast it away. Those will be difficult hours in your life, when you tend to become weary of God's word, when all is in revolt, when no prayer passes your lips anymore, when the heart refuses to listen any longer.

As certain as your faith is alive, all of this must happen. It must happen so that your faith is tested and strengthened [Heb. 4:15], so that you will be able to cope with increasing tasks and struggles. God works on us through these temptations. God never plays a game with you, you can be confident of that, but the Father of us children wants to make fast our hearts. That is the reason why all of this will come over you. And even if the temptation is very confusing, if our resistance threatens utter collapse, indeed, even if defeat has already arrived, then we may and should cry out with the final remnant of our faith: I believe, dear Lord, help my unbelief. The dear Lord is after all the Father who tests us and strengthens us in such a way. The dear Lord is after all Jesus Christ who has suffered all temptations like us, yet without sin, to be an example and a help for us. The dear Lord is after all the Holy Spirit who wants to sanctify us in this struggle.

Your faith will be tested through sorrow. You do not yet know much about this. But God sends sorrow to us children when we need it the most, when we become too overly sure on this earth. Then a great pain, a difficult renunciation, a great loss, sickness, death, enters our life. Our unbelief rears up. Why does God demand this of me? Why has God allowed this to happen? Why, yes, why? That is the great question of unbelief that wants to suffocate our faith. No one can avoid this calamity. Everything is so perplexing, so dark. In this hour of being forsaken by God, we may and shall say: I believe, *dear* Lord, help my unbelief. Yes, dear Lord, also in the dark, also when in doubt, also in the state of being forsaken by God. Dear Lord, you still are my dear Father who makes all things work for my benefit. Dear Lord Jesus Christ, you yourself have cried out: My God, why have you forsaken me? [Mark 15:34] You wanted to be where I am. Now you are with me. Now I know that you won't leave me, even in the hour of my need. I believe, dear Lord, help my unbelief.

Your faith will bring you not only temptation and suffering, but above all struggle. Today's confirmation pupils are like young soldiers marching into war, into the war of Jesus Christ against the gods of this world. This war demands the commitment of one's entire life. Should our Lord God not be worthy of this commitment? The struggle is already being fought, and you shall now join it. The idolatry and fear of human beings confront us everywhere. But do not think that great words here can accomplish anything. It is a struggle with fear and trembling, for the hardest enemy stands not opposite us but within ourselves. You shall know that precisely those who stood and still stand in the midst of this struggle have most deeply experienced this: I believe, dear Lord (yes, dear Lord!), help my *unbelief*. And if we, despite all temptation, do not flee but stand and fight, then this is not due to our strong faith and our courage in battle, our valor, but rather it is the sole fact that we cannot flee anymore, because God holds on to us so that we can no longer pull away. God leads the struggle within us and against us and through us.

"Help my unbelief." God answers our prayers. Amid temptation, suffering, and struggle, God has created a sanctuary of peace. This is the Holy Eucharist. Here there is forgiveness of sins; here is the conquest of death; here are victory and peace. It is not we who have won it. It is God who has done it through Jesus Christ. Righteousness, life, peace belong to God. We exist in unrest, but rest is with God. We exist in strife, but victory is with God. You are called to the Lord's Supper. Come and receive in faith forgiveness, life, and peace. Ultimately, only this remains for you in the world: God's Word and sacrament. Amen.

# Death Is Swallowed Up in Victory

### Sigurdshof, Remembrance Sunday,
### November 26, 1939

═══════════•《◈》•═══════════

This sermon was a homily for the celebration of the Lord's Supper on Remembrance Sunday, when congregations especially remembered those who had died. The service was held at Sigurdshof, a farm belonging to the von Kleist estate in Tychow, where Bonhoeffer and his students moved after they had to vacate the parsonage at Gross-Schlönwitz. The house at Sigurdshof had no electricity, and water was obtained from a pump at the edge of the forest. During the winter, they were snowed in there. World War II had begun that summer, and the Confessing Church was at such a low point that the ordination course was deprived of all support. Yet, despite these conditions, Bonhoeffer preached on this text—given here in the King James Version, which is closest to Luther's Bible—in which the apostle Paul recalls Isaiah 25:8 and Hosea 13:14, that death is swallowed up and the faithful are redeemed from its power. Bonhoeffer begins with two lines from Luther's Easter hymn "Christ Jesus Lay in

Death's Strong Bands," and toward the end mentions an account of the death of a nineteenth-century pastor, Johann Christoph Blumhardt. The statement of faith that follows comes from the Apostles' Creed, confessed by Christians worldwide.

An English fellow prisoner, Payne Best, reported Bonhoeffer's last known words, on April 8, 1945, on being taken away to Flossenbürg, where he faced his own death by execution. They stand as a testament to his faith that death had been swallowed up in victory: "This is the end— for me, the beginning of life."

1 Corinthians 15:55: *Death is swallowed up in victory. O death, where is thy sting: O grave, where is thy victory?*

It was a strange and dreadful strife, when life and death contended.
The *victory* remained with life, the reign of death was ended

You are invited to a *victory celebration*—to the celebration of the greatest victory won in the world, the victory of Jesus Christ over death. *Bread and wine*, body and blood of our Lord Jesus Christ are the *signs of victory*, for Jesus lives and is present in these signs today, the same Jesus who, almost two thousand years ago, was nailed to the cross and laid in the grave. Jesus arose from the dead, burst asunder the rock before the tomb, and remained the victor. Today, you are to *receive the signs of his victory*. And later, whenever you receive the blessed bread and blessed chalice, you should know: *just as certainly* as I eat this bread and drink this wine, *just as certainly* has Jesus Christ remained the victor over death, and *just as certainly* is he the living Lord who meets me.

We *do not like to speak of victories in our lives*. It is too large a word for us. We have suffered too many defeats in our lives. Too many hours of weakness and too many crude sins have reduced victory to nothing. But, isn't it true, *the spirit within us longs* for this word, yearns for the final victory over sin, over the anxious fear of death in our lives. And now God's word does not speak to us about *our* victory. It does not promise us that from now on *we* will be victorious over sin and death. It does say with all power, however, that someone has won this victory, and that this one will also win the victory over us when we have him as our Lord. It is not we who are victorious but Jesus.

Today, *we proclaim and believe this, against everything that we see around us*, against the graves of our loved ones, against the dying nature outdoors, against the death that the war casts over us once again. We see the reign of death, but we preach and believe in the victory of Jesus Christ over death. Death is swallowed up in victory. Jesus is victor, resurrection of the dead, and eternal life.

It is like a *mocking song of triumph* over death and sin that the Holy Scripture sings here: O Death, where is your sting? O Hell, where is your victory? Death and sin puff themselves up and instill fear in humankind, as if they were still the rulers of the world. But it is only an illusion. They have long since lost their power. Jesus has taken it from them. Since then, anyone who is with Jesus no longer needs to fear these dark lords. Sin, that sting of death with which death causes us pain, has no more dominion. Hell no longer has any power over us who are with Jesus. They are powerless. They still rage like a vicious dog on a chain, but they cannot get at us, because Jesus holds them fast. He remains the victor.

But, we ask ourselves, if that is the case, why *does it appear so completely different in our life?* Why does one see so little of this victory? Why do sin and death rule so terribly over us? Indeed, this very question is God's question to you: I have done all this for you, and you live as if nothing has happened! You submit yourselves to sin and fear of death as if they could still enslave you! Why is there so little victory in your life? Because you do not want to believe that Jesus is the victor over death and sin, over your lives. Your *unbelief* brings about your defeat. But now the victory of Jesus is proclaimed again to you today in the Lord's Supper: the victory over sin and death for you, too, whoever you may be. Seize it in faith. Today, Jesus will once again forgive all your heavy and manifold sins. He will make you wholly clean and innocent. From now on, you need not sin anymore. Sin need not rule over you any longer. Jesus will rule over you, and he is stronger than every temptation. Jesus will be victorious in the hour of your trial and fear of death, and you will confess: Jesus has become the victor over my sin, over my death. Whenever you abandon this belief, you will have to sink and succumb, sin and die. Whenever you seize this belief, Jesus will keep the victory.

On Remembrance Sunday we are asked, at the graves of our loved ones: for what are you, too, willing to die? *Do we believe* in the *power of death* and sin, or do we believe in the *power of Jesus Christ?* There can be only one of these two beliefs. In the past century, there was a man of God who during his life had often preached the victory of Jesus Christ and done wonderful things in his name. As he lay in great torment and distress on his deathbed, his son bent over toward his ear and called to the dying man, "Father, *victory is won.*" When dark hours and when the darkest hour comes over us, then we want to hear the voice of Jesus Christ calling in our ear: *victory is won.* Death is swallowed up in victory. Take comfort. And may God grant that then we will be able to say: I believe in the forgiveness of sins, the resurrection of the body, and the life everlasting. It is in this faith that we want to live and die. It is to that end that the Lord's Supper helps us. Amen.

# FOR FURTHER READING

*Dietrich Bonhoeffer Works in English.* Complete annotated edition in 16 volumes, Victoria J. Barnett, Wayne Whitson Floyd Jr., and Barbara Wojhoski, general editors. Various translators and volume editors. Minneapolis: Fortress Press, 1996–.

Vol. 1 *Sanctorum Communio: A Theological Study of the Sociology of the Church*, 1998

Vol. 2 *Act and Being: Transcendental Philosophy and Ontology in Systematic Theology*, 1996

Vol. 3 *Creation and Fall: A Theological Exposition of Genesis 1–3*, 1997.

Vol. 4 *Discipleship* (appeared in an earlier translation as *The Cost of Discipleship*), 2001

Vol. 5 *Life Together/Prayerbook of the Bible*, 1996

Vol. 6 *Ethics*, 2005

Vol. 7 *Fiction from Tegel Prison*, 1999

Vol. 8 *Letters and Papers from Prison*, 2010

Vol. 9 *The Young Bonhoeffer: 1918–1927*, 2003

Vol. 10 *Barcelona, Berlin, New York: 1928–1931*, 2008

Vol. 11 *Ecumenical, Academic, and Pastoral Work: 1931–1932*, 2011

Vol. 12 *Berlin: 1933*, 2009

Vol. 13 *London: 1933–1935*, 2007

Vol. 14 *Theological Education at Finkenwalde: 1935–1937*, forthcoming

Vol. 15 *Theological Education Underground: 1937–1940*, 2012
Vol. 16 *Conspiracy and Imprisonment: 1940–1945*, 2006

*Love Letters from Cell 92: The Correspondence between Dietrich Bonhoeffer and Maria von Wedemeyer.* Edited by Ruth-Alice von Bismarck and Ulrich Kabitz. Translated by John Brownjohn. Nashville: Abingdon, 1994.

*Dietrich Bonhoeffer, Theologian, Christian, Man for His Times: A Biography,* by Eberhard Bethge. English translation revised and edited by Victoria J. Barnett. Minneapolis: Fortress Press, 2000.

*Dietrich Bonhoeffer 1906–1945: Martyr, Thinker, Man of Resistance,* by Ferdinand Schlingensiepen. English translation by Isabel Best. London: T & T Clark/Continuum, 2010.

The International Bonhoeffer Society, English Language Section, publishes a newsletter 2–3 times a year, with recent scholarly articles on Bonhoeffer's work, as well as conference proceedings, announcements of meetings, and an updated bibliography. For information, go to dietrichbonhoeffer.org.

# SOURCES

*Barcelona, Berlin, New York: 1928–1931, Volume 10,* Dietrich Bonhoeffer
Works. Minneapolis: Fortress Press, 2008.
God Is with Us, see "Sermon on Matthew 28:20," 490–95.
Waiting at the Door, see "Sermon on Revelation 3:20," 542–46.

*Ecumenical, Academic, and Pastoral Work: 1931–1932, Volume 11,* Dietrich
Bonhoeffer Works. Minneapolis: Fortress Press, 2012.
National Memorial Day, see "Sermon on Matthew 24:6–14," 419–27.
The Promised Land, see "Sermon on Genesis 32:25–32; 33:10,"
428–33.
God Is Love, see "Baptism Sermon on 1 John 4:16," 440–42.
Lazarus and the Rich Man, see "Sermon on Luke 16:19–31," 443–50.
Risen with Christ, see "Sermon on Colossians 3:1–4," 350–57.
The Things That Are Above, see "Sermon on Colossians 3:1–4,"
457–65.

*Berlin: 1932–1933, Volume 12,* Dietrich Bonhoeffer Works. Minneapolis:
Fortress Press, 2009.
Overcoming Fear, see "Sermon on Matthew 8:23–27," 454–61.
Gideon: God Is My Lord, see "Sermon on Judges 6:15–16; 7:2; 8:23,"
461–67.
The Joy of Ascension, see "Sermon on 1 Peter 1:7b–9," 468–71.

Who Do You Say That I Am? see "Sermon on Matthew 16:13–18," 477–81.

*London: 1933–1935, Volume 13,* Dietrich Bonhoeffer Works. Minneapolis: Fortress Press, 2007.
Ambassadors for Christ, see "Sermon on 2 Corinthians 5:20," 321–26.
Turning Back, see "Sermon on 2 Corinthians 5:10," 326–31.
As a Mother Comforts Her Child, see "Sermon on Wisdom 3:3," 331–36.
Come, O Rescuer, see "Sermon on Luke 21:28," 337–41.
My Spirit Rejoices, see "Sermon on Luke 1:46–55," 342–47.
Beginning with Christ, see "Meditation on Luke 9:57–62," 347–49.
Repent and Do Not Judge, see "Sermon on Luke 13:1–5," 365–70.
Come unto Me, see "Sermon on Matthew 11:28–30," 371–75.
. . . and Have Not Love, see "Sermon on 1 Corinthians 13:1–3," 375–81.
What Love Wants, see "Sermon on 1 Corinthians 13:4–7," 382–87.
Must I Be Perfect? see "Sermon on 1 Corinthians 13:8–12," 387–91.
A Church That Believes, Hopes, and Loves, see "Sermon on 1 Corinthians 13:13," 392–96.
My Strength Is Made Perfect in Weakness, see "Sermon for Evening Prayer on 2 Corinthians 12:9," 401-4.
Lord, Help My Unbelief, see "Sermon on Mark 9:23–24," 404–8.

*Theological Education at Finkenwalde: 1935–1937, Volume 14,* Dietrich Bonhoeffer Works. Minneapolis: Fortress Press, forthcoming in 2013.
Forgiveness, see "Sermon on Matthew 18:21–25," unpaginated.
The Betrayer, see "Sermon on Matthew 26:45b–50," unpaginated.

*Theological Education Underground: 1937–1940, Volume 15,* Dietrich Bonhoeffer Works. Minneapolis: Fortress Press, 2012.
Loving Our Enemies, see "Sermon on Romans 12:17–21," 465–71.
The Gift of Faith, see "Confirmation Sermon on Mark 9:24," 476–80.
Death Is Swallowed Up in Victory, see "Communion Homily on 1 Corinthians 15:55," 487–91.